AIX

Also by Simon Trowbridge

Non-fiction

PETER HALL'S ROYAL SHAKESPEARE COMPANY:
The artists of the RSC during the era of Peter Hall,
Trevor Nunn and Terry Hands, 1960 to 1999

RAMEAU:
A Life

THE MUSIC OF BRUCE SPRINGSTEEN
AND THE E STREET BAND

THE RISE AND FALL OF
THE ROYAL SHAKESPEARE COMPANY:
An Illustrated History

THE COMÉDIE-FRANÇAISE
FROM MOLIÈRE TO ÉRIC RUF

THE COMPANY

Fiction

CEASE TO WEEP

ÉLODIE DUQUETTE

Aix

A History of the
Aix-en-Provence Festival
1948 to 2018

SIMON
TROWBRIDGE

ENGLANCE *PRESS*

New paperback edition
published by Englance Press in 2025

First published by
Englance Press, Oxford, in 2024

ISBN 978-1-7384215-6-5 (pbk.)

ISBN 978-1-7384215-3-4 (hbk., with colour illustrations)

Copyright © 2024, 2025 Simon Trowbridge

All rights reserved. No part of this book may be reproduced, copied, adapted, displayed, stored, distributed or transmitted in any form.

In such a night as this,
When the sweet wind did gently kiss the trees
And they did make no noise, in such a night
Troilus methinks mounted the Trojan walls
And sighed his soul toward the Grecian tents
Where Cressid lay that night.

In such a night
Did Thisbe fearfully o'ertrip the dew,
And saw the lion's shadow ere himself,
And ran dismayed away.

In such a night
Stood Dido with a willow in her hand
Upon the wild sea banks and waft her love
To come again to Carthage.

In such a night
Medea gathered the enchanted herbs
That did renew old Aeson.

                WILLIAM SHAKESPEARE

Contents

Preface 11

PART ONE: GABRIEL DUSSURGET 13

One *Lily and Gabriel* 14
i Prelude 14
ii Discovering Aix 17

Two *Creating the Festival* 20
i A Dream Made Real 20
ii 1948: The First Festival 22
iii 1949: Mozart's Don Giovanni 24

Three *A Golden Decade* 28
i 1950/51: Mozart's Così and Messiaen's Turangalîla 28
ii 1952: Mozart's Figaro and Britten's Michelangelo 31
iii 1953/54/55: Rossini, Gounod and Gluck 34
iv 1956: Rameau's Platée 36
v 1957/58/59: Bizet's Carmen and Boulez's Mallarmé 38

Four *Expansion* 42
i 1960/61: Purcell's Dido and Monteverdi's Poppea 42
ii 1962: Stravinsky and Milhaud 46
iii 1963/64/65/66: Mozart's Idomeneo, Berlioz's Faust, Verdi's Falstaff and Debussy's Pelléas 47

Five *The End of the Festival's First Era* 51
i 1967/68/69: Decline 51
ii 1970/71/72: The Ministry Steps In 53

PART TWO: BERNARD LEFORT 57

Six *A Celebration of Song* 58

i Mission Statement 58
ii 1974: Mozart and Verdi 60
iii 1975: Campra's Le Carnaval de Venise 62
iv 1976/77: Mozart Rethought, Stockhausen Embraced 65

Seven *Premature Departure* 71
i 1978/79: Handel's Alcina and Mozart's Figaro 71
ii 1980/81: Rossini's Sémiramis and Tancrède 75

PART THREE: LOUIS ERLO 79

Eight *Old Rameau, Young Mozart* 80
i Mission Statement 80
ii 1982: Les Boréades 81
iii 1983/84: Rameau, Mozart, Boulez and Berio 86

Nine *An Improved Theatre* 91
i 1985: The Return of Monteverdi, Strauss and Purcell 91
ii 1986/87/88: Campra, Lully at Last 94

Ten *Ancient and Modern* 101
i 1989: Purcell and Shakespeare 101
ii 1990: The Return of Rameau 105
iii 1991: A New Management Model and Britten's Dream 108

Eleven *Funding Woes Deepen* 114
i 1992/93: Stravinsky and Handel 114
ii 1994/95/96: Erlo's Last Seasons and the Appointment of Stéphane Lissner 118

PART FOUR: STÉPHANE LISSNER 127

Twelve *Renaissance* 128
i Laying New Foundations 128
ii 1998: The Fiftieth Edition, Year One of the Académie 132
iii 1999: Le Domaine du Grand Saint-Jean 137
iv 2000: Ulysses 139
v 2001/02: Janáček, Britten and Eötvös 144

Thirteen *Lissner Part Two* 151
i 2003: Strikes Wreck the Festival 151

    ii 2004: Handel, Prokofiev, and Hosokawa 153
    iii 2005: Mozart's Così 155
    iv 2006: Lissner's Final Season 159

PART FIVE: BERNARD FOCCROULLE 163

Fourteen *In Lissner's Shadow* 164
    i 2007: Janáček's De la maison des morts 164
    ii 2008/09: Dusapin's Passion, the Ring Concludes 167
    iii 2010/11: The Académie Returns to the Grand Saint-Jean 169

Fifteen *A Festival of New Operas* 173
    i 2012: Benjamin's Written on Skin 173
    ii 2013: Cavalli, Verdi, Strauss, Mendonça 175
    iii 2014: Aix en Juin, Les Intermittents 177
    iv 2015: Rattle and Dove 181
    v 2016/17/18: The Foccroulle Era Comes to an End 183

Appendices 189
Directors 190
Festival Venues 191
Opera Productions 1948-2023 194
World Premieres 241
The Académie: World Premieres 246
The Académie: Laureates 249

Notes 252

Index 260

Preface

A music festival that began by presenting one opera, Mozart's *Così fan tutte*, performed on a trestle stage erected in the corner of an old courtyard, before spectators who sat on wooden chairs beneath a towering plane tree, grew rapidly to become one of Europe's most important. The singers that first year, 1948, were young and unknown, and the musicians were students from the Paris Conservatoire; but the conductor was the Austrian maestro Hans Rosbaud, an indication that the fledging festival meant business. One year later, a theatre had been built in the courtyard and Rosbaud conducted a distinguished orchestra.

 The Festival international de musique d'Aix-en-Provence flourished because of the flair of its founding artistic director, Gabriel Dussurget, a man of impeccable artistic taste who made the Festival after his own image and who ran it for twenty-four years as a private enterprise organised and funded by Aix's Casino. Gabriel Dussurget established the reputation of the operas of Mozart, Monteverdi and Purcell in France, resurrected the music of Rameau and Campra, and supported Pierre Boulez and other living composers. He created a troupe of outstanding young singers, most of whom went on to enjoy major international careers. And then there was the beguiling appeal of the town itself, its beauty, Mediterranean climate, and way of life. These elements, combined, made the Festival d'Aix unique.

 The romance of Aix didn't end when Dussurget stepped down in 1972 and the Festival became a national organisation funded by local and national government. The Festival kept its singular character and pioneering spirit throughout the very challenging period, 1974 to 1997, when government funding was insufficient.

 The Festival d'Aix remains true to the key artistic principles of the

Dussurget era. It prizes innovation above commercialism. It places the music of 1580 to 1799 and 1900 to 2023 above the grand opera repertoire that dominates most opera houses. It commissions new operas with a commitment that no other festival or opera house can match. From Hans Rosbaud in the 1950s to Simon Rattle in the present era, it forms lasting relationships with conductors who offer adventure as well as prestige. It supports young singers and rarely imports the superstars of opera. Every summer, it creates a community of artists and backstage staff. In 2023, during a public discussion, Simon Rattle said that Aix was special because it supported artists and enabled them to do their 'best work'. Other artists have spoken about how well the Festival manages stress, creating a working environment that fosters fellowship and values a human approach. The most important development since the time of Dussurget, Stéphane Lissner's creation of the Académie européenne de musique in 2008, has survived the test of time. Among the graduates of the Académie are Stéphane Degout, Sabine Devieilhe, Julie Fuchs and Léa Desandre. Former members of the Académie return regularly to Aix.

Of course, Aix has changed with the times. Gabriel Dussurget was not a man of the people. Because the Festival of the 1940s and 50s didn't take public money, he didn't need to worry that opera was a niche art form; and he didn't engage with most of the people of Aix, who viewed the Festival as an annual occupation. With State funding came the obligation to endeavour to be inclusive, and this would change how the Festival was managed, and, eventually, its (social) aspirations and objectives. This book, though, is primarily about the artistic *raison d'etre* of the Festival d'Aix, its artists, repertoire, style, and character.

Part One

The NIGHTS of GABRIEL DUSSURGET

ONE

Lily and Gabriel

1904-1948

i PRELUDE

In early January 1948, a red Georges Irat sports car rumbled and growled down the somnolent streets of the ancient town of Aix-en-Provence. On board were three remarkable people: the comtesse Lily Pastré (the driver of the motor), Gabriel Dussurget, and Dussurget's partner Henri Lambert. They were looking for a Provençal town in which to establish a summer festival of opera and music. A town with an old courtyard that could be converted into an open-air theatre.

Lily Pastré and Gabriel Dussurget made for an odd pairing. Lily Pastré was a formidable woman in her late fifties. For many years this heiress to the Noilly-Prat Vermouth business empire had used her considerable wealth to support the arts in both Paris and her native Marseille. She was unconventional and singular. Her passions included music and fast cars. She was one of the last of the *salonnières* who had sustained and promoted young artists and intellectuals since the 18th century. During the war, her grand home overlooking Marseille, the Château de Montredon, was a haven for refugee artists, many of them Jewish, who had fled Paris and the Occupied Zone. These refugees included the pianists Youra Guller and Clara Haskil.

During these years, the Château de Montredon was a community of singers, musicians and other artists, and the house was full of music. For Lily Pastré and the artists she harboured, art offered consolation and hope: to keep performing music and plays (especially those works banned by Vichy or the Germans) was an act of defiance. An open-air performance of Shakespeare's *A Midsummer Night's Dream* was given before the public at Montredon in July 1942. Jean Wall and Boris Kochno directed, Christian Bérard designed the beautiful costumes (made from Lily's curtains), and Manuel Rosenthal conducted music by Jacques Ibert. Edmonde Charles-Roux played one of the fairies. This remarkable production, created by banned Jewish artists and performed by a largely Jewish orchestra, risked provoking a Vichy regime that, in the summer of 1942, had started to round up Jewish people in large numbers. An abandoned brickworks factory (a grim redbrick industrial pile) in the commune of Aix-en-Provence at Les Milles, converted into an internment camp, was where Jewish men, women and children were incarcerated before being deported to the death camps. While the names of the creators of the production weren't made public, the authorities surely knew what was happening at Montredon. The German consul was in the audience. No action, however, was taken, either at the time or after the Germans occupied the Free Zone.

Gabriel Dussurget, one of Lily Pastré's house guests at Montredon over Christmas and the New Year 1947/48, was a debonair man in his early forties. He was born in Aïn M'lila in Algeria. As revealed in his indiscreet memoirs, *Le Magicien d'Aix*, published after his death, his first sexual encounter was with Maurice Escande[1] of the Comédie-Française.[2] Escande was lodging with the well-to-do Dussurget family while on tour with the Comédie: the troupe performed Racine's *Britannicus* at the Roman theatre at Timgad (1919). Shortly afterwards, Dussurget moved to Paris to finish his schooling. He mixed in homosexual circles, meeting writers, musicians and other artists. On passing his *baccalauréat*, in or around 1923, he briefly tried to follow a conventional path, working as a French teacher at a school in London despite having little English. He went to see *Tosca* at Covent Garden, his first opera, and met a young man during the interval who became a friend – this was Benjamin Britten. (I wonder whether Dussurget misremembered the date in his memoirs, for Britten didn't spend time in London until he started lessons with Frank Bridge at the age of fourteen in 1928.)

Back in France, to appease his family, Dussurget worked for a Paris bank, but only for a few months. One of the curious things about

Dussurget is that for the first thirty-odd years of his life he achieved nothing at all outside of the personal sphere. His family was wealthy. At the age of twenty-four he came into his inheritance and there was no need to work. He eschewed work and followed a path of pleasure. In 1928, he met Henri Lambert. Together they consumed art, especially theatre and opera, in Paris, Salzburg and Venice, where they rented a palazzo for part of the year.

It wasn't until the beginning of the war that Dussurget, who now needed to work to avoid being deported to Germany under the forced labour scheme (Vichy's *Service du travail obligatoire*), found a role that would initiate his distinguished working life. He co-founded, with Lambert, a concert agency, the Bureau des concerts de Paris; and, with the Comédie-Française's Jean-Louis Barrault, Madeleine Renaud, Pierre Bertin and Julien Bertheau, a drama school at the Théâtre Daunou. The agency was soon representing artists of the calibre of the composers Francis Poulenc and Olivier Messiaen, the cellist Maurice Gendron, the pianist Yvonne Loriod, and the violinist Ginette Neveu, whose tragic death in a plane crash at the age of thirty-nine robbed the world of one of its greatest musicians. Messiaen composed *Vingt regards sur l'Enfant Jesus* on Dussurget's piano because he didn't have one of his own.

Dussurget supported Messiaen and his other clients skilfully, managing their careers during the Occupation. He needed to adhere to the demands of the German censor and the anti-Jewish legislation; he was helping his artists to continue to work, which meant organising concerts that were attended by the German occupiers and their mistresses. Some *resistants* viewed this as collaboration. Star performers and ensembles came under pressure to perform in Germany. The German Ambassador Otto Abetz's chosen method was to charm and befriend the artists he admired, inviting them to attend parties at the German embassy and country weekends at the Château de Chantilly. Some went, others kept their distance. The occupying authorities expected Germany's great orchestras and theatre companies to be invited to Paris by their French counterparts. Somehow Dussurget managed to negotiate his way through this minefield. Rather like Lily in Marseille, he managed to keep on the right side of the Germans without collaborating with them.

The concerts he organised, at either the Salle Gaveau or the Théâtre Sarah-Bernhardt, featured a wide range of works, from masterpieces of the Baroque era to cutting-edge premieres. After the Liberation, Dussurget was appointed by De Gaulle's provisional government to chair one of the *comités d'épuration*,[3] a highly sensitive task because it involved investigating individuals in music charged with collaboration.

In February 1945, Dussurget organised a concert at the Salle Gaveau of English music, the first half named *Introduction à la Musique Anglaise* and the second *Hommage à Henry Purcell*. Later that year, he was a co-founder of Roland Petit's innovative, youthful, Ballets des Champs-Elysées at the Théâtre des Champs-Élysées on avenue Montaigne. Boris Kochno was the artistic director. Dussurget and Lambert selected the young dancers and managed the company. The company received great acclaim but folded when Petit and Kochno fell out and Petit decided to depart. The owner of the Théâtre des Champs-Élysées asked Dussurget to direct the theatre. In 1947, Dussurget programmed Mozart's *Così fan tutte*, casting young singers and inviting the Austrian maestro Joseph Krips to conduct the opera. With Krips came the Vienna Philharmonic.

ii DISCOVERING AIX

The immediate post-war period was a time when people's need for renewal found expression in artistic innovation and the establishment of new institutions beyond Paris. The French and Occitan worlds had never felt so connected. The Cannes Film Festival, the most glamorous and internationally focused of these innovations, was launched in 1946. Jean Vilar's theatre Festival d'Avignon, created in 1947, had a different ethos, egalitarian and socialist, but was, in its own intellectual and philosophical way, just as glamorous. It had long been known that the dry hot nights and old stone courtyards and arenas of Provence provided wonderful settings for theatre performances and concerts in the open-air – the Chorégies d'Orange Festival, in that city's Roman arena, had been active since 1869, and the Comédie-Française's performance of *Œdipe roi* in the Roman arena at Nîmes in 1922 was reviewed by *The Times* of London[4] – but the Avignon Festival was the first permanent institution with a national profile to be created there since the war.

Dussurget's experience of bringing *Così fan tutte* to the Théâtre des Champs-Élysées had provoked in him the aspiration to establish a Mozart festival in France. He knew Lily Pastré because they moved in the same artistic circles. At Christmas 1947, they joined forces. Inspired by that magical *A Midsummer Night's Dream* of 1942, she was thinking along the same lines and spoke to Dussurget about establishing a festival of music in Marseille, ideally at Montredon. For Dussurget, this coming together with Lily Pastré was a godsend. She had the local contacts and the financial clout. They agreed to set to work immediately. Dussurget, though, felt that Marseille was too big and raucous. They agreed to consider smaller towns. Reading Dussurget's acidic and rather cruel comments about the countess's bohemian eccentricities and physical appearance in his memoirs, provokes the thought that he did not consider her to be an equal partner.

Dussurget was something of an aesthete. He especially loved in Mozart's music its refinement and elegance of expression. He had attended the Salzburg Festival throughout the 1930s and found the idea of a French Salzburg irresistible. Although it was winter, and the plane trees bare, when Dussurget, Lambert and Lily Pastré arrived in Aix and saw the beautiful Cours Mirabeau, followed by the courtyard of the Archbishop's Palace (cour de l'Archevêché), they knew that they had found their town. The courtyard offered the ideal space for a music theatre. It was large enough but felt intimate, and Dussurget was right to predict that, because of the high walls that enclosed the space, the acoustics would be very good. While Dussurget knew that Aix had the beauty and climate for open-air music-making, he sensed that it would need to be won over. Aix was an aristocratic town; its great families protected their privacy and even its shopkeepers were difficult to charm.[5] He was inspired by the notion of staging Mozart's three Da Ponte operas in Aix. All three were concerned with the Mediterranean world, and one, *Figaro*, was indelibly classically French. Aix combined classical elegance with the sensuality of the South. It was a town in which the characters created by Da Ponte and Mozart would feel at home. However, while Mozart's operas would be given special prominence, they would only form one element in the festival of music that Dussurget was planning.

A centre of art and learning since the Middle Ages, it was good for

Dussurget, too, that Aix had a rich cultural heritage and had produced three of France's greatest creative artists, the composer André Campra, the novelist Émile Zola and Zola's boyhood friend the painter Paul Cézanne. While Zola settled in Paris for good, Cézanne spent most of his life in Aix and died there in 1906. He offered the town one hundred of his paintings, but the director of the Musée d'Aix (today's Musée Granet) from the 1890s to the 1920s, Henri Pointier, refused to place a single Cézanne in the collection. It wasn't until 1949 that the town looked to make amends, but it was too late. The paintings were now too expensive. The mayor travelled to Paris and came back with a lithograph.

Aix is a town of drenching light and ochre walls cut in two by lime-green shadows; of dry windblown heat and azure skies; of olive-skinned arms and legs and designer sunglasses; of students riding scooters and old women walking little dogs on narrow pavements. It attracts tourists in the summer but is not a tourist trap. In 1948, it was smaller and quieter. The A8 autoroute did not exist. The apartment buildings that cover the elevated land beyond the cathedral, surrounding Cézanne's studio at Lauves and blocking sight of Mont Sainte-Victoire, had yet to be built. Likewise, the large university campuses on either side of the avenue Pierre Brossolette. Aix was essentially its old quarters on either side of the Cours Mirabeau. The 17th century Mazarin quarter of honey-stoned *hôtel particuliers*, their facades adorned with decorative lintels and elegant *portes-fenêtres* surrounded by carved borders, and the medieval quarter centred on the cathédrale Saint-Sauveur: narrow streets snaking between old houses; facades in shades of ochre; little painted statues of the Virgin Mary occupying high niches; faces of saints and lunatics frozen in stone (*mascarons*); squares shaded by tall plane trees; and the fountains that grace quiet corners. The fact that in 1948 Aix's grandeur was, here and there, a little frayed at the edges only added to its charm. Understandably, few people at this time wanted to think about its accidental role as a deportation hub in the most tragic and notorious episode of the Occupation.

The former Archbishop's Palace beside the cathedral housed in its 17th century rooms, then as now, the Musée des Tapisseries. The large inner courtyard was being used as a service yard for deliveries and maintenance work. There was a plane tree and a fountain. It was Dussurget's gift to see beyond this.

TWO

Creating the Festival

1948-1949

i A DREAM MADE REAL

Following their tour of the town, Lily Pastré, Dussurget and Lambert discussed options in Les Deux Garçons, a Parisian-style brasserie on the Cours Mirabeau. They agreed to immediately begin work. They hoped to open the festival that summer, just six months away. They didn't make their way to the Hôtel de Ville to seek a meeting with the mayor. Instead, they astutely identified the society that ran Aix's municipal casino (the Société du Casino Aix-Thermal) as the key influential local body to get on side. If the Casino agreed to organise and finance the Festival, it could quickly become a reality. The Casino, then based in an imposingly ugly Art Deco edifice on the avenue Bonaparte, near to the place de la Rotonde and the Cours Mirabeau,[1] produced popular entertainments in its own theatre and owned hotels and restaurants. It supported the town through tourism and was legally obliged to divert a percentage of its profits into artistic projects of quality.[2] Lily Pastré made a phone call, and a meeting was organised for later that day. The Casino's head, Jean Bertrand, introduced them to his director of entertainments, Roger Bigonnet. Bigonnet was intrigued by the notion of championing Mozart in the Midi, where Verdi was king. After a few weeks of reflection, he accepted Dussurget's proposal, meaning that the Casino would fund and organise the Festival, with Bigonnet taking on the role of general administrator. Dussurget would be artistic director with complete authority over creative matters. This suited Dussurget far better than having to answer to the Ville d'Aix: no attempt was made for many years to make the municipal authority a stakeholder in the festival that took place in its town. For the inaugural festival, Bigonnet authorised a July opening and a duration of one week. Dussurget hadn't envisaged mounting an opera during the first festival since he didn't feel they would be ready to do it justice, but Bigonnet thought that an opera was necessary to get the festival noticed. *Così fan tutte* was chosen. There would be at least three orchestral concerts. And so it was that the first lyric festival in France was founded by Lily Pastré, Gabriel Dussurget, Henri Lambert, and Roger Bigonnet.

Bigonnet shared Dussurget's ambition to make the festival international. Dussurget sought the approbation of the relevant government ministries in Paris, for this was clearly in the festival's interest as long as there was no interference. Some of the politicians Dussurget spoke to were dismissive of the idea of establishing a classical music festival in the provinces. Mozart's operas were not well known. Aix, they proclaimed, was a provincial backwater. Stars won't work there, and the public won't attend. Dussurget explained that his vision for the festival was that it should be a place where young and up-and-coming artists would be discovered. Thankfully, Jacques Jaujard (Director General of Arts and Letters at the Ministry of Education) and Louis Joxe (Director General of Culture at the Ministry of Foreign Affairs) were both supportive. Next, he looked for backing within the arts community. Having run his agency for some years he knew how to negotiate these waters. However, the task proved to be frustrating and inconclusive. There was as much opposition as support. Poulenc was in the latter camp.

Dussurget went to the Conservatoire and was relieved to secure its student orchestra (Orchestre des cadets du conservatoire): the student players and their young director, Pierre Michel Le Conte, were full of enthusiasm. But Le Conte was very inexperienced. Dussurget admired the outstanding Austrian conductor Hans Rosbaud, having heard his Mozart concerts on the radio. Rosbaud agreed to become the festival's music director, conducting two of the orchestral concerts as well *Così fan tutte*. Le Conte would conduct the third concert. Because Rosbaud had been the director of the Orchestre philharmonique de Strasbourg during the Occupation, there was some opposition to his appointment. But Rosbaud had earned admiration in Strasbourg because he had supported his players while keeping his distance from the Nazi party. It was later revealed that his brother Paul, a scientist working in publishing, had risked his life spying for the British (providing intelligence on the Germans' V2 and atomic bomb programs) as well as by organising the escape of Jewish colleagues. The Americans placed Hans Rosbaud in charge of the Münchner Philharmoniker in 1945.

ii 1948: THE FIRST FESTIVAL

Start small but think big might have been Dussurget's motto in 1948. A makeshift stage, just a small semi-circular platform with drapes under a basic canopy, created by Dussurget's friend the designer Georges Wakhévitch, was constructed in one corner of the courtyard, with a service shed behind serving as the backstage. Hard wooden chairs of the type used by cathedrals were placed in several blocks on the level ground. The old plane tree rose from a gap between the rows. It was rough and ready, and somewhat amateurish. Rosbaud stood before a small chamber orchestra of student players, for there was no room for anything grander. On all sides, the old stone walls of the courtyard, and, above, the sky, a luminous pale blue at dusk, deepening through violet into indigo and then black, speckled with stars. Swallows singing, as if part of the orchestra.

Rosbaud was Dussurget's trump card. He gave the festival an instant cachet. He was a progressive who championed contemporary music, and Dussurget intended to place performances of contemporary music at the heart of the Festival's programme of concerts. He had conducted works by Mahler (who, with his spectacles and dark hair, he resembled), Bruckner and Berg long before these masters became fashionable. He had premiered pieces by Schönberg, Bartók and Boulez. He was restricted during the Nazi era, but, before and after, his range was broader and more eclectic than that of his great Austrian or German contemporaries including Herbert von Karajan, and in this sense he was the precursor of later conductors such as Simon Rattle.

The Rosbaud described by Dussurget in *Le Magicien d'Aix* was paradoxical. His approach was extremely exacting, but he coached the singers patiently and gently. Dussurget related that, on occasions, he clashed with Rosbaud over casting decisions. He made some disparaging comments about the conductor's motives that I won't repeat here because Rosbaud can't reply. When these casting disagreements occurred, Dussurget didn't back down, and was even prepared to lose his music director. Luckily, Mme Rosbaud loved her summer sojourns in Aix, so he always came. The revealing point here is Dussurget's strength of character in keeping absolute control over artistic policy and casting. Edmonde Charles-Roux, whose mother was Lily Pastré's close friend, found Rosbaud 'irresistible, humble and in love with his orchestra'.[3]

The inaugural festival ran smoothly enough. The production of *Così fan tutte* was staged by Marisa Morel. Dussurget's young singers were mostly underpowered. He admitted that they were no more than honest.[4] Only the Italian mezzo Jolanda Gardino would forge a notable career. Edmonde Charles-Roux remembered the first night fondly. The production was improvised but charming. A north wind was blowing, and the people of Aix were reluctant to attend. Most of the spectators came from Marseille.[5]

More significant than the opera, perhaps, was a chamber concert devoted to the music of Rameau, given by the harpsichordist Pauline Aubert, the violinist Paolo Borciani, the cellist Franco Rossi, and the singers Ninon Alexander and Julien Giovannetti in the *grand salon* of the Musée des Tapisseries. The pieces were the Quatrième and Cinquième Concerts and the Cantatas *Orphée* and *Aquilon et Orithie*. Dussurget's advocacy of Rameau, a great master then pitifully undervalued, would be one of the features of the Festival going forward.

Also in the Musée des Tapisseries, the pianist Jean Doyen played Mozart, Dukas and Ravel (*Le Tombeau de Couperin*). Dussurget organised chamber concerts in venues throughout the town. A concert in the place des Quatre-Dauphins was devoted to Darius Milhaud. Dussurget invited the organist Bernard Gavoty to give a recital in the cathedral, hoping that he would write about the Festival in *Le Figaro*, for Gavoty wrote reviews under the pseudonym Clarendon. Gavoty would write about the Festival, but not until the 1949 edition. Eager to reference Cézanne, Dussurget wanted to place some concerts at the painter's family home, the Jas de Bouffan. The property's owner would only allow the Festival to use the park, so Clara Haskil gave a recital of Mozart's sonatas under the trees, accompanied by the ceaseless drone of the cicadas. Dussurget was discovering that performing classical music in a town that wasn't wholly on side, taking over places that had never been used for concerts, was risky. During a concert of Mozart's chamber music in the beautiful courtyard of the Hôtel Boyer d'Eguilles, residents in the buildings across the narrow street listened to their radios at full volume and refused to stop.

iii 1949: MOZART'S DON GIOVANNI

The 1948 festival did not receive national coverage, but it laid down a marker. Dussurget and Bigonnet made extraordinary progress in time for the 1949 edition, creating a programme that had the scale and stature to attract attention at home and abroad. A shrewd impresario, Bigonnet told Dussurget that it was necessary to make a 'grand statement'. Even though Bigonnet will be mentioned only occasionally in this narrative, his importance should not be underestimated.

The artist and designer Cassandre was commissioned to transform the courtyard of the Archbishop's Palace into an opera theatre (the Théâtre de l'Archevêché) while preserving, as far as possible, its character and atmosphere. The stage was constructed against the righthand side wall of the courtyard (as viewed from the entrance), the wall with the fountain; facing it, filling most of the rest of the courtyard, he placed raked stalls and a balcony. This configuration would be used for the next twenty-three years. The stage had width but limited depth. The pit could only accommodate a small orchestra.

The 1949 edition lasted for three weeks. Crucially, Dussurget was able to secure two renowned orchestras, Rosbaud's Orchestre de Sudwestfunk de Baden-Baden and the Orchestre de la Société des concerts du Conservatoire de Paris (the future Orchestre de Paris), beginning its twenty-two years as the Festival's resident opera ensemble. Ernest Bour shared conducting duties with Rosbaud. Also invited were the Lausanne Chamber Orchestra, under Victor Desarzens, the Nuovo Quartetto Italiano, the Calvet Quartet and the Pasquier Trio. New performance spaces included the Château de la Mignarde, a magnificent 18th century mansion and park, where Rosbaud and Bour conducted the Orchestre de Sudwestfunk in works by Bizet, Chabrier, and Johann Strauss.

Edmonde Charles-Roux was a member of the organising team. She remembered that during the early years of the Festival the staff members were inseparable.[6] They worked all hours, rarely getting to bed before five in the morning. There were no offices. Meetings took place in the café des Deux-Garcons, in full view of journalists and the public. The large attic of the Musée des Tapisseries, stifling and dusty, was hastily converted into a workshop where the artists went for their costume fittings. The ethos was to support the artists, to keep them happy. This was not always easy. Because of an argument over tempi, two members of the Nuovo Quartetto Italiano abandoned their colleagues and began to walk to Marseille. The festival team chased after them in a car.

The journalists who arrived in Aix that July discovered an enterprise that was well organised and presented despite the difficulties. As Dussurget had predicted, Aix beguiled them as it had beguiled him. The opening concert, given at the Théâtre de l'Archevêché by Bour and the Orchestre de la Société des concerts du Conservatoire (henceforth abbreviated to Orchestre des concerts du Conservatoire in these pages), consisted of Mozart's Symphony no. 35 and Concerto for Piano no. 24 in C minor, alongside two lesser-known pieces – the *Idomeneo* suite and the Concert Aria 'Mia speranza adorata' (K416). Robert Casadesus and Clara Ebers, of the Hamburg Opera, were the distinguished soloists. René Dumesnil admired the quality of the playing and the acoustics. Dussurget's bold and imaginative concert programming continued. A solo recital by Casadesus featured pieces by Rameau (from his keyboard Suites) and Debussy (the second book of Preludes). This illuminating pairing predated Víkingur Ólafsson's album *Debussy-Rameau* by seventy years. 'The tone achieved by Robert Casadesus was marvellous,' wrote Dumesnil, 'and it seems that this sorcerer has the art to charm the birds, for a goldfinch (others say a warbler, but it doesn't matter) mingled his voice with the trills of the pianist, his rival.' The great guitarist Andrès Ségovia gave a recital of works by Bach, Scarlatti, Sor, Albenez and Couperin.

The festival's centrepiece was a new production of *Don Giovanni* by Jean Meyer, designed by Cassandre and conducted by Rosbaud. Meyer, a member of the Comédie-Française, had emerged as a leading director during the war. Like Peter Hall, he was a classicist with a modern outlook. He set the production in a late 18th century lost to danger and decadence and brought to the opera form the same questioning intelligence that marked his work at the Comédie. Dussurget, then, had persuaded one of the finest young directors of the era to come to Aix to stage the Festival's first signature production. He had also assembled a strong cast of young singers: Renato Capecchi (Don Giovanni), Marcello Cortis (Leporello), Clara Ebers (Anna), Suzanne Danco (Elvira) and Emmy Loose (Zerlina). Meyer and Cassandre dressed the men in the dandyish attire of the *Muscadins* and used candlelight imaginatively. The costumes and wigs were beautifully made by the Parisian design houses used by the Comédie-Française. The visual beauty and attention to detail that marked Aix's productions under Dussurget were revealed for the first time. Bigonnet allocated more money to the Festival than his masters at the Casino were comfortable with, but the budget was still tight. Many people worked for free. Others came to accept that they wouldn't be paid until much later, if at all, but stayed anyway. Dussurget and Bigonnet had a remarkable gift for achieving the highest standards on a shoestring.

Rosbaud's direction of the music matched Meyer's concept. Edmonde Charles-Roux told Laure Adler that Rosbaud took the music very seriously but not himself. He was a musician like the others. This approach resulted in a congenial and creative working environment.[7]

Aix's *Don Giovanni* was widely acclaimed. Renato Capecchi was only twenty-five, a deliberate choice by Dussurget. Clarendon, in *Le Figaro*, believed that he was too young to inhabit the soul of the seducer, but others felt that a youthful Don Giovanni transformed the opera. François Mauriac wrote: '[Capecchi] wore the frock coat and wig of the marquis de Sade. Almost an adolescent, with an insect-like thinness, he made me feel all the morbidity of the character, his icy ferocity.'[8]

The 1949 edition established the Festival d'Aix as a major summer music festival. And surely Edmonde Charles-Roux was right in her belief that the miracle of Aix, as she called it, was partly the consequence of the moment of its creation. It was intimately connected to people's determination to make the most of a future that only a few years before had seemed impossible. 'It was suddenly as if the mistral had swept everything away and Aix had once again become a place of freedom.'[9]

It appears that Lily Pastré was already slowly and quietly withdrawing from any active participation in the Festival. Decades later, in an interview,[10] Edmonde Charles-Roux commented that the countess was out of tune with Dussurget's determination to create one of the great festivals and the pace with which he operated. She had envisaged, perhaps, a kind of continuation of the community she had built at Montredon during the war; a festival that would be the creation of a close-knit community of friends, with the relaxed ethos of amateur music-making despite the calibre of the people involved. The first festival partly conformed to this model. From 1949 onwards, though, the Festival was professionally run and internationally focused. Because of its success, it became an enterprise. Edmonde Charles-Roux was saddened by the effect this had on Lily, recalling that there were surly people who took her for a mad woman.[11] This is indeed sad, for, without her, it is unlikely that there would have been a festival at Aix.

THREE

A Golden Decade

1950-1959

i 1950/51: MOZART'S COSÌ AND MESSIAEN'S TURANGALÎLA

Dussurget and Bigonnet decided that the opera programme for most editions of the Festival would consist of one new production and two revivals. This policy of revivals kept good work alive while being cost-effective. Dussurget invited great painters to design the productions. He told Edmonde Charles-Roux, who had accepted the role of director of communication: 'We should strive to rediscover the spirit of the Ballets russes by bringing together the finest painters and composers.' In 1950, Balthus, who had assisted his friend Cassandre on *Giovanni*, designed Jean Meyer's new production of *Così fan tutte*. Balthus had created the décor for Jean-Louis Barrault's production of Albert Camus's *L'État de siège* at the Théâtre Marigny in Paris in 1948.

We learn from Dussurget's memoirs that both Meyer and Rosbaud rejected Balthus's painted backcloth. 'Leave, then,' Dussurget told them.[1] Rosbaud decided to stay, but Meyer, wanting a design that served his concept, understandably withdrew. Dussurget asked one of his singers, Marcello Cortis, to take over as director. Balthus's set, a beautiful dream-like depiction of the bay of Naples, was applauded every night.

However, none of this was publicly announced. Meyer was still credited, and critics reviewed the production as his work. This may suggest that Meyer had completed the staging before the dispute.

Meyer's *Don Giovanni* was revived alongside *Così* and the productions shared the same singers, most of them returning from 1949: Suzanne Danco (Donna Elvira and Fiordiligi), Emmy Loose (Zerlina and Despina), Renato Capecchi (Don Giovanni and Guglielmo), Léopold Simoneau (Don Ottavio and Ferrando), Eugenia Zareska (Dorabella), Marcello Cortis (Leporello and Don Alfonso), Raphaël Arié (the Commander), and Eraldo Coda (Masetto).

Yves Florenne, of *Le Monde*, believed that Aix could claim its own Mozartian style, a style characterised by elegance and liveliness. For the first time, an English newspaper sent a reviewer to Aix. The reviewer, A.P. (Andrew Porter?), didn't enjoy the open-air setting, commenting that the playing 'mounted so directly to the stars that little of it was audible to the audience'. The dark comedy of Meyer's staging didn't work for him. 'Don Giovanni is a mincing, affected fop, but worse than that a clown playing to his adoring audience.' This critic did admire Suzanne Danco and Simoneau but thought that Rosbaud's interpretation of the score was 'dull' and complained about 'provincial standards'.[2]

The concert programme was strong, featuring neglected masterpieces of the Baroque and new works. At the Théâtre de l'Archevêché, Wilhelm Kempff performed concertos by Bach, Mozart, and Beethoven; Nadia Boulanger conducted 'musiques oubliées' (works by Haydn, Bach, Monteverdi, Rameau, and Graun); Pizzetti's Requiem was juxtaposed with Bartók's Divertimento for Strings; and both Monteverdi's *Orfeo* and Vivaldi's *Giustino* were given in concert. Bour conducted. There were two European premieres: Poulenc's Concerto pour piano, with the composer at the piano (Charles Munch conducted), and – the orchestral event of the Festival – Messiaen's great *Turangalîla-Symphonie*. Roger Désormière conducted the Orchestre national de la RTF.

In 1951 Dussurget upped the ante as far as the opera programme was concerned. For the first time he mounted three new operas at the Théâtre de l'Archevêché. Alongside Mozart's *Die Entführung aus dem Serail*, he placed an *opera buffa* by Mozart's Italian contemporary Domenico Cimarosa, *Le Mariage secret*, and a contemporary comedic work, *Le Téléphone* by Gian Carlo Menotti, presented as a double bill. The Orchestre des concerts du Conservatoire was conducted by Rosbaud, Gian Andrea Gavazzeni, and Jean Gitton. In only the fourth edition of the Festival, by choosing to give the European premiere of a new opera, albeit one slight in quality, Dussurget was making a clear statement about his vision for Aix. It was clever programming.

Dussurget placed one director in charge of all three. Like Jean Meyer, Pierre Bertin had risen to prominence at the Comédie-Française. A very experienced comic actor and director, his style combined wit, invention, and lightness of touch. Dussurget's policy of inviting great painters to design Aix's Mozart productions continued with the arrival of André Derain to design *Die Entführung*. Derain created vibrantly coloured stage pictures that were theatrically conservative. His reputation was still suffering because of his trip to Germany during the war and the accusation of collaboration that followed. Edmonde Charles-Roux saw that he was anguished. 'He carried his trip to Germany like a cross,' she said. Dussurget was apolitical. He believed in understanding, reconciliation and second chances, where they were warranted, hence his invitation to Rosbaud and his German orchestra and to figures tainted by accusations of collaboration. Edmonde Charles-Roux – a member of the Resistance during the war – shared that view.[3]

Bertin played the non-singing role of Selim Bassa himself. The singers were Victoria de los Ángeles (Constanza), Emmy Loose (Blondine), Ernst Haefliger (Belmonte), Angelo Mercuriali (Pedrillo), and Fritz Ollendorff (Osmin).

The 1951 season was notable for the emergence of the twenty-four-year-old soprano Graziella Sciutti, who played Lucy, opposite Michel Roux, in Menotti's two-hander *Le Téléphone*, and Elisatta in *Le Mariage secret*. This was the young Italian's stage debut. The consensus view was that Aix had witnessed a revelation, for Graziella Sciutti was that relatively rare thing in opera, a natural actor. Both pieces were received as entertaining fripperies, expertly realised by Bertin and his singers. Fritz Ollendorff, Pierrette Alarie, Eugenia Zareska, Gérard Souzay, and Ernst Haefliger completed the cast of *Le Mariage secret*. A young professional designer, the highly regarded François Ganeau, created the sets.

The edition's opening concert took place in the Jardin Campra, at the rear of the cathédrale Saint-Sauveur and next to the Théâtre de l'Archevêché.[4] Gunter Wand conducted the Orchestre de chambre Gürzenich de Cologne in Beethoven's Symphony no. 1, Mozart's *Serenata notturna*, and Cherubini's Sinfonia. These forces also performed symphonies by Haydn and Mozart, the Oxford and the Haffner, in the gardens of the Château du Tholonet. At the Hôtel d'Espagnet (Hôtel Maurel de Pontèves dit d'Espagnet), on the Cours Mirabeau, the Quintette Boccherini performed music by Pugnani, Guerrini and Boccherini.

For the first time, the Festival journeyed into the Luberon. The Collegium Musicum Italicum, Rome, under Renato Fasano, performed works by Albinoni, Cimarosa, Vivaldi, Marcello, and Pergolese, at the Château de Lourmarin. A 'Fête de Nuit', on the beautiful terraces of the Château d'Ansouis, before the facade of the château, gloriously illuminated, featured pieces by Adam, Gluck, Debussy, and Johann Strauss. Rosbaud conducted the Orchestre des concerts du Conservatoire.

ii 1952: MOZART'S FIGARO AND BRITTEN'S MICHELANGELO

At the beginning of the 1952 season, the distinguished writer and critic Robert Kemp wrote of Aix: 'This is our Salzburg.'[5] This must have pleased Dussurget greatly, but, in truth, he was engaged in a project that would make Aix unique amongst Europe's music festivals. Dussurget would make both early and contemporary music synonymous with Aix; he would champion the stage works of Monteverdi, Vivaldi, Rameau and Purcell (works then rarely played in full in France and never in Strasbourg); and he would give exposure to the avant-garde as well as the pioneers of the early years of the century. The festival thrived because of his astute casting of young singers, the quality of the guest artists and ensembles, and the broad range of his programming. In making decisions, Dussurget followed his own taste and instincts, later admitting that he had never been a scholar of music.[6] In England, there was recognition of Dussurget's achievement. *The Times* gave this assessment:

> France was late in entering the field of the holiday music festival, but has already found, as in the other arts of civilized living, how to contrive something uniquely attractive. The Aix festival, now in its fifth year, resembles Edinburgh in being international and in using Mozart's operas as one pillar in the

structure of its programme. But it is much less strenuous.[7]

The 1952 edition was the first to have an English component. Dussurget programmed Purcell's *Ode to Saint Cecilia* in the cathédrale Saint-Sauveur and invited the Boyd Neel Ensemble to play music by Byrd, Gibbons, Locke, and Leonard Berkeley. The very young soprano Jacqueline Delman made her debut. Most significantly, Benjamin Britten and Peter Pears gave a recital in the courtyard of the Hôtel de Ville.

Aix's first cycle of the Da Ponte operas was completed by *Le nozze di Figaro*. Rosbaud conducted the Orchestre des concerts du Conservatoire. This time, instead of turning to an established director in Paris, Dussurget chose Maurice Sarrazin. Sarrazin had recently founded the Grenier de Toulouse company and was at the forefront of the new theatre movement. Antoni Clavé's imaginative sets and costumes were more theatrically effective than Derain's. He dressed Chérubin in a red military jerkin: it stood out against the green décor. Sarrazin wanted wooden boards, solid walls, and three dimensions despite the limited space. Clavé achieved this. Sarrazin's direction was admired for its theatrical lucidity and sensitivity to the music.

Graziella Sciutti returned to play Suzanne. Robert Kemp, writing in *Le Monde*, called Sciutti's sparkling Suzanne magnificent. Aix regulars Michel Roux and Marcello Cortis sang Figaro and Bartholo. The critic of *The Times*, however, found the singing and playing 'wooden' and the director's concept 'misconceived' because it failed to indicate the class distinctions. On the production's revival a year later, Yves Florenne admired the performance of Jacqueline Delman as Chérubin. Graceful, mischievous, and ready to die for love, he compared her to a Shakespearean heroine.[8]

The final opera at the Théâtre de l'Archevêché was Gluck's *Iphigénie en Tauride*. This was the first French-language opera to be performed at Aix, but its appearance had not been expected. Gluck's operas were rarely performed at this time. Dussurget had made a bold choice. The critics, though, approached the premiere as a duty rather than a pleasure.

To conduct the opera, Dussurget appointed a young maestro from Italy who was on the verge of stardom: Carlo Mario Giulini. Dussurget went to Milan to offer Giulini the role at short notice after the conductor initially engaged, Roger Désormière, fell ill. Giulini was passionate about the score: the orchestra, and the listeners, responded. The director was Jan Doat. André Masson designed the production. Giulini became artistic director of La Scala the following year, but he would return to Aix.

The concert programme was typically varied and included the second performance of Henri Dutilleux's meditative, lyrical, Symphony no. 1 following its premiere in Paris earlier that year (Jean Martinon conducted the Orchestre de Sudwestfunk de Baden-Baden), and a new collaborative orchestral work called *La Guirlande de Campra* that Dussurget had commissioned in honour of Aix's son André Campra. Seven French-based composers (Honegger, Daniel-Lesur, Roland-Manuel, Tailleferre, Poulenc, Sauguet and Auric) each wrote a variation on a theme from Campra's opera *Camille*. This agreeable celebration of French music was performed by the Orchestre des concerts du Conservatoire. Rosbaud conducted.

In the Cathedral, alongside the Purcell, the Orchestre des concerts du Conservatoire and the Ensemble vocal de Paris performed Couperin's *Motet de Sainte Suzanne* and works by Handel and Vivaldi. Andrès Ségovia gave a solo recital at the Hôtel de Ville. In the place de Saint-Jean-de-Malte, the Nuovo Quartetto Italiano's programme included quartets by Mozart, Schubert, and Kodaly. It was here that the Boyd Neel Ensemble gave two concerts. The critic of *The Times* wrote evocatively: 'The breathless stillness of the summer night encouraged in the players a quiet style of playing. The audience sat in darkness beneath the trees, the front of the church was floodlit, and the sounds of the orchestra floated up into the indigo sky.'[9]

Dussurget and Benjamin Britten had maintained a friendship since before the war. Dussurget stayed with Britten and Pears when he was in London. Britten and Pears drove down to the south of France in Britten's Rolls-Royce. They stayed with Dussurget in his house on the Chemin de Repentance and attended some of the concerts before their own recital in the beautiful open-air setting of the courtyard of the Hôtel de Ville.[10]

It was a cleverly constructed programme: Britten's arrangements of the French folk songs 'La Belle est au jardin d'amour' and 'Le Roi s'en va-t-en chasse'; Dowland's 'In Darkness Let Me Dwell' and Purcell's 'Man is For Woman Made'; and Schubert's 'Auf der Brück', 'Grabe an Silmos', 'Im Früling', 'Nacht und Traüme', and 'Der

Müsensohn'. The recital's main work was Britten's song cycle *Seven Sonnets of Michelangelo*, composed in 1940. Between songs, Poulenc was heard to say: 'Mais le jeu de piano... merveilleux.'[11] Dussurget related, in his memoirs, that a black cat appeared on the podium and rubbed itself for a long time against Pears's legs. The singer didn't miss a beat.

For once, the French and English critics were in agreement. Yves Florenne felt that the music was being created in the moment and admired how Britten's score, in its tender subtlety and ambiguous voluptuousness, matched Michelangelo's words.[12] 'The stillness of the open air,' wrote *The Times*, 'produced a keener, finer acoustic condition than any hall, and the subtlety of [Britten's] art was appreciable to the last nuance.'[13]

iii 1953/54/55: ROSSINI, GOUNOD AND GLUCK

1953 to 1955 were years of consolidation. Rossini entered Aix's repertoire in 1953. *Le Barbier de Séville* played alongside *Le nozze di Figaro*. It was obvious programming to run the two operas together, but, surprisingly, Dussurget didn't cross-cast them. Giulini conducted *Le Barbier*, and as was logical, Sarrazin directed. Derain designed. The cast, led by Aix's own Capecchi and La Scala's Cesare Valletti, was strong. A revival of *Così fan tutte* completed the programme at the Théâtre de l'Archevêché. The American soprano Teresa Stich-Randall began her long and distinguished Aix career as Fiordiligi. Graziella Sciutti played Despina. Simoneau, Capecchi, and Cortis, returned to the roles they had created in 1950. Dussurget had built a company of young singers, singers who had charisma and real acting ability. Others would soon join the troupe, among them Rolando Panerai, Teresa Berganza, and Michel Sénéchal. Dussurget loved his singers, and they loved him back. This meant a lot to him. In his memoirs he remembered that the singers were inseparable.[14] Teresa Stich-Randall told an interviewer: 'What created the style of Aix-en-Provence was a different spirit compared to Strasbourg or Vienna or anywhere else. Of course, we came to Aix from all walks of life knowing how to sing Mozart, but the Mozart of Aix was simply more joyous. During this era everything was a dream at Aix, the public, the atmosphere.'[15]

Dussurget increased the number of contemporary works performed. These concerts often took place in the courtyard of the Hôtel Maynier d'Oppède, in the shade of the plane trees. Honegger's *Concerto da camera*, Stravinsky's *Dumbarton Oaks*, Darius Milhaud's *Cinq études* for Piano and Orchestra and *Les Amours de Ronsard*, and Schönberg's Chamber Symphony no. 1, were all presented in 1953. In 1954, Dussurget premiered a new French opera, *Les Caprices de Marianne* by the composer Henri Sauguet, based on Alfred de Musset's play. Jean Meyer returned to direct, and Graziella Sciutti sang the role of Marianne. The work was slight, for in its libretto and music it failed to acknowledge the bitterness and pain that resided beneath the surface of Musset's enigmatic work.

Dussurget was content to programme the occasional, carefully selected, 19th century opera. The operas of the middle decades of the 19th century, with their large forces, were unsuited to the small stage and orchestra pit of the Théâtre de l'Archevêché, so he looked for an alternative venue. In examining this repertoire, Dussurget preferred French operas to the more popular Italian. Because of its Provençal setting, he chose Gounod's *Mireille*, a work based on Frédéric Mistral's poem *Mirèio*. Dussurget conceived a grand project for the work, for it was decided to present it at the spectacular natural setting of Les Baux-de-Provence, below the fantastical, fractured, white rocks of the Val d'Enfer. André Cluytens conducted the Orchestre des concerts du Conservatoire. Already one of the great singers of his generation, Nicolai Gedda, in his debut season at Aix, played Vincent. The production, directed by Jean Meyer and designed by Georges Wakhévitch, amazed in its spectacle but not its music, for how could Gounod's delicate score survive in this vast open space? Nevertheless, it was a glorious idea, brilliantly realised.

Cluytens, or rather his wife, made demands that exasperated Dussurget, and he would make an example of them in his memoirs. Cluytens had directed the Opéra de Lyon during the Occupation and had been too close to the Germans. Denounced by one of the theatre's workers, he was investigated by the *comité d'épuration* chaired by Dussurget. Cluytens's wife, in tears, begged Dussurget to pardon him. Dussurget and his colleagues on the comité found Cluytens guilty but declared that he should be rehabilitated. Therefore, his career continued. Mme Cluytens didn't thank Dussurget when she arrived in Aix with her husband. She rejected the house that had been reserved for the couple and rejected twelve more that she was taken to see. In the end, the couple stayed at the Hôtel du Pigonnet, where, according to Dussurget, her demands drove the manager mad.[16]

The 1954 edition saw the arrival of Herbert von Karajan, at the head of the Philharmonia Orchestra of London. Karajan's programme, at Les Baux-de-Provence, included Britten's *Variations on a Theme of Frank Bridge*. Karajan demanded a fee of 3,000 dollars.[17] On the appointed day, the members of this grand orchestra, larger than the norm for Aix, arrived at the train station and were taken to their hotel in a fleet of coaches. In 1955, revivals of *Le nozze di Figaro* and *Così fan tutte* played alongside a new staging, by Meyer, of Gluck's *Orphée*, starring Gedda in the title role. The Italian baritone Rolando Panerai, appearing for the first time at Aix, was an outstanding Figaro in *Le nozze*. Singing Chérubin was another of Dussurget's discoveries, the young Spanish soprano Pilar Lorengar. The programming of contemporary works continued with a concert in the courtyard of the Hôtel Maynier d'Oppède: Rosbaud conducted Honegger's *Pastorale d'été*, Berg's *Kammerkonzert* for piano, violin and thirteen wind instruments, Webern's *Five Movements* for strings, and Milhaud's *La Création du Monde*.

iv 1956: RAMEAU'S PLATÉE

In 1956, Dussurget celebrated the bicentenary of Mozart's birth by reviving the Festival's most acclaimed production, the 1949 *Don Giovanni*. Antonio Campo starred as Giovanni. Teresa Stich-Randall played Donna Anna; Suzanne Danco and Marcello Cortis reprised the roles of Elvira and Leporello; and the American soprano Anna Moffo made her debut as Zerlina. Mozart's music dominated the concerts given by the two resident orchestras and the Nuovo Quartetto Italiano in the place des Quatre-Dauphins.

The edition's main event, though, was the staging of an opera by Rameau. Dussurget had been an admirer of Rameau's music since seeing *Castor et Pollux* at the Paris Opéra in 1930. This was years before the revival of interest in the French Baroque spearheaded by pioneers of period instruments and historically informed performances. Before these pioneers there was Dussurget. Dussurget set out to rectify the neglect of Rameau by introducing his music to the public at Aix, starting with two of his cantatas during the inaugural season. Now, he placed one of Rameau's forgotten masterpieces on his main stage. *Platée* had been suggested by Roger Désormière, and Désormière would have conducted the opera had he not fallen ill.

Most of Rameau's operas were never staged. The common view of his operas was that they were harmonically advanced, but dramatically inert, remnants of the *ancien regime*. The two works that had been staged in France in recent times, *Castor* and the *opéra-ballet Les Indes galantes*, mounted successfully at the Paris Opéra in 1952, were produced using re-orchestrated and edited scores, but at least they modified people's view of Rameau. Dussurget wanted to present *Platée* as faithfully as the current scholarship would allow. *Platée* was neither a *tragédie lyrique* nor an *opéra-ballet*. It came out of Rameau's work for the Paris fairs and was the cruellest of comedies, a satire on both the ruling class and the ruled, that parodied French and Italian musical styles along the way. It was first performed in 1745, during the Dauphin's wedding to the Infanta of Spain, a famously ugly young woman whom it was assumed, wrongly, that Rameau was ridiculing.

The score was reconstituted from the original manuscripts by the musicologist Renée Viollier. Dussurget worked for weeks in Paris with his chef de chœur, Elisabeth Brasseur, and the members of the Chœur du Conservatoire. Michel Sénéchal played the title role. A fine character actor as well as a fine singer, he made the part his own. Nicolai Gedda sang Thespis, André Huc-Santana Jupiter, David Thaw Mercure, and Janine Micheau La Folie. Neither Rosbaud nor the musicians of the Orchestre des concerts du Conservatoire were familiar with Rameau's art, but the production was a success. Director Jean-Pierre Grenier and designer Jean-Denis Malclès, celebrated for his work at the Comédie-Française and his collaborations with Jean-Louis Barrault and Jean Anouilh, staged the work with style and panache. Yves Florenne praised the brilliance of the spectacle but devoted much of his review to Rameau, recognising that *Platée* was a unique opera that combined comedy with profound and beautiful music.[18]

The Times sent a special correspondent to review the production. The correspondent found it beautifully done but didn't rate the music. His review revealed that Rameau's admirers faced an uphill battle in their quest to achieve international recognition for the composer: 'Musically speaking [*Platée*] is insignificant, but it has been revived with a blend of imagination and scholarship, and it deserves a good airing before being put back in the dusty cupboard with the rest of Rameau's operas.'[19] *The Guardian*'s correspondent, Colin Mason, felt that few of the singers had 'much command of the operatic vocal style of the period' when compared to their English counterparts, but admired the choreography and the dancing. He felt that the work was 'amusing' and could 'probably be seen several times with enjoyment'. As for the Festival, he wrote: 'The generally careful and purposeful planning of these concerts, the excellent operatic policy, and the consistent and intelligent support of modern music, combine to give the Aix programme an admirable unity and balance.'[20]

To accompany *Platée*, Dussurget mounted another comic opera of the French Baroque, *Zémire et Azor* by Grétry (1771). Sarrazin directed. It didn't fare as well. 'Rameau's loose change would have enriched poor Grétry,' wrote a critic.

v 1957/58/59: BIZET'S CARMEN AND BOULEZ'S MALLARMÉ

In the three seasons that ended the decade, Dussurget provided a summation of the previous twelve years by reviving all three of the Da Ponte operas and Rossini's *Le Barbier de Séville*. *Die Zauberflöte* joined the repertoire in 1958 and there was a fascinating rarity – Haydn's *Le Monde de la lune* in 1959 (both designed by Malclès). He also embraced the avant-garde: the last two of the three years belonged, in large part, to Pierre Boulez. Dussurget had no fear of journalists who were new music sceptics, such as the correspondent of *The Times* who wrote of 'M. Pierre Boulez unleashing a serialist composition in the peaceful courtyard of the Hôtel Maynier d'Oppède'.[21]

The 1957 season was unusual because there was little contemporary music. Dussurget went for the spectacular by mounting Bizet's

Carmen in the outdoor setting of Le Tholonet. Jean-Pierre Grenier and François Ganeau threw everything at the vast stage, including horses and children, and achieved a grand effect by lighting the hillside of rocks and trees that rose behind the stage. Pierre Dervaux of the Paris Opéra conducted the Orchestre de l'Association des Concerts Pasdeloup.

The setting overwhelmed most of the singers but not Jean Madeira's Carmen. 'Miss Jean Madeira rode the whirlwind,' wrote Jeremy Noble in *The Observer*, 'and I don't mean side-saddle. This must be the sexiest interpretation of Carmen on record.'[22] With such a Carmen, the production was a success, but Noble felt that it was 'a bit of a circus' and wondered whether Bizet (and Gounod) were too populist and provincial for an international festival. Dussurget was ahead of the critic of *The Observer* in recognising that *Carmen* was a masterpiece but didn't follow through by staging it at the Théâtre de l'Archevêché with the seriousness that was applied to Mozart. Noble admired the singing of Graziella Sciutti and Teresa Stich-Randall in that year's revival of *Le nozze di Figaro* but was dismissive of Rosbaud and the orchestra. He believed that Rosbaud was one of the two best interpreters of contemporary scores in Europe but found his conducting of Mozart's operas 'run-of-the-mill and stodgy'. Rosbaud's intellectual, rigorously analytical approach, was anti-romantic at a time when Mozart was usually performed romantically.

The French critics particularly admired the 1957 revival of *Così fan tutte*, the last to be conducted by Rosbaud. The young Spanish mezzo-soprano Teresa Berganza played Dorabella, alongside the Fiordiligi of Teresa Stich-Randall. It was Teresa Berganza's operatic debut. She had been recommended to Dussurget by her teacher at the Madrid Conservatoire. He auditioned the twenty-four-year-old and cast her on the spot. The revival became known as the *Così fan tutte* of the two Teresas. One critic mixed his metaphors: they were 'two jewels shining equally', they were 'birds of paradise'. Also new at Aix, were the Peruvian tenor Luigi Alva (Ferrando) and the striking Italian soprano Mariella Adani, aged twenty-two. Adani trained at the academy of La Scala. She played Despina in *Così*, as well as Chérubin in *Le nozze di Figaro*. She would return every year until 1967, singing, principally, Despina and Zerlina in *Don Giovanni*.

One of the invited ensembles, Louis Auriacombe's Orchestre de chambre de Toulouse, performed Rameau's Concert no. 6 and Jean-

Marie Leclair's *Scylla et Glaucus* suite alongside neoclassical works by Albert Roussel and Jean Rivier, at the Château de Fonscolombe, in the countryside north of Aix, a new venue for the Festival.

In 1958, Dussurget more than made up for the scarcity of new music in the previous year's edition. Rosbaud was a mentor of Pierre Boulez. He had premiered some of his pieces at Baden-Baden, including the mesmerising *Le Marteau sans maître* for voice and six instruments, which he repeated at Aix during the 1955 festival. In 1958, the concerts given by the Orchestre de Sudwestfunk de Baden-Baden were dominated by 20th century works. At the Hôtel Maynier d'Oppède, Rosbaud conducted pieces by Dallapiccola and Schönberg; and Boulez conducted his *Improvisation I sur Mallarmé* for soprano and percussion instruments alongside Stravinsky's Symphony for Wind Instruments, Stockhausen's *Kontrapunkte* pour dix instruments, and Webern's Symphony op. 21. At the Théâtre de l'Archevêché, where masterpieces by Mozart and other classical composers were expected, Dussurget and Rosbaud selected works by Schönberg, Henze, and Bartók; and Georg Solti, making his Aix debut, led the orchestra in Bartók and Ravel (plus Beethoven). Karajan, Giulini and now Solti – Dussurget had brought the era's three most influential maestros to Aix. Finally, at the cloître Saint-Louis, a new venue for the Festival, Rosbaud conducted Stravinsky's *Le Sacre du printemps*. The cloître Saint-Louis, built in the 19th century on the site of the Couvent des Dames Carmélites, forms part of the Lycée Vauvenargues on boulevard Carnot (named Lycée Carnot before 1962).

Other periods weren't ignored. At the cloître Saint-Louis, the Orchestre Jean-Marie Leclair performed Couperin's *Le Parnasse ou L'Apothéose de Corelli* and Rameau's Concert no. 4. Wilhelm Kempff played sonatas by Brahms and Chopin, and Beethoven's *Bagatelles*, op. 126.

Serious illness forced Rosbaud to withdraw from the 1959 festival. He asked Boulez to take over his concert with the Grand orchestre de l'Institut national belge de radiodiffusion, in Parc Rambot. The programme consisted of Webern's *Six pièces* for orchestra, Berg's *Trois fragments de Wozzeck* for soprano and orchestra (soloist: Helga Pilarczyk), Henri Pousseur's *Rimes pour diverses sources sonores*, and Hindemith's Concerto for Orchestra. Boulez didn't rate the Hindemith (an understatement), but it didn't show. The concert was a huge personal success, launching his career as a conductor of symphony orchestras. The distinguished music critic Claude Rostand wrote of Boulez's seductive power and unexpected mastery.[23] For the piece by the young Belgian composer Henri Pousseur, the orchestra was divided into three units and electronic music was amplified through loudspeakers. Strange sounds drifted between the chestnut trees of Rambot Park. The Grand orchestre de l'INR's second concert, conducted by Edgard Doneux, included Britten's *The Young Person's Guide to the Orchestra*.

The season saw the juxtaposition of early and new music. For the first time, Dussurget invited specialist early music ensembles to Aix. The concert of French, Italian, English and Spanish music given by Pro Musica Antiqua of New York in the courtyard of the Hôtel Maynier d'Oppède included works by Monteverdi, Josquin des Prez, Guillaume de Machaut, Guillaume d'Amiens, Francesco Landino, Guillaume Dufay, Juan del Encina, and Thomas Campion. The Ensemble baroque de Paris performed pieces by Albinoni, Telemann, and Vivaldi, in Parc Rambot.

Haydn's opera-buffa *Le Monde de la lune*, to a libretto by the great playwright Carlo Goldoni, was first performed at Esterhazy in 1777. Aix's production was the opera's first full outing since its premiere. Goldoni's text concerned the duping of a tyrannical father by his daughter's pursuer, disguised as an astronomer. The father is duped into believing that he has been transported to the moon. Haydn's score predicted Mozart's opera-buffas. Dussurget formed a partnership with the Holland Festival to produce the opera – it was Aix's first co-production. Aix regulars Giulini, conducting the Orchestre de la chambre de Hollande, and Sarrazin realised the production with commitment and flair. *Le Monde de la lune* was performed alongside revivals of *Così fan tutte* and *Die Zauberflöte*. As Papagena, Dussurget chose a recent graduate of the Conservatoire who had been in the chorus at Aix, Christiane Eda-Pierre.

FOUR

Expansion

1960-1966

i 1960/61: PURCELL'S DIDO AND MONTEVERDI'S POPPEA

Gabriel Dussurget's success at Aix was recognised in 1959 when André Malraux, Minister of Culture under De Gaulle, appointed him to the new position of *conseiller artistique* (effectively artistic director) of the Paris Opéra. He worked alongside the *administrateur* (general director). Dussurget would fulfil this role for the next ten years.[1]

Hans Rosbaud was seriously ill and unable to return to Aix. He died in 1962. His stature as a conductor of both classical and contemporary music had helped the Festival to develop a distinctive style. Despite their arguments over casting and design, Dussurget's appreciation of Rosbaud's artistry never wavered. He agreed when Poulenc told him that Rosbaud was greater than Karajan.[2]

Dussurget remained committed to 20th century music, but, with Rosbaud gone, there would be fewer modern works in the repertoire until the 1962 season. Britten, Stravinsky and Poulenc were favoured. The French composer Henry Berraud was commissioned to write an opera, continuing a (misfiring) policy that had been initiated with Henri Sauguet's *Les Caprices de Marianne* in 1954. In general, the concert programme throughout the 1960s was less extensive and less radical than it had been during the previous decade.

The first two seasons of the new decade were dominated by the Baroque. For the 1960 season, on the recommendation of Ernest Bour, Dussurget engaged the young maestro Michael Gielen to share the conducting of the Mozart operas with Alberto Erede. Erede also conducted the concerts given by the Orchestre des concerts du Conservatoire. Dussurget continued his advocacy of Campra's neglected music. The programme of the Ensemble instrumental de Provence, under Clément Zaffini at the Hôtel Maynier d'Oppède, included orchestral extracts from Campra's opera *Idoménée* as well as the Concerto for Strings by Stravinsky; and Bernard Wahl's Orchestre de chambre de Versailles performed the Suite from the opera *Fêtes vénitiennes*, the Motet *Exurge Domine*, and the Cantata *Didon*. This orchestra gave three further concerts dominated by early music (Lully, Rameau, Handel, Gabrieli, Telemann). The ensemble I Musici from Rome gave two concerts at the cloître Saint-Louis. They performed Britten's *Simple Symphony*, but the concerts were dominated by Italian works for strings by Vivaldi and the less well-known Torelli, Pergolese, Bonporti, and Giordani.

Gérard Souzay and Dalton Baldwin performed a fine programme of songs by Purcell, Schubert, Fauré, Ravel, and Strauss, at the Hôtel Maynier d'Oppède. At the cloître Saint-Louis, Arthur Rubenstein played Beethoven (the 'Appassionata' sonata), Brahms, Schumann, and Chopin.

Where new productions were concerned, the new decade saw a challenge to Mozart at the Théâtre de l'Archevêché. In 1960, there were two double-bills, Poulenc's *La Voix humaine* preceding Gounod's *Le Médecin malgré lui*, and Vivaldi's *La senna festeggiante* preceding Purcell's *Dido and Aeneas*. The first double-bill, combining Molière with Cocteau, was a delicious prospect, especially since Jean Meyer, a Molière specialist, directed the former and Cocteau the latter. It didn't quite fulfil its promise. Cocteau's production, starring Denise Duval, was a transfer from the Opéra-Comique.

Purcell's *Dido and Aeneas* was given in Britten's realisation. Pierre Dervaux conducted the Orchestre des concerts du Conservatoire. Dussurget went to see the comtesse Geneviève Thibaut de Chambure, then director of the Musée instrumental du conservatoire de Paris, and formerly Conservator of the Royal Library at Buckingham Palace. Her personal collection of ancient instruments was the finest in Europe. She lent Dussurget the instruments he needed to realise Purcell's masterpiece and would later support William Christie and others. Aix's production was the French stage premiere of this work from circa 1688. It was one of the triumphs of Dussurget's directorship; and a personal triumph for one of his singers, Teresa Berganza. Yves Florenne declared that the work was a unique masterpiece. He saw in *Dido* an impossible union of Racine and Shakespeare, a musical dream in which *Bérénice* was haunted by the witches of *Macbeth*. The music pierced and overwhelmed as if brand new. Florenne admired the singing of Teresa Berganza, Gérard Souzay, Henny Steffek and Jane Berbié, and commended Pierre Dervaux for the intensity of tragic expression achieved by the orchestra. The director, Michel Crochot, ensured that Purcell's intimate tragedy was not overburdened by directorial effects. His designer, Suzanne Lalique, best known for her work at the Comédie-Française, where she collaborated regularly with Jean Meyer, delivered traditional sets and costumes of an elegant simplicity. The interplay of tulle and shadows created a sense of mystery.

Revivals of Meyer's *Don Giovanni* and Sarrazin's *Le nozze di Figaro* completed the programme at the Théâtre de l'Archevêché. The revival of *Giovanni* was notable for the Aix debut of the great baritone Gabriel Bacquier, who was superb in the title role. It was the first Aix production to be broadcast internationally by Eurovision. Bacquier was courted by the great European houses, from Covent Garden to La Scala, but he returned to Aix regularly to sing Alfonso, Falstaff and Golaud. In *Figaro*, Teresa Berganza played Chérubin for the first time. Teresa Stich-Randall, Antonio Campo, Rolando Panerai and Marcello Cortis reprised the roles of the Countess, Almaviva, Figaro and Bartholo.

Having served Purcell so well in 1960, the following year Dussurget turned his attention to Monteverdi and fulfilled a longstanding aspiration to fully stage *L'incoronazione di Poppea*. *Poppea* was handed to the production team behind *Dido*, Michel Crochot and designer Suzanne Lalique, who adopted the same approach – stately and refined, with classical décor and costumes in white and bronze, but not devoid of psychological insights or tragic intensity.

Aix used Gian Francesco Malipiero's edition of a work only rediscovered at the end of the 19th century. There had been performances of different (incomplete) editions of the score by student and other amateur groups, but Aix was the first mainstream opera institution to mount a full production. Dussurget beat Glyndebourne by a year and the Vienna State Opera by two years.

The critics concentrated on the importance of the occasion, the rediscovery of a masterpiece. *Le Monde* declared that in *Poppea* and *Dido* everything had been said, for Monteverdi and Purcell were close to Shakespeare. The production benefited from an excellent cast – Jane Rhodes, making her Aix debut, as Poppea, Robert Massard, as Nero, Teresa Berganza, as Ottavia, and Roland Panerai revealing his range as Otone. Bruno Bartoletti conducted the Orchestre de la chambre de Hollande.

While *Le Monde* had nothing but praise for the performance, *The Times* had reservations. The reviewer's points on the shortcomings of the Malipiero edition were fair, although he did not suggest an alternative. 'Malipiero's realisation for strings of the accompaniment to *Poppea* obscures, with the best intentions in the world, the amazing variety of moods and musical styles in which the long sequence of scenes is set.' The reviewer found Bartoletti's conducting limp. As for the singers: 'Unfortunately the performances showed little understanding of the stylistic problems involved. Neither Miss Jane Rhodes nor Mr Robert Massard could supply the vocal agility or, still more important, the sensitivity to harmonic and rhythmic detail that Monteverdi's essentially intimate style demands.'[3]

The tone was condescending. Ten years on from the establishment of the Festival d'Aix, some English reviewers were still making comparisons with Glyndebourne and claiming the superiority of the latter's Mozart productions. Glyndebourne and Aix were too different to be compared effectively, the former mounting operas in a private stately home for an exclusive audience, the latter a music festival in a Mediterranean city, with an open-air theatre and other venues; but it would take many years before this subliminal national bias dropped away. Andrew Porter, writing in 1960, acknowledged that Dussurget had a rare gift for discovering voices, citing Graziella Sciutti, Pilar Lorengar, Consuelo Rubio, Teresa Berganza, and Léopold Simoneau, but continued: 'All of these subsequently went on to Glyndebourne, and there learnt a truer, more refined Mozart style. [...] It is a pity for Panerai that he has never had a Glyndebourne engagement, for he is a singer of great promise. [...] The French have no sound tradition of Mozart. My advice to M. Dussurget is to engage one of the young Glyndebourne producers.'[4]

At this time, French and English ideas on opera performances rarely aligned. One difference is noticeable. Whereas English reviewers of the era tended to give preference to purely musical matters, their French counterparts gave equal weight to acting and the quality of the direction and design.

A second work by Monteverdi, *Il combattimento di Tancredi e Clorinda*, preceded a revival of *Dido and Aeneas*. It was a rewarding pairing. The opera programme was completed by revivals of *Così fan tutte* and *Die Zauberflöte*, conducted by Gielen, and the premiere of Henry Berraud's light opera *Lavinia*, directed by Daniel Sorano. Serge Baudo conducted.

Baroque music once again featured heavily in the concerts at the cloître Saint-Louis and the courtyard of the Hôtel Maynier d'Oppède. The Ensemble baroque de Paris performed music by Scarlatti, Mondonville, Telemann, Mozart, Rameau, and Vivaldi. The Ensemble instrumental de Provence, under Clément Zaffini, juxtaposed pieces by Marcello, Besard, Vivaldi, Haydn, and Cimarosa, with Britten's *Variations on a Theme of Frank Bridge*.

ii 1962: STRAVINSKY AND MILHAUD

Dussurget made the 1962 season a celebration of Marius Milhaud and Igor Stravinsky. In the Théâtre de l'Archevêché, Milhaud's *Les Malheurs d'Orphée* preceded Stravinsky's *Les Noces*. To play this music, Dussurget engaged Pierre Dervaux and the Orchestre des solistes de l'Association des Concerts Colonne. The orchestra also gave two concerts in the courtyard of the Hôtel Maynier d'Oppède during which Milhaud's *Six symphonies pour petit orchestre* and *La Création du monde* and Stravinsky's *L'Histoire du soldat* were the central works. Bartók's *Sonate pour deux pianos et percussion* was also played.

Dussurget had programmed music by Aix's Milhaud over the years, but *Les Malheurs d'Orphée* was the first of his operas to be produced. This short chamber opera of 1926 was staged by the director of the moment Michel Crochot, collaborating with Jean-Denis Malclès. The work, an updating of the death of Orphée set in the Midi, could have been written especially for the open-air Théâtre de l'Archevêché. Stravinsky's *Les Noces*, for singers, chorus, dancers and an instrumental ensemble of four pianos and percussion, was the first modernist masterpiece presented on Aix's main stage. It was premiered by the Ballets russes in Paris in 1923. Dussurget invited the

Russian dancer and choreographer Georges Skibine, his colleague at the Paris Opéra, to stage the work. Both Skibine and his father Boris, murdered during Stalin's Great Purge in 1937, had been members of Diaghilev's company. The pianists were the renowned soloists Geneviève Joy (wife of Henri Dutilleux), Pierre Barbizet, Jacques Février and René Gorget-Chemin. The evening combined French élan with Russian mystery and emotion. René Dumesnil admired the harsh poetry of Stravinsky's score, its mixing of the burlesque with the tragic, and commended the singing of the Chœur du Conservatoire (directed by Elisabeth Brasseur) and the soloists, especially Mady Mesplé who, in the role of the bride, conveyed an underlying anxiety.

This was Mady Mesplé's second season at Aix. In 1956 she played Zémire in *Zémire et Azor* and Lucy in the revival of *Le Téléphone*. Dumesnil also admired the other singers – Christiane Gayraud, Michel Hamel, and André Vessières – but found Natalie Goncharova's design too fussy. The choreography needed more space than the small stage could provide.

iii 1963/64/65/66: MOZART'S IDOMENEO, BERLIOZ'S FAUST, VERDI'S FALSTAFF AND DEBUSSY'S PELLÉAS

The next four seasons were dominated by masterpieces from across the history of opera. In 1963, Richard Strauss's *Ariadne auf Naxos* opened the season, but the spotlight fell on Mozart's opera seria *Idomeneo*, conducted by Peter Maag. Teresa Stich-Randall sang the role of Ilia. A great opera, rarely seen anywhere since its 1781 premiere: unsurprisingly, the faithful and typically handsome production by Michel Crochot and Suzanne Lalique (with choreography by Skibine) was considered revelatory.

Equally significant was a concert performance of Hector Berlioz's *La Damnation de Faust*. *Faust* was one of Dussurget's most important repertoire choices, for Berlioz's music was then neglected. To perform the work, Dussurget created a new ensemble, the Orchestre philharmonique du Festival d'Aix, made up of musicians from the Orchestre des concerts du Conservatoire and the Orchestre des solistes de l'Association des Concerts Colonne. Pierre Dervaux conducted. This orchestra also performed Verdi's Requiem in the cathédrale Saint-Sauveur. A memorial concert was given for Poulenc, who had died that January. The revivals that year included *Die Zauberflöte*. Dussurget invited John Pritchard, who at that time was the principal conductor of the London Philharmonic Orchestra as well as a Glyndebourne man through and through, to conduct the performances.

In 1964, Dussurget programmed Verdi's *Falstaff*, the only new production that year. Verdi's operas were not among Dussurget's personal favourites, and their scale made them a challenge to realise effectively at the Théâtre de l'Archevêché. The Shakespearean *Falstaff* was an exception, dramatically sublime as well as relatively small in scale. And not often played in France. A production at the Opéra-Comique, created in 1952, had quickly been dropped from the repertory. Verdi's first appearance as an opera composer at Aix was a big moment. Dussurget ensured that the production would be a labour of love by handing it to Dervaux and his regular director Crochot and by casting the outstanding Italian bass-baritone Wladimiro Ganzarolli in the demanding title role. Ganzarolli received acclaim for the subtlety of his acting.

Dussurget continued his advocacy of Berlioz by programming *L'Enfance du Christ* in the cathédrale Saint-Sauveur. Robert Casadesus and Zino Francescatti performed sonatas for violin and piano by Beethoven, the 3rd, 6th and 7th. At Parc Rambot, Jean Rivier's Concerto pour basson was premiered.

Monteverdi's *Orfeo* had been given in concert in 1950; in 1965 it was staged. Unusually for Aix, the production was imported. Directed by Sandro Sequi, with sets by Alfred Silbermann and choreography by Clotilde Sakharoff, it had been created at the Opera da Camera di Milano and had previously been seen in France at the Théâtre Montansier in Versailles in 1964. Gianfranco Rivoli conducted the Orchestre des concerts du Conservatoire. The cast was led by Robert Kerns (Orfeo), Christiane Eda-Pierre (Euridice), and Jane Berbié (La messaggera).

That year, some of the concerts took place in the courtyard of the École des Arts et Métiers. Dussurget's Berlioz project continued with performances – by the Orchestre des concerts du Conservatoire under Serge Baudo – of *Le Spectre de la Rose*, *Roméo et Juliette*, and *Les*

Troyens. Perhaps the most significant event was the return of the avant-garde with the visit of a programme of pieces organised by Boulez's Domaine Musical concert society in Paris. The musicians were the string players Gérard Jarry, Serge Collot, and Michel Tournus; the pianist Claude Helfer; and the clarinettist Guy Deplus. Their programme included Boulez's Sonata for Piano no. 1, Schönberg's *Cinq pièces pour piano* and String Trio, Berg's *Quatre pièces pour clarinette et piano*, Stravinsky's *Trois pièces pour clarinette seule*, and Webern's String Trio. A second visit would take place in 1966.

Dussurget formed a collaboration with the Festival de Saint-Maximin-la-Sainte-Baume (east of Aix in the Var) which would continue for a number of years. Here in 1965, at the Couvent Royal, the Orchestre de chambre de La Sarre performed works by Telemann, Couperin, and Louis Marchaud.

Dussurget had wanted to stage Debussy's *Pelléas et Mélisande* for some years and realised this ambition in 1966. The arrival at Aix of *Pelléas* was an important milestone in the history of the Festival. It was the first landmark 20th century opera to be staged. The designer of the production was Jacques Dupont, another veteran of the Ballets russes. Unusually, Dussurget decided that Dupont should take charge of the *mise en scène* too. Dupont's use of tulle curtains and traditional costumes and wigs was effective but old-fashioned. Serge Baudo's interpretation of Debussy's score was admired. He ensured that the delicate sonorities were not lost in the open-air. William Workmann and Eliane Lublinand sang the title roles, but it was the presence and voice of Gabriel Bacquier, as Golaud, that elevated the performance.

It was another good year for the music of the Baroque. Dussurget invited the period instruments ensemble Collegium Aureum to give a concert at the Couvent Royal, Saint-Maximin-la-Sainte-Baume. They performed a suite of dances from Rameau's *Dardanus*, a significant concert. Also at Saint-Maximin-la-Sainte-Baume, the Deller Consort sang works by Purcell, Marin Marais, Michel Pignolet, De Montclair, and Robert de Visée. 'I was amazed by the unclassifiable nature of his voice,' Dussurget wrote of Alfred Deller. 'It was both that of a child and a mythical creature.'[5] In the cathedral, the Schola Cantorum of the University of Arkansas juxtaposed music by Jean Mouton and Josquin des Prez with Britten's *Hymn to Saint Cecilia* and Poulenc's Mass in G major. At Le Tholonet, the Orchestre de chambre de Versailles, under Bernard Wahl, performed Britten's *Serenade for Tenor, Horn and Strings*.

FIVE

The End of the Festival's First Era

1967-1973

i 1967/68/69: DECLINE

At the end of 1963, a crisis within the administration of the Société du Casino Aix-Thermal resulted in Roger Bigonnet's retirement. It seems that some of the executives, including the president, Jean Bertrand, had become worried about the management of the artistic budget, believing that too much money was being spent, money that hadn't been authorised. Bertrand had supported Bigonnet and the Festival since the very beginning, so his volte-face suggests that their relationship had broken down. Bigonnet's departure was a major blow that contributed to the decline in intensity that marked Dussurget's final years in charge. Dussurget had relied heavily on Bigonnet's flexible management of the entire enterprise, as well as his enthusiasm. He was in many ways the public face of the Festival since Dussurget did not seek the limelight. Renowned within a tight and exclusive classical music circle as the magician of Aix, he was largely unknown to the public. *Le Monde* would later call him 'a man of the shadows'.[1] It was a small miracle that Bigonnet had been able to keep his colleagues at the Casino on side for so long.

The excitement of establishing the Festival had created a unique first decade. It was difficult to maintain the sense of magic. The productions of Mozart's *Don Giovanni, Così fan tutte, Le nozze di Figaro* and *Die Entführung aus dem Serail*, so important during the Festival's first seasons, had been revived constantly for over fifteen years: inevitably, they had started to look dated (some more than others) and had lost vitality. It seems that Dussurget was too attached to them. The Meyer/Cortis/Balthus production of *Così fan tutte* was re-designed, by François Ganeau, in 1963 (and would be re-directed, unsuccessfully, by Daniel Leveugle in 1971). Finally, in 1968, there was a completely new production of *Le nozze di Figaro*, directed by Jean-Laurent Cochet and designed by Pierre Clayette. The most radical of Aix's productions of Mozart was replaced by a conventional staging. The setting was one of Aix's great houses, with a view of Sainte-Victoire in the distance. Worryingly, this *Figaro* was the only new opera production offered during the three seasons from 1967 to 1969.

The concert programme remained strong. In 1967 the Orchestre des concerts du Conservatoire was dissolved and reconstituted, by Malraux, as the Orchestre de Paris. The orchestra continued its association with Aix. In 1968, it performed Charpentier's *Leçons des Ténèbres* and Gilles's Requiem in the cathedral and gave two concerts at Le Tholonet: an all-Mozart programme and a French evening consisting of Berlioz's *Symphonie fantastique*, Debussy's *L'Après-midi d'un faune* and Ravel's *Daphnis et Chloé*. The conductors were Jean-Pierre Jacquillat, Lorin Mazel and Baudo. Also at Le Tholonet, the Borodin Quartet was outstanding in quartets by Borodin, Shostakovich, Haydn, and Beethoven.

In 1969, the Ensemble instrumental de France performed works by Mozart at the Château d'Ansouis and was joined by the Maîtrise Gabriel Fauré de Marseille for Britten's *Ceremony of Carols* and Kodaly's *Quatre pièces religieuses* in the cathedral. At Le Tholonet, the Groupe instrumental de Paris performed Messiaen's *Quator pour la fin du temps* and Schönberg's *Ode à Napoléon*. The Quatuor Via Nova gave a concert at the beautiful Abbaye de Silvacane in La Roque-d'Anthéron (Mozart and Schubert). Karajan returned to Aix at the head of the Orchestre de Paris. His concert at the Théâtre de l'Archevêché consisted of Mozart's Concerto for Three Pianos, K245, and Berlioz's *Symphonie fantastique*. However, a strong concert programme could not carry the Festival. It was the operas that received the attention and drew large numbers of patrons to the Festival, particularly from abroad.

Because of Dussurget's close working relationship with Bigonnet, the fact that the Casino essentially owned the Festival had been an advantage for him in the period up to Bigonnet's departure. It meant he could keep the Ministry of Culture and the Ville d'Aix at arm's length and didn't have to deal with politically motivated interference from these powerful bodies. The weakness of his reliance on the Casino, however, now revealed itself. Jean Bertrand took over the general direction of the Festival. The financial health of the Société du Casino Aix-Thermal was his priority. He reduced the Festival's spending on all things, including the salaries of the principal artists. And he believed that the Festival's artistic policy should reflect the interests of the clientele of the Société du Casino Aix-Thermal. These two factors had a direct impact on what Dussurget could do artistically, although he found a way through before 1967. As well as the question of adequate funding to create new work, the Théâtre de l'Archevêché required refurbishment and modernisation.

ii 1970/71/72: THE MINISTRY STEPS IN

In 1969, the Ministry of Culture and the Ville d'Aix reacted to the perilous state of the Festival by providing it with significant subsidies of 100,000 francs each, supplementing the core funding of 500,000 francs allocated by the Casino from an eight per cent tax refund. The State also provided an extra 200,000 francs through the National Fund for Historic Monuments and paid the salaries of the musicians of the Orchestre de Paris while they were in Aix (approximately 450,000 francs). In 1971, the Ministry increased its subsidy to 500,000 francs. The extra funding, though, did not result in an increase in standards. The Ministry issued a protocol that required the organisers of the Festival to seek policy approval from all the bodies providing financial support and began negotiations with the Casino to take over control of the Festival. The Casino resisted. While it was unable or unwilling to allocate the money needed for the Festival to prosper, it didn't want to give up the jewel in its crown.

In July 1972, Pierre Gay, Aix's Deputy Mayor for Culture, gave a speech in which he declared: 'The Festival d'Aix cannot continue as a private enterprise. The child has grown up. The municipality now has an imperative duty to make every effort to enable the Festival to prosper and to expand its audience in our town and region.' The Ministry shared the view that the Festival had failed to engage with local people. There had always been a disconnect between the Festival and the town. A festival of classical music and opera was easily dismissed as the reserve of the *haute bourgeoisie* because this was essentially true. It was the same in Salzburg and Glyndebourne. The Ministry, though, expected state-funded arts organisations to at least strive to be welcoming to all sections of society. The festival's lack of a common touch was thrown into sharp relief in 1972, when the Relais culturel d'Aix and France-Musique organised the first of what would become an annual summer festival of free concerts in the streets and the squares called *Musique dans la rue*. It took place before the Festival d'Aix in June. This rather brazen encroachment onto the territory of the Festival may not have happened had the latter been firing on all cylinders. Because it was free, fun-loving, and broadcast on radio, it was embraced by the townspeople, particularly the young. It was unfairly contrasted with the Festival d'Aix since the latter's concerts in the squares had to be ticketed and were expensive. Nevertheless, the Festival made the mistake of publicly objecting to *Musique dans la rue*. A potential new audience had been created in quick time, and it was doubtful whether Dussurget would be the right artistic director to grasp this moment of change even if funding was provided to reduce ticket prices.

These were hard years for Dussurget. The halcyon days of the 1950s seemed a very long time ago. He was able to mount one new production in 1970, Rossini's *L'italiana in Algeri*, but it wasn't enough. He brought the English Opera Group's productions of Britten's *Curlew River* and *The Prodigal Son* to the Festival, but they were performed only once and not in Aix. The Basilique Sainte-Marie-Madeleine in Saint-Maximin-la-Sainte-Baume was a magnificent venue for these church parables, but it would have been better if they had been placed at the centre of the Festival in the cathédrale Saint-Sauveur. The critic Jacques Lonchampt admired the English Opera Group and was moved by the poetry, refinement, and humanity of Britten's score, citing the dissonances achieved by the sinister Tempter, the use of masks and the Gregorian and East Asian timbres in the instrumentation. It was a strong year for contemporary music, for as well as these austere masterpieces by Britten, there was the premiere of a masterpiece by Henri Dutilleux: *Tout un monde lointain…* for cello and orchestra. Serge Baudo conducted the Orchestre de Paris. Mstislav Rostropovich was the soloist.

In 1971, Dussurget premiered Jacques Charpentier's *Béatrice de Planissoles*, an opera with a libretto in Occitan. The director was Dominique Delouche. Jacques Charpentier conducted. There were revivals of *Die Zauberflöte* and *Falstaff* alongside Daniel Leveugle's new production of *Così fan tutte*. This last was critically savaged and cited as an example of Aix's decline.

In March 1972, Dussurget announced that he would step down at the end of the 1972 season. The Ministry of Culture's negotiations with the Casino had yet to conclude, since the Casino was still not prepared to concede control. The Ministry had the option of withdrawing funding but chose not to take a step that would have meant the annulation of the 1972 edition. There is no evidence that any of the parties required Dussurget to resign. He had been worn out by the uncertainty of the last few years, as well as the artistic compromises, and faced a future in which he would not be able to run 'his' festival in the way he wanted. Hopefully, though, he had come to accept that, after over a quarter of a century, it was time to hand over to other people. The 1972 festival consisted of revivals of *Don Giovanni*, *Le nozze di Figaro*, *Les Malheurs d'Orphée*, and *Pelléas et Mélisande*.

There was no festival in 1973 while negotiations continued. The Ministry increased the pressure, and the managers of the Casino finally accepted the inevitable. Jacques Duhamel, Minister of Culture since 1971, wanted the Théâtre de l'Archevêché to stay at the heart of the Festival and allocated the funding needed for its modernisation (around 200,000 francs). The work needed to be completed in time to allow the reinauguration of the Festival in July 1974. As well as the renovation of the building, the pit was enlarged so that it could accommodate an orchestra of 120 musicians, and the stage deepened by nearly ten metres. This would allow a broadening of the repertoire. Capacity remained much the same at 1,600 places.

Much of Cassandre's theatre of 1949 was bulldozed into rubble and dust – his Italian style proscenium was retained – to leave a wasteland of stones, metal, capsized seats, and threadbare theatrical drapes; for some, it was as if the Dussurget era was being metaphorically dumped. Then, for a brief time, the courtyard was once again an open area over which *boules* clattered and rolled in the dust.

With Dussurget's departure, innovation survived, but it was less apparent in the selection of works, particularly in the concert programming. Under Dussurget, Aix was a music festival that gave equal weight to orchestral music, chamber music, instrumental recitals, and operas. Post-Dussurget, Aix gradually became a festival of operas with some concerts attached.

Part Two

The NIGHTS of BERNARD LEFORT

SIX

A Celebration of Song

1974-1977

i   MISSION STATEMENT

In December 1973, a new beginning for the Festival d'Aix was announced at a press conference at the Hôtel de Sully in Paris. Going forward, the Festival would be run by a new Association, established under a law of 1901, led by representatives of the State and the Ville d'Aix. The key players were Pierre Gay (Aix's Deputy Mayor), Marcel Landowski (Director of Music at the Ministry of Culture), and Jean Salusse (Director of the National Historical Monuments Fund). The man chosen to lead the Festival into this new era was the singer-turned-opera manager Bernard Lefort.

Bernard Lefort was appointed, initially, for four years. The creation of limited contracts and accountability was one of the first innovations of the Festival's new (political) masters. While affection and admiration for the long Dussurget era would linger for some time, there was no denying the malaise of Dussurget's final years.

Lefort was born in Paris in 1922. He trained at the Paris Conservatoire and specialised in light baritone roles, notably in Paris at the Théâtre du Châtelet and the Opéra during the 1950s. When illness forced him to retire as a singer in 1960, he began a second career as an artistic director of opera theatres and music festivals, running, in quick succession, the Lausanne Festival, the Opéra de Marseille, and the Festival d'automne à Paris.

Lefort understood the art of singing intimately and was a fine teacher. As an artistic director and administrator, he was highly organised, creative, and strong-willed, and had a proven track record at the highest level. His first standout statement was: 'The Festival d'Aix must be a grand celebration of *Song*. Song must reign here in absolute mastery, and each production will be consecrated to it either completely or in part.' However, he also said: 'Aix must once again become a place of work and creation. Productions made here will in no way resemble what can be seen elsewhere.' Lefort would engage leading directors and give them the freedom to create work that was distinctive. It would take time for original work to dominate. Lefort's first two seasons would rely on co-productions with other houses.

Dussurget's focus had been on discovering new talent and forming a company. While not ignoring these goals, Lefort shifted the balance in favour of engaging established superstars. Concerning the desire for inclusiveness (the Ministry of Culture's policy of democratisation), he lowered ticket prices and formed an association with the *Musique dans la rue* organisers. The aim was to make the Festival less elitist. The old festival of dinner jackets and ball gowns would be changed by the courting of new audiences. Jazz and folk music would enter the repertoire. And, to increase interest in the Festival and raise additional funds, Lefort made agreements with television and radio to broadcast more of the Festival's shows.

Recognising a gap in Dussurget's programming, Lefort prioritised 19th century *bel canto* operas while continuing his predecessor's advocacy of the Baroque repertoire. Mozart's three Da Ponte operas would be given new productions. He reduced the number of revivals. He would benefit from the reconfigured and improved Théâtre de l'Archevêché. However, he believed that the Festival also needed a second, larger, open-air theatre. Dussurget's artistic collaborators had demonstrated remarkable theatrical guile and panache in making the most of the original Théâtre de l'Archevêché, but the process had always been highly demanding and stressful, and the cramped spaces had been hazardous for performers to negotiate. While Dussurget had chosen striking locations within Aix's orbit to mount the occasional large-scale work, Lefort was seeking a permanent solution. Even after the recent modifications to the stage and pit, the Théâtre de l'Archevêché was too small to accommodate the large forces that were the norm when staging the works of Verdi, Wagner, and other 19th century opera composers. The policy of co-productions with other houses would be restricted as a result. Initiating the process to acquire a new theatre, Lefort identified as a possible location the site of the former black marble quarry outside Aix, near Le Tholonet.

ii 1974: MOZART AND VERDI

Lefort organised the 1974 season in only eight months. He devised a decent programme, focused on song as he had promised, that initiated his survey of 19th century Italian opera, continued Aix's love affair with Mozart, Monteverdi and Purcell, marked the fiftieth anniversary of Gabriel Fauré's death, and showcased international star singers from different worlds – among them Birgit Nilsen, Montserrat Caballé, Elisabeth Schwarzkopf and the American folksinger Joan Baez. Regrettably, the Orchestre de Paris's long service as the Festival's resident orchestra came to an end, although it did give a concert under Colin Davis at Le Tholonet: the works were Mozart's Symphony no. 39 and Mahler's *Das Lied von der Erde* (with the singers Joséphine Veasey and Stuart Burrows). Lefort didn't secure a permanent replacement. The Fauré celebrations were centred on the composer's complete *mélodies* (in recitals by Elly Ameling, Gérard Souzay and Dalton Baldwin) and ended with a performance of his Requiem in the cathédrale Saint-Sauveur: Michel Plasson conducted the Paris-based Orchestre lyrique de l'ORTF and the Ensemble vocal de Provence. Lovro von Matačić's Orchestre national de Monte-Carlo accompanied Birgit Nilsen in extracts from the operas of Wagner, including the final scene of *Götterdämmerung*. Geoffrey Parsons, Hugues Cuenod, and Éric Tappy performed songs by Purcell and Monteverdi at the Église du Saint-Esprit (rue Espariat). Montserrat Caballé sang *bel canto* arias at Le Tholonet, while Elisabeth Schwarzkopf and Geoffrey Parsons performed songs by Schubert, Schumann, and Brahms, at the cloître Saint-Louis.

The 1974 *Musique dans la rue* festivities, preceding the Festival d'Aix, attracted over 100,000 spectators. Lefort wisely opened the Festival with a street production that, in its aesthetics and joyful festival atmosphere, was a continuation of *Musique dans la rue*. This double-bill of two short comic operas, Mozart's *Le Directeur de théâtre* (*Der Schauspieldirektor*) and Pergolesi's *La serva padrona*, was created in the place des Quatre-Dauphins on a makeshift stage built between two of the facades of the square's 18th century houses (the designer was Roger Harth). It paid homage to the 1948 production of *Così fan tutte*, itself a *spectacle de tréteaux*.

Mozart's dramatically slight *singspiel*, concerning an exasperated director and two competing singers, was written during the period of *Le nozze di Figaro* and has music of similar quality. Pergolesi's *La serva padrona*, although seldom seen in over two hundred years, was something of a legendary work in France, for performances of this effervescent forty-minute *intermezzo* by an Italian troupe at the Opéra in the 1750s provoked the *Querelle des bouffons*, a heated public debate that pitted admirers of Rameau and French music against admirers of Italian music, and which featured shouting matches and fistfights in the auditorium as well as the printing of hundreds of poisonous pamphlets. Jean Le Poulain (soon to join the Comédie-Française) directed and played the non-singing role of the Music Director. Jean-Claude Casadesus conducted the Orchestre lyrique de l'ORTF. The American sopranos Faye Robinson and Constanza Cuccaro, both new to Aix, sang the female roles. The men were Jean-Christophe Benoit, Umberto de Pergolèse, and Jean-Pierre Chevalier. These simple comedies did not trouble the mind but, in such a beautiful setting, in the Aix night, they delighted the senses.

The other operas, staged at the Théâtre de l'Archevêché, were Verdi's *Luisa Miller*, a co-production with the Opéra du Rhin, Strasbourg, and Mozart's *La clemenza di Tito*. *Luisa Miller* opened the renovated theatre. The spectators streamed in to discover that the charm of the space had just about been preserved while the ugly tiered seating gave excellent views of the stage from all sections of the auditorium. Director Nicolaus Lehnoff and conductor Alain Lombard's interpretation of this rarely performed work was cool and considered – a startlingly classical reading of an opera by Verdi. Lehnoff used austere, monochrome, sets, and emblematic imagery (an open space with three black trees; an all-white room). There was delicate playing by the Orchestre de Strasbourg. Both the staging and the musical interpretation were too dull and undramatic for Stanley Sadie, writing in *The Times*, and, like many of the reviewers, he judged the singing to be of variable quality.[1] Lefort had announced that José Carreras and Ingvar Wixell would star, but both withdrew. The Japanese soprano Yasuko Hayashi sang Luisa and

Ottavio Garaventa Rodolfo, supported by Jacques Mars, Nadine Denize, Pierre Thau, and Armand MacKane.

Antoine Bourseiller's high-concept staging of *Tito*, from the Opéra de Marseille, was an exercise in abstract expressionism: copper-coloured panels and high platforms; some characters shirtless, others booted; a virile atmosphere that was more fascistic than Mozartian. The staging divided opinion. The concept did not help conductor Alberto Erede, conducting the Orchestre lyrique de l'ORTF. The decision to cast tenors and not sopranos or mezzo-sopranos in the castrato roles of Sesto and Annio destabilised the musical balance. The singers were Noëlle Rogers, Christiane Château, Éric Tappy (as Tito), Gyula Littai, Alan Titus, and Robert Lloyd (highly praised in the small role of Publius). The stage was bigger than before but still not big enough: the chorus, a vital dramatic element, had to sing offstage. Neither show had the impact of the Mozart-Pergolesi performances.

The rectangular place des Cardeurs was cleared of restaurant terraces and cars to create a spectacular enclosed space for the concert given by Joan Baez. 1,500 people attended. Lefort was delighted that just as many people filled the cathédrale Saint-Sauveur for a concert of orchestral pieces and cantata arias by Bach given by the Orchestre Pro Arte de Munich under Kurt Redel. He was rightly content with his first season. He had reignited interest in the Festival and laid a foundation on which he could build.

iii 1975: CAMPRA'S LE CARNAVAL DE VENISE

Instead of funding Lefort's new theatre, the Ministry of Culture asked the festivals of Provence to consider forming a regional hub of shared spaces. The alternative option was to create a temporary performance space at a suitable location in the countryside around Aix, as Dussurget had done at Les Baux. Lefort decided on the first option and formed an association with the Festival d'Arles so that he could stage 1975's showcase production, Montserrat Caballé in Rossini's rarely performed *Elisabetta, regina d'Inghilterra*, in that city's Roman theatre. The curved rows of stone steps, rising steeply, could accommodate some 3,000 spectators. Behind the stage and lighting rig, ancient white stone columns rose between green-flamed cypress trees; and the elegant clock tower of Saint-Trophime overlooked the site. It felt wrong, a dilution, a surrender of identity, to place even a single production at Arles, a rival city with its own strong cultural and geographical character on the edge of the Camargue.

Elisabetta was a co-production with the Opéra du Rhin. The critics found the opera theatrically dull and, for long passages, musically mediocre, with too many self-borrowings, and assumed that Lefort had chosen the piece as a vehicle for Montserrat Caballé. She was in superb voice, as was the English National Opera's Valerie Masterson, who replaced the indisposed Ileana Cótrubas as Mathilde. The venue, open on all sides with no enclosing walls to create a soundbox, frustrated the musicians of the Orchestre de Strasbourg under Gianfranco Masini. Jean-Claude Auvray's staging was conventional, with old costumes borrowed from La Scala, but in the darkness, once the cicadas had fallen silent, Auvray successfully conveyed the cold and gloom of the Tower of London.

The 1975 season opened with André Campra's *Le Carnaval de Venise*, a work not seen since its premiere in Paris in 1699. This was an important event, on a par with Dussurget's resurrection of Rameau's *Platée* in 1956. To direct, Lefort invited Jorge Lavelli, whose recent production of *Faust* at the Paris Opéra had been greatly admired. Lavelli had made his name in the 1960s as a director of contemporary plays, only turning to opera – a form of theatre he had previously disparaged – at the end of that decade. His opera productions of the early 1970s were admired for their lucidity: he created order out of the chaos of the opera form. He did not impose a concept on Campra's *opéra-ballet*, a work that juxtaposed French courtly elegance with the flamboyance of Italian street theatre, but treated it on its own terms, expressing the work's *commedia dell'arte* elements poetically: the images were both theatrical and dreamlike. *Le Monde*'s critic Jacques Lonchampt detected the influence of the Elizabethan stage in the wit and humanity of Campra's *Le Carnaval* as interpreted by Lavelli. As in the RSC's *Comedy of Errors* of 1962 (among other examples), Lavelli's theatre was a box of illusions: light projectors were visible, and the players put on their costumes on stage. For their set, Lavelli and his designer Claudio Segovia used a bare stage and the wall of the courtyard that marked the rear of the stage.

Jean-François Fegnard's libretto begins with an intriguing prologue. Cleaners and stagehands are working, without urgency, to prepare an abandoned theatre for a play. The gods, frustrated by the delay, descend, and in an instant a magnificent theatre is created. The play, concerning two wrongly aligned couples in Venice during carnival, can now be presented.

Hence, Lavelli was able to begin his production with the striking image of a sweeper pushing an old wooden wheelbarrow across an empty stage. The deities stepped from the palace's high windows onto ladders. The players donned their carnival masks and costumes of white, gold, deep red and black.

The leading roles were played by Roger Soyer (Léandre), Christiane Eda-Pierre (Isabelle), Michel Philip (Rodolf), and Christiane Château (Léonore). Michel Plasson conducted his Orchestre du Capitole de Toulouse. The dance sequences were choreographed (in a modern style) by Norbert Schmucki.

The season's third new opera production, the second at the Théâtre de l'Archevêché, and the second to be co-produced with the Opéra du Rhin, was another *bel canto* work, *L'elisir d'amore* by Donizetti. The production, by Werner Duggelin, was too fussy for such a simple tale. The show was a personal triumph for a veteran of the Dussurget era, Gabriel Bacquier, playing Dulcamara. Armin Jordan conducted a Strasbourg orchestra that was still struggling to play at its best in the open-air. Michel Guy, the Secretary of State for Culture, attended the opening, and Lefort paid tribute to the Festival's co-founder, Roger Bigonnet, who had died in January.

Lefort revived the Mozart-Pergolesi double bill in the place des Quatre-Dauphins, and once again turned the place des Cardeurs into a venue for a free concert. This was the year that jazz came to the Festival d'Aix. Bass, drums, piano and the soulful voice of the legendary Ella Fitzgerald turned the night air blue and pulsated around the ancient square, packed to the far walls with smiling faces. Elsewhere, the concert programme fell heavily in favour of early music. Michel Plasson and the Orchestre du Capitole de Toulouse performed instrumental extracts from Rameau's *Castor et Pollux* in the église de la Madeleine. In a recital of French and English music, given in the cloître Saint-Sauveur by the distinguished instrumentalists Trevor Pinnock (harpsichord), Jordi Savall (viol), and Stephen Preston (flute), and the soprano Judith Nelson, the central works were

Rameau's early Cantata *L'Impatience*, Purcell's Suite for Harpsichord no. 5, and Marin Marais's Sonate *La Maraisienne*. The concert included rarities by Thomas Arne, John Jenkins and Thomas Attwood. Hugues Cuenod and the lutenist Joël Cohen performed songs by Dowland and Guillaume de Machaut at the Château d'Ansouis.

Lefort continued the Berlioz cycle initiated by Dussurget by inviting Alain Lombard to conduct *Roméo et Juliette* in the cathédrale Saint-Sauveur. The singers were Nadine Denize and Roger Soyer. Also in the cathedral, Carissimi's *Jephté* and madrigals by Monteverdi were performed by the Ensemble vocal et instrumental de Lausanne under Michel Corboz. The pianist Christian Ivaldi and the singers Hugues Cuenod and Jean-Christophe Benoit gave a recital of songs by Erik Satie at the Commanderie de la Bargemone in Saint-Cannat.

iv 1976/77: MOZART RETHOUGHT, STOCKHAUSEN EMBRACED

The programme for 1976 at the Théâtre de l'Archevêché consisted of Verdi's *La Traviata*, in a production by Jorge Lavelli, and the first *Don Giovanni* of the post-Dussurget era. The returning Orchestre du Capitole de Toulouse was in the pit for both productions.

Reviewing *La Traviata* for *Le Monde*, Gérard Condé thought that Michel Plasson's musical direction was too metronomic, lacking emotion and constraining an able cast of singers. In contrast, Lavelli 'highlighted all that is implied in the drama – the hypocrisy of society and people, solitude, the closed world of the bourgeoisie'. His designer, Max Bignens, created a box set in wood, deliberately claustrophobic and coloured symbolically for each act, red, white, and black. The idea seemed to be that Violetta was metaphorically imprisoned, while the fragility of her position was conveyed by the intrusion of street prostitutes into her gilded world, a reminder of what she really was. The young Hungarian soprano Sylvia Sass, unknown in France until this moment, was outstanding as Violetta.

The spotlight fell on the new *Don Giovanni*, the beginning of a four-year plan to mount the three Da Pointe operas. To direct the production, Lefort, who to his credit wanted a new beginning and not an act of homage to the old *Giovanni*, invited another of France's leading younger directors, Jean-Pierre Vincent, head of the Théâtre national de Strasbourg. Vincent's collaborators were the actor-director Jean Dautremay and the designer Patrice Cauchetier. Inevitably, veteran patrons of the Festival compared Vincent's production to its predecessor and found it wanting, a rejection of the Aix style of presenting Mozart. But that style was the style of the 1950s. Vincent, directing his first opera production, brought to the assignment the same rigorously intellectual approach he used when directing a play. He placed the opera in the same philosophical landscape occupied by Diderot and Rousseau, and his interpretation of the leading characters was compelling and modern, if not new. Richard Stilwell's Giovanni was jaded and cynical. Similarly, Stafford Dean's Leporello was not the traditional buffoon but a sardonic and sinister schemer. The permanent setting – a cyclorama of clouds and a few statues – had to serve for all scenes. Its romanticism was ironic. Its starkness was striking. The roles of Anna, Elvira and Zerline were played, respectively, by Yusuko Hayashi, Elena Mauti-Nunziata, and Sylvia Lindenstrand. Robert Lloyd was a formidable Commadore. Jésus Lopez-Cobos conducted.

The season's final opera was Luigi Cherubini's *Médée* of 1797. Lefort decided to use Arles's antique theatre for the second time despite the openness of the location, its vulnerability to the mistral. It provided an ideal setting for this opera based on plays by Euripides and Pierre Corneille. Under Dino Yannopoulos's direction, the distinguished soprano Leonie Rysanek excelled in the title role, supported by Constanza Cuccaro (Glauce), Nadine Denize (Neris), Veriano Luchetti (Jason), and Dimiter Petkov (Créon). Serge Baudo conducted the Orchestre de Lyon.

Songs for voice and piano dominated the concert programme. Intimate recitals were given at the cloître Saint-Sauveur by, among others, Robert Lloyd and André Raynaud (Schubert, Finzi, Verdi, Gibbs), Gérard Souzay and Dalton Baldwin (Purcell arranged by Britten, Gounod, Brahms, Samuel Barber), Bernard Kruysen and Noël Lee (Debussy), and Sylvia Lindenstrand and Janos Solyom (Purcell, Laci Bodelman, Berg's *Sept lieder de jeunesse*). Montserrat Caballé and Jessye Norman both sold out the Théâtre de l'Archevêché. In the cathedral, Serge Baudo conducted the Orchestre de Lyon in the rewarding pairing of Puccini's *Missa di Gloria* and

Arthur Honegger's *La Danse des morts,* to words by Paul Claudel.

In 1977, the Festival's relationship with the Orchestre du Capitole de Toulouse continued. The other resident orchestra was the highly regarded English Chamber Orchestra, a coup for Lefort. Charles Mackerras made his Aix debut conducting the ECO and a fine cast of young singers in *Così fan tutte.* Aix's first and most iconic opera was entrusted to Jean Mercure, director of the Théâtre de la Ville in Paris. He followed Jorge Lavelli by using the windowed wall of the courtyard as his set. It was a beautiful if somewhat austere setting for some of the more intimate scenes. His was a sombre reading, elegantly staged, that suggested that the two young women – Valerie Masterson and Sylvia Lindenstrand, equally beguiling – were vulnerable rather than fickle; and that, in the end, although they played the game, they would make their own choices. During the overture, they changed the phrase 'Così fan tutte' written on a blackboard to 'Così fan *tutti*'. The men were played by Knut Skram and Francisco Araiza. Gabriel Bacquier gave a masterclass as Alfonso without upstaging his young colleagues. His scenes with Norma Burrowes's sparkling Despina were magical.

The interpretation of the music had never been stronger. 'Charles Mackerras sustains the spirit of the music with unremitting verve and particular understanding,' wrote William Mann in *The Times.* 'On the whole this *Così fan tutte* was the most completely musical performance of the opera that I have ever heard and the most enjoyable.' High praise indeed from one of England's most important critics, a writer who valued the genius of the Beatles as much as the genius of Mozart. Of Mercure's direction, Mann wrote:

> His attitude is sensitive and correct. The six characters are presented as real people, the drama thought through, the events shown neatly with some illuminating imagery. In 'E la fede' Alfonso juggles two oranges which he throws to the soldiers who exchange them similarly: the oranges are their sweethearts, and at the end of the opera Mercure decides that the boys and girls cannot resume their *status quo ante partners* (I agree with him, though many devotees do not). Mercure wanted us to laugh without hypocrisy: we did. Mackerras wanted us to hear Mozart. We did too.[2]

Mann's review marked the moment that English reviewers finally stopped comparing Aix unfavourably with Glyndebourne. This *Così* was worthy of any of the leading opera theatres of Europe, but its initial reception in Aix was somewhat subdued.

Valerie Masterton and Sylvia Lindenstrand joined Robert Lloyd in performances of Bach's *Magnificat* and Mozart's *Exultate Jubilate* in the cathedral, one of several concerts given by the English Chamber Orchestra. The conductor was Ralf Weikert.

The other opera at the Théâtre de l'Archevêché was Donizetti's *Roberto Devereux*. Montserrat Caballé starred as Elizabeth I, opposite José Carreras. These two outstanding voices dominated a traditional production by Alberto Fassini. Julius Rudel conducted the Orchestre du Capitole de Toulouse. One of the singers, Grace Bumbry, withdrew at the last minute. Lefort engaged Janet Coster to replace her: she had to learn the part in eight days. Lefort showed his mettle by revealing the circumstances of the crisis at a press conference:

> I hired Mrs Bumbry by contract in October 1976. She was to arrive here on 9 July. However, in February she signed another contract to sing on 9 July in the United States. She therefore knew that she could not come to Aix but said nothing about it. Opera houses are increasingly falling victim to these savage processes. Let it be known that I am suing Mrs Bumbry as I sued, three years ago, Ingvar Wixell, who should have appeared in *Luisa Miller*. I won that lawsuit and I will win the one against Mrs Bumbry, from whom I will seek damages of 250,000 francs.[3]

To make matters worse, freak thunderstorms wrecked one of the four performances of the opera. The drenched spectators were ushered into the cathedral where they were told that the performance would continue. However, after half an hour it was announced that this had proven to be impossible, although whether this was because of technical problems or, as was rumoured, because Montserrat Caballé had demurred to wing it in the cathedral, was not made known. There were angry scenes.

Instead of reviving Mozart-Pergolesi for a third time, Lefort asked Jean Le Poulain and Roger Harth to create a new entertainment in the place des Quatre-Dauphins. The two works chosen were Domenico Cimarosa's *Il maestra di capella* and Donizetti's *Il campanello di note*. Le Poulain came up with a neat way of connecting the two pieces. In Cimarosa's slight *intermezzo*, a pompous fool of a conductor causes musical mayhem rehearsing an orchestra. At the end of Le Poulain's production, Jean-Christophe Benoit, playing the conductor, was taken away by nurses. The night's real maestro, Ralf Weikert, then jumped onto the podium to conduct Donizetti's pitch-perfect comedy. A girl marries an old apothecary; her jealous former lover disrupts the wedding night by assuming disguises and repeatedly ringing the doorbell. Stafford Dean, Lajos Miller, and Faye Robinson sang the principal roles; Jean-Simon Prévost played the spoken part of the apothecary. Roger Harth placed cabinets and rows of apothecary bottles around the square.

The 1977 season ended with the premiere of a major work of the avant-garde, Karlheinz Stockhausen's *Sirius*. The festival had ignored contemporary music for three years, so Stockhausen's residency at the cloître Saint-Louis – he ran a three-week academy for young musicians, named the Sirius Centre, leading up to the performance of the work – was something of a relief. The project, funded by the government, was instigated by Michel Guy, and organised by Jean Maheu, with the agreement of the Festival.

Stockhausen drew on science-fiction, astronomy, his own dreams, and the cycles of life and nature, in the creation of a vast musical tapestry. Some commentators interpreted the work as a modern mystery play. Perhaps more intriguing is the presence of masonic ideas. The score combines electronic music – endless circles of complex polyphony – with four solo instruments: trumpet, bass clarinet, bass, and the soprano voice, each representing a different element, season, or human characteristic. However, the meaning of the work was a mystery to its composer. Introducing the piece, he said: 'It's an organic process rather than a work of mine. I prepared this process, and the work came out of it. I followed the sounds as a hunter follows the track of an animal. It's up to each person to give meaning to this music.' The music 'imitates the perpetual mutation of nature by a process, made possible by the synthesizer, of the metamorphosis of sounds'. The electronic music was pre-recorded on eight-track tape. As well as a tape deck, Stockhausen's equipment included four transmitters, five microphones, eight loudspeakers and a mixing console. The soloists were trumpeter Markus Stockhausen, soprano Annette Meriweather, bass clarinettist Suzanne Stephens and bassist Boris Carmeli.

The centre, renamed Centre Acanthes, would run training sessions and masterclasses during the Festival until 1986. The festival collaborated with the Centre, co-producing one or two of its concerts each season. After 1986, the Centre Acanthes moved to Avignon, Metz, and finally to IRCAM in Paris.

SEVEN

Premature Departure

1978-1981

i 1978/79: HANDEL'S ALCINA AND MOZART'S FIGARO

For the 1978 edition, centred on two masterpieces of the English Baroque, Lefort formed an association with Scottish Opera and the conductors Raymond Leppard and Charles Mackerras.

Handel's *Alcina*, little known at the time in France, was staged by Jorge Lavelli, returning to Aix following his acclaimed productions of Campra's *Le Carnaval de Venise* and Verdi's *La Traviata*. Leppard conducted the Scottish Chamber Orchestra and a very fine cast: as Alcina and her sister Morgana, Christiane Eda-Pierre and Valerie Masterson (confirming her status as the young star of the Lefort era) were beautifully matched, while, as Ruggiero, Teresa Berganza made a triumphant return to the theatre where she had made her name; Bradamnante and Oronte were played by Ann Murray and Philip Langridge.

Lavelli and his designer Krystina Zachwatowicz utilised the whole width of the stage and the wall of the courtyard, transformed, the fountain, and lighted windows, barred. The staging was highly stylised. Alcina's realm was conveyed by shiny black surfaces and screens, funeral shrouds, and plants with dagger-shaped leaves; her previous victims, transformed into animals, were imprisoned in cages. The characters wore simple black costumes. Alcina and Morgana's faces were ashen and mask-like, the faces of their servants even more so. Lavelli took as much care over how the characters moved, synchronising with the music, as Leppard did over the notes themselves: as a result, an extraordinary unity of expression was achieved. The disguised Bradamante, on a quest to rescue Ruggiero, was the only character dressed in white. The symbolism, if obvious, was dramatically effective. 'This must surely be the most striking production yet of a Handel opera,' wrote Stanley Sadie in *The Times*. 'Musically it was even more distinguished. Justly chosen tempos, numerous sensitive details of timing, accompaniment carefully balanced and always unobtrusively supporting to the singer.' Sadie particularly admired the way Christiane Eda-Pierre sang the tragic music of the second half, humanising Handel's villainess; and Valerie Masterson's 'warm, ringing tone and spirited style'; as for Teresa Berganza, she 'relished everything she did, acting with zest, singing with accuracy and rhythmic precision, and graceful in the lyrical aria'.[1]

The production of Purcell's *Dido and Aeneas*, preceded by his *Ode to Saint Cecilia*, was less successful. A co-production with Scottish Opera, it was given in a routine staging by John Copley and designer Stefanos Lazaridis. The designs were both garish and bland, the stage too cluttered and the costumes difficult to wear comfortably. With Mackerras at the podium, the musical interpretation was first-rate. Janet Baker, making her debut in the role in France, was magnificent. The opening night was accident-prone. The audience members were fractious, irritated by the intrusive television cameras. They were confused by the non-opera that opened the evening. A robe worn by one of the singers got caught on a sharp object and had to be ripped off.

The season's 'street' production, in the place des Quatre-Dauphins, was a staging of Donizetti's comic opera *Don Pasquale*. Jean-Louis Thamin directed; Gianfranco Rivoli conducted the Orchestre philharmonique de Radio-France. Gabriel Bacquier savoured the playing of the title role; spectators savoured seeing and hearing the great actor-singer at such close quarters. That year's popular music concert in the place des Cardeurs was given by Ray Charles and the Raelettes.

Between the 1977 and 1978 editions, Lefort had been offered and had accepted the directorship of the Paris Opéra. He would take up the position in June 1980, but would remain in charge of the Festival d'Aix until 1981. He told *Le Monde* during the 1978 festival that he hoped his successor would be selected by the end of 1979, to give enough time for a smooth transition. In the same interview, he revealed that the building of a new theatre remained the top priority. The festival had outgrown the Théâtre de l'Archevêché: its seating capacity was too small, meaning that ticket prices were too high. The festival had to cover sixty-five per cent of its outgoings from ticket sales. It needed, he said, a theatre with around 3,500 seats. Progress had been made. A site at the old black marble quarry near Le Tholonet had been agreed upon. The Ville d'Aix had purchased the site and approved Lefort's plan. The cost of building the new theatre would be around twenty million francs. Lefort's next task was to talk to the government. As long as his successor had the necessary prestige and ambition, Lefort believed the theatre would be built, and quickly.[2] In fact, by the end of 1980 the plan had been abandoned in favour of the building of a new theatre as part of the redevelopment of the Sextius-Mirabeau quarter. (This was finally realised in 2007 with the opening of the Grand Théâtre de Provence.)

The most eagerly anticipated production of the Lefort era was Jorge Lavelli's *Le nozze di Figaro*, opening the 1979 festival. The first night audience was disappointed. Lavelli's cold reading of the work challenged people's perceptions of the opera. He lifted the drama out of the pre-French Revolution 18th century and placed it at the beginning of the 20th, thereby negating the impulses that lay behind Beaumarchais's play. He looked beneath the surface and between the notes and decided that the characters were not as they appeared to be and directed his singers accordingly. In Lavelli's productions of Campra, Verdi and Handel, the *mise en scène* was in sync with the music, but here there was a tension, a feeling that his direction was fighting against the music. This was particularly true of the bizarre last act, an exercise in heavy-handed irony. The characters were now dressed in 18th century dress, but with chalked faces, more like puppets than people. The production was at least thought-provoking.

Where Mozart was concerned, the Festival's core audience was, at this time, notably conservative. Some spectators booed when Lavelli and his designer Max Bignens (responsible for the glass and steel décor) walked on stage during the curtain calls. In *Le Monde*, Jacques Lonchampt declared, with sadness, that the production was a failure. Whereas Mozart subtly suggested psychological motivations, Lavelli underlined them.[3] Mihaï de Brancovan, writing in *La Nouvelle revue des deux mondes*, condemned the production, and criticised Lefort's policy of engaging theatre directors with limited experience of opera. He named Giorgio Strehler, Peter Hall and Jean-Pierre Ponnelle as three directors Aix should be courting.[4] William Mann at least admired the performance of the music:

> M. Lefort is a self-confessed anglophile. For this year's *Nozze di Figaro* he booked Valerie Masterson as the Countess, Ann Murray as Cherubino and Neville Marriner with the Academy of St Martin in the Fields. British admirers could only be content with the charming, touching and true portrayals by the ladies and by the spry, involved playing and [musical] direction – perhaps too few graces and too many urgent tempi from Mr Marriner. There were also some painful musical cuts such as neither Lefort nor Marriner ought to have countenanced. This was a fine and enjoyable *Nozze di Figaro* fighting for its life, with the audience's enthusiastic support, against the murderous attacks of a brilliant but determinedly contrary producer.[5]

The Délégation musicale régionale and the Centre de pédagogie lyrique, organized a course to accompany rehearsals of *Le nozze di Figaro*, led by Lavelli, Max Bignens, plus musicologists and journalists.

The second opera at the Théâtre de l'Archevêché was Massenet's *Werther*. Teresa Berganza, cast as Charlotte, was forced to cancel. Her replacement was Nadine Denize. Neil Shicoff sang the title role, with Christine Barbaux as Sophie, Jean-Marie Frémeau as Albert and Jules Bastin as Bailli. Jean-Claude Casadesus conducted the Orchestre de Lille. Lefort chose another young director, Jean-Claude Fall, who was staging his first opera. The choice confirmed what people already knew, that Lefort didn't want traditional productions. Fall and his designer André Acquart interpreted the work poetically as a waking dream, with abstract décor (a high wall with three unreachable windows, an image of imprisonment), and the mysterious presence of men and women dressed in black, representing loss and mourning.

Porporino, about the famous castrato and his rival Feliciano, was based on a novel by Dominique Fernandez. Roger Blanchard selected suitable arias by Nicola Porpora, Johann Adolf Hasse, and Alessandro Scarlatti. Ralf Weikert conducted the Orchestre de Lille.

Patrick Guinand directed. The show was a vehicle for the wonderful voices of James Bowman and Bruce Brewer. 'Both clomped about the stage,' wrote William Mann, 'in capacious uniforms topped with plumed helmets, struck attitudes, and tore off elaborate cadenzas. The effect was more absurd than evocative.'

The concert given in the cathedral by Stanislas Skrowaczewski and the Academy of St Martin in the Fields was generally considered to be the highlight of that year's concert series. They were joined by the Chorale Elisabeth-Brasseur in a performance of Schubert's Mass in A-flat. The soloists were Jules Bastin, Philip Langridge, Ann Murray, and Valerie Masterson. Her voice is 'an arrow of light' wrote *Le Monde*.

The three-week-long programme of the Centre Acanthes, now in its second year, and fully established as a vital event in the contemporary music calendar, took place at the Conservatoire Darius-Milhaud in the Hôtel de Caumont. The subject was the music of György Ligeti. Ligeti ran the course, with Gilbert Amy, Katia Labèque, Marielle Labèque, and William Pearson. Over eighty young composers and musicians from around the world were admitted. The French premiere of Ligeti's *Le Grand Macabre*, at the cloître Saint-Louis, closed the Festival. With contemporary music not featuring at all in the main festival programme, the concerts of the Centre Acanthes were essential.

Soon after the end of the 1979 edition, it was announced that Louis Erlo, head of the Opéra de Lyon, had been appointed to succeed Lefort in 1981. Erlo was the choice of the Ministry of Culture and the Ville d'Aix. At the beginning of the year, Alain Joissains, mayor of Aix, had wanted Jorge Lavelli to be offered the role.

ii 1980/81: ROSSINI'S SÉMIRAMIS AND TANCRÈDE

During his final two seasons, at the Théâtre de l'Archevêché, Lefort mounted two operas close to his heart – Rossini's rarely seen *Sémiramis* in 1980, and *Tancrède* in 1981, both based on texts by Voltaire. That year, he also surprised by staging a contemporary opera, Claude Prey's *Les Liaisons dangereuses*, written in 1974. Jean Mercure's elegantly spare *Così fan tutte* and Jean-Pierre Vincent's *Don Giovanni*, re-thought, were revived. The resident ensemble at the Théâtre de l'Archevêché was the Scottish Chamber Orchestra. Lefort, who was working full-time at the Paris Opéra, only programmed the operas in 1981. The concert series was curated by Jean-Louis Pujol.

Sémiramis, a co-production with the Paris Opéra, the Teatro Comunale de Gênes, and the Teatro Regio de Turin, lasted for well over three hours. Rain fell during the last act on the opening night, but few people ran for cover. Montserrat Caballé (Sémiramis) and Marilyn Horne (Arsace) were on dazzling form. But this was more than a diva show. Pier Luigi Pizzi's stylised production, with monumental white sets and mostly white costumes (Arsace wore a helmet with red plumes), matched the power and elegance of Rossini's music. Jésus Lopez-Cobos conducted.

Tancrède, conducted by Ralph Weikert, was even longer. Most of the action took place off-stage. Jean-Claude Auvray's sombre production used classical imagery – columns and a distant view of mountains, in the style of Claude Loraine – and a stylish colour scheme of blue and gold. Unlike Pizzi, he treated the opera on its own terms as a celebration of the female voice. The stars were Marilyn Horne and Katia Ricciarelli. The critic of *The Times*, John Higgins, described how the mistral, chilly at one in the morning, caused the backdrop to inflate. 'It needed strong arms,' he wrote, 'to keep the banners of the Syracuse army from flying off into the night. But after nearly four hours of music the audience was intact, totally involved and finally hugely enthusiastic.'[6]

Claude Prey's *Les Liaisons dangereuses*, after the novel by Choderlos de Laclos, was presented in the courtyard of the Hôtel de Valbelle (rue Mignet), a new festival venue. A more appropriate location could not have been found for Prey's tense chamber opera, for this was music that deconstructed 18th century elegance into a sinister 20th century sound world. Pierre Barat directed Peter Gottlieb as Valmont, Irène Jarsky as Mme de Merteuil, Anne-Marie Blazat as Cécile, Micaëla Etcheverry as Tourvel, and Jean-Pierre Chevalier as Danceny. The production was co-produced with the Paris Opéra, the Centre lyrique de Wallonie, and the Théâtre municipal d'Avignon.

The concerts given during these two editions were unadventurous but at least one of the orchestras involved was outstanding – the

Academy of St Martin in the Fields. In the cathedral, the Uppsala University Choir performed the requiems of Mozart and Fauré, and *a cappella* pieces by Mozart, Pizzetti, Ingvar Lidholm, Frank Martin, Poulenc, and Schönberg. Anders Edy conducted. Valerie Masterson, Ann Murray, Malcolm King and Georges Gautier were the soloists in performances of Mozart's *Vesperae solennes de Dominica* and *Krönungsmesse*. Teresa Berganza, Marilyn Horne and Katia Ricciarelli gave recitals.

The Centre Acanthes's programme of workshops and talks at the Hôtel de Caumont was devoted to the music of Henri Dutilleux and Witold Lutosławski in 1980, and Mauricio Kagel in 1981. At the cloître Saint-Louis, Gilbert Amy conducted the Nouvel orchestre philharmonique de Radio-France in performances of Witold Lutosławski's *Novelette* and Dutilleux's *Timbres, espace, movement*, and Kagel presented a new work, *Le Tribun*, written for the Harmonie municipale d'Aix-en-Provence.

While Lefort's repertoire choices were conservative, dominated by Mozart, Rossini, Donizetti and Verdi, the productions were often progressive. Most of Lefort's eight editions were made by great singers, scholarly conductors and radically-minded directors. The concert programmes were dominated by vocal music to such an extent that instrumental chamber music was rarely present, but Lefort had made it known at the very beginning of his tenure that he would prioritise singers. The most significant weakness, if one compared Lefort with Dussurget, was the absence of modern and contemporary music (the Centre Acanthes was crucially important for students and professionals but its impact on the attendees of the Festival was minimal). Of the twenty-one operas chosen by Lefort, only *Les Liaisons dangereuses* was written after 1900. However, Lefort would surely have broadened the repertoire had he stayed longer at Aix.

Part Three

The NIGHTS of LOUIS ERLO

EIGHT

Old Rameau, Young Mozart

1982-1984

i   MISSION STATEMENT

Louis Erlo had directed the Opéra de Lyon since 1969. His achievement would be recognised in 1996, when the house was given the status of a national company.

Appointed to succeed Bernard Lefort as Aix's artistic director in 1979, Erlo had the luxury of plenty of time to plan and organise the 1982 edition of the Festival. He invited Jean-Louis Pujol to stay on as his deputy. Erlo had attended the Festival d'Aix since the early 1950s. He valued its history and special atmosphere. In the 1982 festival programme, he wrote: 'My first concern is not to disturb the mysterious balance of so many intangible things that make Aix a place where one hears music more accurately than elsewhere, where music finds its fulfilment.' This meant remaining faithful to the composers who were synonymous with Aix: Mozart, of course, but also Rossini, Monteverdi, Purcell, Campra, and Rameau. He intended to return Rameau and Monteverdi, unperformed during the Lefort era, to the position they had enjoyed under Dussurget.[1] Rameau's tragedies and Mozart's less well-known operas would be prioritised.

Erlo also wrote: 'Aix must remain, as throughout its history, a centre of innovation, a place brimming with ideas where singers, musicologists, designers, directors, and conductors work passionately together.' Innovation meant embracing new ideas and methods. Aix's new productions of operas by Rameau and other composers of the Baroque era would use period instruments. John Eliot Gardiner was the crucial figure.

Erlo let it be known that he would not choose operas based on the wishes of star singers (which may or may not have been a criticism of Lefort). He would bring to Aix 'artists of high renown whose style and vocal quality matched the roles on offer' while hoping to be able to emulate his predecessors by discovering and nurturing talented young singers. The young English soprano Joan Rodgers would be the first beneficiary. The paucity of young French singers concerned Erlo more than Dussurget, who had been relaxed about relying on foreign artists. Erlo believed that the lyric theatre in France would only prosper if the country produced more artists of the front rank. To this end, he instigated a training programme during the Festival. For the 1982 edition, he asked Éric Tappy to run two courses for young singers, one on the quintets in the operas of Mozart, and the other on French song.

At Lyon, Erlo was known for programming contemporary works. He told the Ministry of Culture that the performance of contemporary music must once again become a vital part of the Festival d'Aix. The festival, like all the national companies, had a duty to propagate opera as a living art form. He requested funding so that he could run a workshop studio in which new works would be developed and previewed. Funding wasn't immediately allocated, so the project was placed on hold while the Ministry carried out an assessment. In the meantime, Erlo strengthened the Festival's ties with the Centre Acanthes. In 1982 he co-produced the Centre's two shows in parc Jourdan – *Dieu* by Pierre Henry and *Art sans la barre* by Maurice Béjart.

ii 1982: LES BORÉADES

At the beginning of the 1970s, John Eliot Gardiner, intrigued by Rameau's never publicly staged, and long-ignored, final work *Les Boréades*, had sought out the surviving primary sources in the Bibliothèque nationale de France.[2] These included an incomplete score with corrections written in Rameau's hand, a clean copy of Rameau's lost complete manuscript made by the Opéra's copyist Jean-Georges

Durand, and the part-books, approved by Rameau and used during the work's aborted rehearsals in 1763. Gardiner was astounded by what he discovered. In its quality, temerity, and modernity, *Les Boréades* was not, as many scholars had thought, a musty relic of old age; it was vibrant and sensual; and, from first note to last, it encapsulated the quiddity of Rameau's art. Gardiner began the painstaking work of creating a performing edition. The source manuscripts were not fully notated. As was usual for the time, many details of instrumentation and ornamentation, as well as the figured bass, were either absent or unclear. The part-books provided Gardiner with clues, but to complete the realisation he needed to make his own scholarly decisions. Gardiner premiered the work in a concert given at the Queen Elizabeth Hall in London in April 1975.[3]

The music world sat up. Gardiner now worked towards producing *Les Boréades* on the stage. However, this was only achieved after, in Gardiner's own words, 'false starts, legal menaces and difficulties'.[4] In 1976, the Bibliothèque nationale transferred the exploitation rights of *Les Boréades* to a commercial publisher. The publisher enforced its exclusive rights and demanded very high royalties.

In 1977, Gardiner's ensemble the Monteverdi Players switched to period instruments and became the English Baroque Soloists. Gardiner wasn't against modern instruments and wasn't motivated by a quest for 'authenticity' for its own sake. Early music, though, because of the particularities of its style, sounded *right* as well as beautiful when played on period instruments, especially in small to mid-size venues. Gardiner and Erlo came together at the right moment. 'When Erlo was appointed director at Aix in 1981,' Gardiner told an interviewer, 'he felt that French neglect of Rameau was such a scandal that he set himself to listen to all the available recordings.'[5] Erlo admired Gardiner's Rameau the most and invited him to lead his exploration of the Baroque era at Aix, beginning with *Les Boréades*. As artistic director of both Aix and the Opéra de Lyon, Erlo could mount *Les Boréades* as a co-production, making the rights affordable. Gardiner became music director of the Opéra de Lyon (from 1983) as well as Artist in Residence at Aix. Gardiner explained his passion for Rameau thus: 'The aspect of Debussy I adore is the very one which means most to me in Rameau: the meticulous intelligence, the sensuousness with which they both set the French language, and, above all, the orchestral colours. They're blood brothers.'[6]

The premiere of *Les Boréades* on 21 July 1982 in the Théâtre de l'Archevêché remains the Festival's most profound and most beautiful achievement. Marc Minkowski, who, aged nineteen, listened to the live broadcast on the radio, would later write that the 'shock was indescribable' and that it 'changed the lives of so many musicians'.[7] The libretto, widely dismissed as weak, was deceptive, being Rameau and Louis de Cahusac's most advanced and elegant treatment of the *tragédie lyrique* form. In *Les Boréades* they integrated the various elements more seamlessly than ever before, thus helping director Jean-Louis Martinoty and designer Daniel Ogier to create a clear and coherent story. With splendid costumes from Rameau's own time and effective choreography by Catherine Turocy and the New York Baroque Dance Company, the work was presented with terrific verve and style. A Watteau painting, split between large panels, became whole when the panels were placed together.

Martinoty avoided the trap of being reverential. He found inspiration in the manners of 18th century France, the narcissism of seeing and being seen (panels became mirrors, in which both performers and audience members were reflected) and the art of ridicule, as well as a growing longing for individual liberty. This mirrored the startling main theme of Cahusac's libretto. There were pointed references to the intellectual dispute over the meaning of music that pitted a reluctant Rameau against the young *philosophes* Diderot, d'Alembert and Jean-Jacques Rousseau, who, played by actors, were on-stage spectators, scrutinising and sometimes intervening. It was such a powerful idea to make Rameau's reputational assassin Rousseau a witness to the triumph of *Les Boréades* and the staggering beauty of the Entrée de Polymnie. Lonchampt wrote about the music's grace, tenderness, harmonic delicacy, orchestral finesse, and grandeur, and doubted whether a piece by Rameau had ever been interpreted as effectively as here, by John Eliot Gardiner, at the head of the English Baroque Soloists and the Monteverdi Choir.

Nicholas Kenyon, reviewing the production on its transfer to Lyon, greatly admired the work and, with reservations, the production:

> This sumptuous extravaganza proceeded from the premise that the story of gods and tempests, passions, and torments, could

not be taken seriously — and so had to be treated with the twin heavy hands of irony and politicisation. When the heroine Alphise was snatched away in the storm, anachronistic revolutionary soldiers effected the deed. Characters continually laughed at themselves and their actions. Cardinals paced up and down meaninglessly. Apollo was made up as Rameau himself, and so on. In fact, though, many of Martinoty's stage pictures were brilliant and striking — the frozen chorus, the drunken feast, the all-seeing eye of Apollo, the lumbering dressing table costumes wittily recreated in Daniel Ogier's designs — and the cast realised his conception of the opera with startling conviction. Jennifer Smith as Alphise, perpetually bewildered with her fate as if she had wandered into a dream, was superb; her consort Abaris (Philip Langridge) was equally cogent.[8]

It was true that the staging was a little too fussy in its inventiveness, the small stage too crowded with figures, and some of the ideas close to caricature and parody. However, the significance of the event, and the beauty of the music, made such quibbles irrelevant.

Internationally, the success of *Les Boréades* (the production was recorded and released by Erato on LP) was the catalyst for a long overdue reappraisal of Rameau's work, admittedly slow burning and not fully embraced even within the classical music community, but a reappraisal all the same. 'Much of the score of *Les Boréades* is so extraordinary,' wrote Gerald Kaufman in *The Guardian*, 'that some of it even sounds like late Stravinsky.'[9] For Edward Greenfield, reviewing the 1975 performance, 'Our whole view of Rameau [...] is at one leap altered': 'What can you say when an opera by Rameau, his final testament in music, never performed before, is suddenly produced from the shelves of a library, and found to be a masterpiece?'[10]

Die Zauberflöte opened the season. Mozart's Masonic opera had always been a difficult work to pull off. The radical Romanian filmmaker and theatre director Lucian Pintilié, based in Paris, was staging his first opera. Pintilié released a press release in which he let it be known that the production had not 'fulfilled the conception he had imagined and worked to achieve'. He wrote of 'significant technical impediments' that had wrecked rehearsals. For a director to go public in this way was extraordinary. Despite Pintilié's unhappiness, which must have affected his collaborators and especially his cast, the production was striking in its strangeness and originally. The performances were first-rate.

The set designed by Radu and Miruna Boruzescu consisted of three wooden galleries, semi-dilapidated, filling the whole height of the theatre. It was like a bullring, a pit, where sinister and deadly things might happen. The bottom gallery housed animal-like creatures. Tamino and Pamina were separated in glass boxes high up on either side of the stage. Released, they searched for each other across the galleries. A central glass box, which rose and fell between the levels, was the domain of Sarastro. The glass boxes presumably represented magic and transformation, but also imprisonment and tyranny. When the Queen of the Night appeared, a thousand tiny stars illuminated the stage. Pintilié's more provocative ideas included having Pamina plunge her head into a tub of water during the water trial and giving Pamina and Tamino the faces of old people once their ordeal was over.

Theodor Guschlbauer conducted the Nouvel orchestre philharmonique de Radio-France. Joan Rodgers, aged twenty-four and making her opera debut, replaced the indisposed Judith Blegen at short notice to sing Pamina. Gauche, tender, and spirited, with a beguiling voice, she was the revelation of the season. Robert Lloyd's commanding presence and glorious bass voice made Sarastro formidable. Venceskawa Freiberger's Queen of the Night was somewhat underpowered, but then she did replace Edita Gruberov at very short notice. Erland Hagegard, Stephan Dickson, and John Tomlinson, as the orator, completed Pintilié's highly committed cast.

The season's third opera, Rossini's *Il Turco in Italia*, staged in the place des Quatre-Dauphins, the setting of Le Poulain's triumphant shows of the 1970s, was slight in comparison, despite inventive staging from Jean-Louis Thamin. The conductor was Maurizio Arena. Jacques Lonchampt reported that the setting, although delightful 'with its sun-kissed houses and tall chestnut trees quivering at the slightest breath', had become a victim of its success: to be well-seated you had to arrive early; those who didn't had a very poor view and yet they had paid the same money.

John Eliot Gardiner conducted the English Baroque Soloists and the Monteverdi Choir in a series of concerts, at the cathedral and the cloître Saint-Louis, designed to complement Rameau's *Les Boréades* and Mozart's *Die Zauberflöte*. The works played included Mozart's Symphony no. 33, Haydn's Symphony no. 48 and *Theresienmesse*,

Monteverdi's *Vespro della Beata Vergine*, and Handel's *Hercules*. Jessye Norman sang *Les Nuits d'été* by Berlioz, and Georg Solti conducted the the Orchestre des jeunes de l'Union européenne in performances of Richard Strauss's *Ein Heldenleben* and Beethoven's Symphony no. 3. The Nouvel orchestre philharmonique de Radio-France, under Luis Garcia Navarro, performed French music at the cloître Saint-Louis: Ravel's *Le Tombeau de Couperin*, Fauré's *Pelléas et Mélisande*, and Milhaud's *Le Boeuf sur le toit* and *Le Carnaval d'Aix*.

iii 1983/84: RAMEAU, MOZART, BOULEZ AND BERIO

In 1983, the tercentenary of Rameau's birth, Erlo and Gardiner followed *Les Boréades* with a production of Rameau's first opera, the tragedy *Hippolyte et Aricie*. Joining *Hippolyte* in the Théâtre de l'Archevêché was the rarely staged *Mitridate, re di Ponto*, composed by Mozart in 1770 when he was fourteen years old. The opera programme was completed by Rossini's *Cenerentola* and a compelling juxtaposition of Luciano Berio's *Passaggio* (1963) with Monteverdi's *Il combattimento di Tancredi e Clorinda*. It was a strong season, not least because contemporary music was placed at the heart of the Festival for the first time in years.

The Ministry of Culture and Ville d'Aix increased their funding commitment to the Festival by fifty per cent: this was only helpful in the short-term. *Le Monde* reported that the budget for 1983 was a little over twenty-two million francs.[11] Government funding only amounted to twenty-five per cent of the total. Income also came from co-producers, sponsors, and external partners (among them the British Council, funding the residency of the English Baroque Soloists and Monteverdi Choir), but ticket sales had to cover an unrealistically large percentage of the whole. Erlo knew that *Cenerentola* would attract a large audience and would not fulfil its revenue potential in the Théâtre de l'Archevêché. Whereas Lefort had used the Roman theatre in Arles, Erlo chose to construct a temporary stage in the garden of the Pavillon Vendôme, in front of the building's beautiful facade. Here he was able to double the seating capacity of the Théâtre de l'Archevêché.

Hippolyte et Aricie is a long opera. People were still in their seats at two in the morning. Adapted from Racine's *Phèdre*, it is the most dramatically compelling of Rameau's operas: at key moments, it possesses a psychological depth that transcends the artificialities of the *tragédie lyrique* form. Rameau's music, sometimes majestic, often bleakly spare and melancholy, matches Racine's words. Gardiner and director Pier Luigi Pizzi, whose décor was classical but stylised (black marble columns, cut-out trees, a white statue of the goddess Diana, a reflective stage, a colour palate dominated by purple, red, white, gold, and black), delivered a fine production, with a powerful performance from Jessye Norman as Phèdre, alongside John Aler, Rachel Yakar, and the great bass-baritone José van Dam. 'The marriage of musical and dramatic expression is as near perfect as one could imagine,' wrote Edward Greenfield in *The Guardian*, 'culminating in the extraordinary scene in Act 3 where Thesée returns to find Hippolyte apparently threatening Phèdre with his sword':

> Pizzi and Gardiner between them seize every opportunity to give such confrontations an involvement rare in classical opera. Standing clear of everyone is Jessye Norman as Phèdre, a monumental figure dressed in flowing scarlet robes until she puts on despairing black for her death scene. Not just self-torture but the biting menace of Phèdre's character comes out superbly in Miss Norman's singing, with the producer cleverly using the very wide but shallow stage of the theatre to give her maximum power both vocally and dramatically.[12]

In just two years, Gardiner had become one of the leading figures of French opera and music. Jacques Lonchampt called Aix the town of Rameau and wrote of Gardiner that he had 'rediscovered the truth and grandeur of *Hippolyte et Aricie*', penetrating the soul of Rameau's music. The English Baroque Soloists were 'wonderfully alert, supple, sparkling and poetic'. They were also stretched to their limits by Rameau's extremely difficult score, something they shared with the musicians of the Paris Opéra who premiered the work under Rameau's intimidating direction in 1733. He was forced to alter one section – the trio of Fates at the end of Act 2, a bravura passage of diatonic enharmony – because the musicians couldn't perform it to his satisfaction.

Aix's production of Mozart's *Mitridate* was the opera's French premiere. The wunderkind's first opera seria, written just six years after Rameau's death, was, like *Hippolyte et Aricie*, adapted from a play by Racine. As with the previous year's staging of *Die Zauberflöte*, Theodor Guschlbauer conducted the Nouvel orchestre philharmonique de Radio-France. Hilary Finch, reviewing the production for *The Times*, commended the 'sheer dramatic intensity of projection' and described how the 'work's long and taxing recitatives were charged with a momentum which crackled between stage and pit'. The singers – Rockwell Blake, Yvonne Kenny, Ashley Putnam, Sandra Browne, Marvis Martin and Joan Rodgers – were inspired by the realisation that they were singing music by Mozart that many members of the audience were hearing for the first time. They received a standing ovation, but when the director, Jean-Claude Fall, took his bow there were boos. 'His split-level *mise en scène*, with its Louis XV chair and model ox dug into a snowy desert, did at times seem as arbitrary as the neurotic flurries of activity from the Arabian-clad protagonists at every available orchestral interlude.'[13]

Rossini's *Cenerentola*, directed by Nicolas Joël, inaugurated the garden of the Pavillon Vendôme as a performance space. Lucia Valentini-Terrani replaced the indisposed Teresa Berganza; Ralf Weikert conducted. Unfortunately, because the space was open-sided, the music floated on the air with negligible clarity or resonance. There were happier audiences in the cathédrale Saint-Sauveur, where relatively neglected choral works by great masters were performed, including Mendelssohn's *Paulus* and Handel's *Israel in Egypt*.

The contemporary music programme included pieces by Pierre Boulez and Luciano Berio, who was the resident artist at the Centre Acanthes, but also a work by Marcel Landowski – his cantata-opera *La Prison*. Landowski had been the director of music at the Ministry of Culture during the 1960s and 70s. With a considerable pot of money at his disposal, he established the Orchestre de Paris and rejuvenated regional orchestras and opera houses. Boulez was one of the modernists who opposed Malraux's decision to appoint Landowski in 1966. *La Prison* was performed by its dedicatees, Galina Vishnevskaia and Mstislav Rostropovich, who conducted the Orchestre de Lille.

Boulez and the Ensemble Intercontemporain celebrated the centenary of Anton Webern's birth at the Théâtre de l'Archevêché. As well as pieces by Werbern, the concert included Boulez's 1965 work *Éclat*. Luciano Berio's *Passaggio*, a messa in scena for soprano, double chorus and orchestra, was staged. In the cloître Saint-Sauveur, Jill Gomez sang Webern's Lieder op. 4, 12, 23 and 25. The students of the Centre Acanthes, conducted by Olivier Guion, performed Berio's *O King*.

In planning the 1984 edition, Erlo decided not to continue with the Pavillon Vendôme. Similarly, the place des Quatre-Dauphins: the residents had had enough of the disruption. It looked as if the Festival was moving away from the street ethos that had seemed so important only ten years before. More surprisingly, Erlo decided to suspend use of Saint-Sauveur until the acoustics could be improved. In 1984, all the concerts took place in the Théâtre de l'Archevêché. As a result, the Festival programme was a little reduced – two operas instead of three and fewer concerts.

All the Festival's stakeholders – the conseil d'administration, mayor Jean-Pierre de Peretti Della Rocca, and the Ministry's Maurice Fleuret – believed that the Théâtre de l'Archevêché should remain at the heart of the Festival. The government authorised the modernisation of the theatre, at a cost of twenty million francs. The work would begin as soon as the 1984 season had concluded. The theatre's rudimentary stage machinery, dating from 1949, would be overhauled. Storage space for sets would be created at either side of the stage, and the stage would be given more depth. The seating capacity of the auditorium would be increased. Once completed, it was hoped that the Festival's productions would be more technically compatible with the theatres of its partners (and Fleuret expected the Festival to increase its co-productions to lower the financial burden placed on the State).

Erlo's rehabilitation of Mozart's early stage works continued in the Théâtre de l'Archevêché, where the Nouvel orchestre philharmonique de Radio-France was again the resident orchestra, with the opera buffa *La finta giardiniera*, written four years after *Mitridate* and premiered in 1775. The original, Italian, full score of *La finta giardiniera* was only discovered in 1978. It was produced at Salzburg in 1980. There are passages of sublime music. Mozart, at times, achieved a dramatic seriousness that the plot and characters didn't deserve.

Aix's production, directed by Gildas Bourdet and Alain Milianti, and conducted by the young Russian-born American Semyon Bychkov, all working at Aix for the first time, was admired. 'Magnificent accompanied recitatives are linked with dramatic dialogues, and arias expressing anger, love or melancholy, intertwine,' wrote Jacques Lonchampt.[14] The set consisted of classical columns in yellow and green marble and white steps backed by a cyclorama of constantly changing clouds. The elegant costumes were by Françoise Chevalier. The production's success was due to the directors' decision to underplay the farcical imbroglios of the plot, and to the young singers who sang and acted beautifully: Roberta Alexander, Christine Weidinger, Joan Rodgers, Anne-Sofie von Otter, John Aler, Gilles Cachemaille, and Anthony Rolfe Johnson.

La finta Giardiniera was co-produced by the opera houses of Lyon, Bordeaux, Lille, and Strasbourg. The season's second opera *Le Barbier de Séville*, was co-produced by Lyon, Marseille, Venice, and Naples. The conductor was Gian-Luigi Gelmetti. Roberto de Simone's production failed on a grand scale. It was cartoon-like, with primary colours and unfunny sequences of knockabout comedy. Aix had been disrupted by last-minute withdrawals during recent seasons. In 1984 it was the turn of Lucia Valentini-Terrani. Ewa Podles replaced her as Rosine.

In contrast, Gardiner's unsentimental reading of Handel's *Messiah* with the English Baroque Soloists and the Monteverdi Choir was acclaimed. The soloists were Judith Nelson, Catherine Denley, Michaël Chance, Wynford Evans, and John Tomlinson. Erlo and Gardiner were right to choose the Théâtre de l'Archevêché for this concert. It fitted Gardiner's unromantic approach. At least one member of the first-night audience missed the *Messiah* he was used to. Score in hand, he muttered angrily throughout the performance and declared at its end: 'Quel désastre.'[15] Contemporary music was restricted to a single concert by the students and teachers of the Centre Acanthes on the theme of percussion, choral singing and analyses. *Cinq concerts à la une*, a collective work by the composers Carlos-Roque Alsina, Gilbert Amy, Nguyen Thien Dao, Hugues Dufourt and François-Bernard Mâche, was premiered.

NINE

An Improved Theatre

1985-1988

i   1985: THE RETURN OF MONTEVERDI, STRAUSS AND PURCELL

The re-built Théâtre de l'Archevêché was the main story of the 1985 season. The alterations of 1974 had been relatively superficial. Now, the architect Bernard Guillaumot designed a new theatre, with modern machinery and adequate space backstage. Because Historic Monuments had allowed the listed wall of the courtyard to be set back by four metres (it was dismantled stone by stone and then re-built), the stage was given more depth.

The auditorium now consisted of three levels (stalls and two overhanging balconies) with places for nearly 1,700 people. The walls of the courtyard were still visible. Crucially, Erlo could now alternate three or four productions during each season. In 1985 there were three operas, Mozart's *Le nozze di Figaro*, Monteverdi's *Orfeo* and Richard Strauss's *Ariadne auf Naxos*, all significant works in the history of the Festival, plus a concert performance of Purcell's *King Arthur*. Erlo organised twenty-six concerts, most of them in the cloître Saint-Sauveur. As had been the arrangement for some time, concerts took place at midday and at six in the evening.

Erlo chose to inaugurate the theatre with the first Mozart/Da Ponte opera of his tenure – *Le nozze di Figaro*. Unfortunately, the production misfired. John Eliot Gardiner was in the pit with the Opéra de Lyon orchestra he had recently reconstituted, so expectations were high. The critical consensus, though, was that the music didn't take flight. Jacques Lonchampt put this down to the newness of the orchestra and believed that Gardiner just needed more time.[1] Gardiner was hampered by the staging. To stage *Le nozze di Figaro*, Erlo invited the Italian Pierluigi Pier'Alli. Pier'Alli was relatively inexperienced in opera but had made a splash at La Scala in Milan directing Schönberg's *Pierrot lunaire* and Wagner's *Lohengrin* (1983). His interpretation of *Le nozze* was centred on the concept of Time. Clocks were placed on the stage. The idea was perplexing rather than illuminating. Why time? Nobody seemed to know. Hilary Finch found the concept naive and self-serving, a negation of the 'essential social and emotional dynamism' of Mozart's masterpiece: 'The new space, now an immense black void, is dotted with isolated figures and dominated by a huge central clockface. Cherubino leaps out of it into the first act; in the second it becomes a mirror (that Narcissus-pool of so many directors), and is flanked by two vertical clock-cases, their cogwheels lurching into action at any possibly significant moment.'[2]

The staging was well executed, but it was fatally out of sync with Mozart's score. Gilles Cachemaille, Lella Cuberli, Diana Montague, Christine Barbaux, and Thomas Hampson, were the unfortunate singers.

Given the choice made for Rameau, and the continuing presence of Gardiner, it was a surprise to find that the production of Monteverdi's *Orfeo* was not being mounted by Gardiner and the English Baroque Soloists. Gardiner had conducted the work at the ENO in 1981, a production that Erlo admired. Perhaps he didn't want to return to the work so soon. His Opéra de Lyon orchestra was in the pit. The conductor was Michel Corboz. He had a fine history with Monteverdi, but his interpretation here divided opinion, perhaps because ears had started to become tuned to period instruments. Hilary Finch noted that the orchestra played sensitively but wondered why they were using 'Edward Tarr's ludicrously plain, literal edition'. Finch found Gino Quilico's Orfeo too Verdi-like but admired the voices of Audrey Michael (Eurydice) and Carolyn Watkinson (the Messenger). The production was directed by the filmmaker Claude Goretta, new to opera. Goretta's focus was on the film version he would premiere at Venice later in the year. Finch thought it was a production made by a cinematographer. 'Shifting sand-dunes, now ochre, now black, and silhouetted against a sky of torrid blue or lowering magenta, form Jacques Bufoir's setting for the breezeblown dancing and mime of the Ballet du Grand Théâtre de Genève.'[3]

The singers were subservient to the director's vision, or perhaps it was Goretta's inexperience in opera that resulted in one unfortunate singer having to deliver a major aria while lying down. However, the images were often hauntingly enigmatic and beautiful (Philippe Hutinet's lighting was exquisite). The barefooted dancers wore light linen chiton tunics in pale colours.

Strauss's *Ariadne auf Naxos*, last staged at Aix in 1963, was entrusted to the Swedish director Göran Järvefelt. The staging was uncontroversial. The distinguished singers, led by Jessye Norman, in magnificent voice, were accompanied by the Nouvel orchestre philharmonique de Radio-France under Semyon Bychkov. Bychkov, in only his second engagement at Aix, confirmed his status as the Festival's young star conductor. The original idea had been to use Pierre Clayette's sets from 1963, but, unsurprisingly, their decrepit condition made them unusable. One suspects that Järvefelt was relieved. He set the work in the 20th century. In the first half, Kathrine Hysing designed a magnificent palace ballroom. The second part took place in front of a curtain depicting the painting 'Isle of the Dead' by Böcklin, an idea stolen from Chéreau's *Der Ring des Nibelungen*. On the arrival of Bacchus, the curtain parted to reveal a seascape. *Ariadne* initiated a mini cycle of operas by Strauss.

The show was a popular success. A concert performance of a Purcell rarity at the Théâtre de l'Archevêché received most of the critical plaudits. Purcell's *Dido and Aeneas* was one of the Festival's most iconic works, but this was the first time that another of the composer's stage works was performed. The spectacular 'semi-opera' *King Arthur*, with words by John Dryden, was premiered at the Queen's Theatre in London in 1691. In Dryden's libretto, King Arthur attempts to recover his fiancée, Emmeline, from the Saxon King Oswald. Historical characters rub shoulders with Cupid and Venus and other mythological gods and goddesses. Merlin is borrowed from the Camelot legend. The principal human characters do not sing. Spoken dialogue is interspersed with songs and musical set pieces.

King Arthur is a very problematic work to stage. The first major modern performance was given by the English Opera Group in

1970. Colin Graham cut up the work, giving the music to the leading characters so that they could sing. This corrupted version didn't achieve acceptance. Erlo and Gardiner decided to present the work in concert, without spoken dialogue. The music was largely unknown in France, so Aix was once again trailblazing. Joining the English Baroque Soloists and the Monteverdi Choir were the singers Jennifer Smith, Nancy Argenta, Lynne Dawson, Ashley Stafford, Mark Tucker, and Stephen Varcoe. Under the title 'L'enchanteur Purcell', Jacques Lonchampt wrote of music 'fine as lace, of a delicate feeling, generally, but sometimes of a biting irony, even somewhat buffoonish'. As with Strauss, there would be more Purcell in the years ahead.

Among the other works performed in concert, were Schumann's *Le Paradis et la Péri* (Théâtre de l'Archevêché), Bach's Mass in B minor (cathédrale Saint-Sauveur) and *Variations Goldberg* (cour de l'Hôtel de Ville), and Mozart's Requiem (cathédrale Saint-Sauveur). Iannis Xenakis was the composer in residence at the Centre Acanthes. The festival presented two concerts of his music at the cloître Saint-Sauveur, the first given by the harpsichordist Elisabeth Chojuacka and the percussionist Sylvio Gualda; and the second by the Arditti Quartet and Claude Heiffer.

ii 1986/87/88: CAMPRA, LULLY AT LAST

The 1985 season had been relatively disappointing. Erlo began the 1986 edition with *Don Giovanni*, a brave choice. The festival's previous production of its signature opera, by Jean-Pierre Vincent in 1976, had not satisfied veteran patrons of the Festival. To break the curse of the 1949 *Giovanni*, the new production would need to be remarkable.

On opening night, just before the opera was about to start, a freak thunderstorm broke above the Théâtre de l'Archevêché, drenching the auditorium, and necessitating a delay of over an hour. The critic David Murray wrote of the 'comic ballet of *ouvreuses* hustling damp customers in and battling back against the stream to escort some more, all issued with wodges from enormous rolls of paper for drying their seats'.[4] The trying conditions did little to encourage vibrant playing from the Orchestre de l'Opéra de Lyon given Stephen Soltesz's rather bland reading of the score. The production, by Gildas Bourdet and Alain Milianti, wasn't a failure, but it wasn't remarkable either. Some scenes were performed in front of an enormous reproduction of Ruben's voluptuous painting 'The Drunken Silenus', suggesting a licentious decadence that never materialised. When the front curtain was lifted, Laurent Peduzzi's design consisted of a courtyard and a kind of hunting lodge in pale wood: its meaning was unclear. Some sequences were skilfully animated. Gino Quilico's Giovanni sang the Champagne aria while perched on Leporello's shoulders. Leporello, played by Jean-Philippe Lafont, was weighed down by Giovanni and four large pieces of luggage. Quilico was cruel and hollow and only able to bond with Leporello. Suzanne Murphy, Marlette Kemmer, and Patricia Rozario struggled a little on opening night. The audience, wrote David Murray, 'booed all the principal sopranos, which at 1.35 am seemed not only ungallant but cruel'.[5]

Mozart's *Idomeneo* fared better. People didn't remember Aix's 1963 production as vividly as they remembered Meyer's *Don Giovanni*. A co-production with Lyon, Nice, Paris, Strasbourg, Frankfurt and the Opéra Royal de Wallonie, it was directed and designed by Pierre Strosser.

The setting consisted of a shingle beach drenched in white light and backed by a turbulent sea and sky. Black reflective panels provided a picture frame. The women wore Japanese yukata gowns in white. The singers moved very slowly or simply stood still for many minutes. Visually, the production had a crystalline, static, beauty; it was achingly chic but Strosser's refusal to animate the characters or the story reduced its power. The Sinfonia Varsovia, under Hans Gras, played Mozart's score in a languorous style. The singers intermittently broke free to create striking moments. Anthony Rolfe Johnson had a problem with his voice (he would be replaced by Philip Langridge during the run). Sylvia Greenberg and Eliane Coelho sang the roles of Ilia and Electra. The charismatic young American Jeanne Piland dazzled both here, as Idamante, and, later in the season, as the Composer in the revival of Göran Järvefelt's production of Richard Strauss's *Ariadne auf Naxos*. The singers of Harry Christophers's The Sixteen were the on-stage chorus.

The third new production was Campra's tragedy *Tancrède*. Erlo conceived the 1986 season as a celebration of Aix's great composer, for, as well as the opera, Campra's Messe de Requiem, one of the revelations of the French Baroque, was performed in the cathedral where Campra had been a chorister. With Gardiner absent, Erlo entrusted both the opera and the mass to Jean-Claude Malgoire's period instruments ensemble La Grande Écurie et la Chambre du Roy and The Sixteen. In bringing *Tancrède* to 'plausible, fanciful life' Jean-Claude Penchenat found inspiration in the staging conventions of the 18th century, but not slavishly. The overhead cloth that fluttered above the stage and auditorium was stylishly effective (designer: Guy-Claude François). David Murray wrote that Jean-Claude Malgoire conducted 'brightly and enthusiastically, with more tenderness in the slower music than one had expected'.[6] François Le Roux was outstanding in the title role, supported by Daphne Evangelatos, Pierre-Yves Le Maigat, Colette Alliol-Lugaz, Gregory Reinhart, and the young soprano Catherine Dubosc. The young *comédiens danseurs* danced in a natural style that suited Campra's music.

Catherine Dubosc's performance, in the cloître Saint-Sauveur, of Alban Berg's *Sept lieder de jeunesse* with Louis Langrée at the piano, was the highlight of the concert programme.

The works of the earliest of the three great masters of the French Baroque, Lully, had long been ignored by the Festival. In 1987, buoyed by the success of the recent stagings of works by Campra and Rameau, Erlo rectified this omission by mounting a production of Lully's opera *Psyché*. The tricentenary of Lully's death had been reached in March.

Full use was made of the new Théâtre de l'Archevêché in 1987, with four operas presented alternately, although only two of them were new creations, *Psyché* and Richard Strauss's *Der Rosenkavalier*. The others were Mozart's *Die Entführung aus dem Serail*, a revival of Georges Lavaudant's acclaimed Opéra de Lyon production of 1982, and Verdi's *Falstaff*, brought in from the Théâtre Royal de la Monnaie de Bruxelles. José van Dam played the title role; Luis Pascal directed. A fifth opera, Gluck's *Iphigénie en Aulide*, was given in concert.

Der Rosenkavalier opened the season, its debut at Aix. Semyon Bychkov conducted the Orchestre philharmonique de Strasbourg, reduced to around eighty musicians. The pit could have accommodated one hundred and twenty. The decision not to fill the pit was perplexing. The playing was fine but somewhat underpowered. Tobias Richter's production allowed the opera to speak for itself, although Gian Maurizio Fercioni's elegant sun-kissed set, off-white and uncluttered, with portes-fenêtres, was more of the Mediterranean than of central Europe. The great final trio was performed to magical effect on a bare stage. Mechthild Gessendorf, Jeanne Piland, Christine Barbaux, and Aage Haugland, sang the leading roles. The unnamed roles were played by members of The Sixteen.

Georges Lavaudant's production of *Die Entführung aus dem Serail* deserved its new staging at Aix. His sombre reading transformed the work. On Jean-Pierre Vergier's uncluttered stage, a section of wall depicted Salim's palace, and the infinity of the sea and sky was conveyed by a single sailing boat. Mariella Devia's Constance was isolated, and Gunther von Kannen's Osman, beneath the bluster, was a dangerous brute. Charles Schmitt brought depth to Selim, while the young Canadian soprano Tracy Dahl, playing Blondchen, revealed a natural talent for comedy. Armin Jordan conducted the Orchestre de l'Opéra de Lyon.

Erlo handed Lully's *Psyché* to the creators of the previous year's *Tancrède*, Jean-Claude Malgoire and Jean-Claude Penchenat. Molière and Lully's *comédie-ballet* of 1671 was the most spectacular, and costly, entertainment of the reign of Louis XIV, with breathtaking stage effects, dances, a spoken text and instrumental music and arias. After Molière's death, Lully commissioned a libretto from Thomas Corneille and reworked his music to create an opera under the same name (1678). Venus is jealous of the beautiful mortal girl Psyche and orders Cupid to punish her. Cupid, though, falls in love with her. The furious Venus schemes against them. At the end, Apollo fixes matters by making Psyche immortal.

Wanting more from the plot, Jean-Claude Penchenat decided to stage the opera as if it was being presented before the Sun King, his mistress Mme de Montespan, and one of her younger rivals, at Versailles, the conceit being that the opera alluded to the king's personal life. Guy-Claude François designed an elegant salon, and the splendid period costumes were by Françoise Tournafond. Dominique Bagouet's stylish choreography added a third layer of commentary since the dancers doubled the leading characters. The actor Bruno Choel played the king. It was a 'game of mirrors' in which the various elements were successfully integrated. However, the framing device divided opinion. The critic of *The Financial Times*, Max Loppert, found it 'frivolous' and compared the production unfavourably to William Christie and Jean-Marie Villegier's *Atys*, staged in Paris earlier in the year.[7] Few opera productions of 1987 would have won that comparison.

Jean-Claude Malgoire's ensemble La Grande Écurie et la Chambre du Roy served Lully's score well, especially the continuo musicians, playing viols and lutes, who were part of the on-stage action, along with the singers of The Sixteen. Ann Monoyios, as Psyche, carried the show, supported by Howard Crook as Cupid and Marie Duisit as Venus. The other roles were sung by Elisabeth Vidal, Elisabeth Baudry, Sophie Boulin, Roger Soyer, René Schirrer, Christian Tréguier, Gilles Ragon, and Jean Nironet.

The concert performance of Gluck's *Iphigénie en Aulide*, given by Gardiner and the Orchestre de l'Opéra de Lyon, was the first account of an opera by Gluck at Aix since the era of Dussurget. Despite intermittent rain showers, Max Loppert considered the performance to be an 'utterly enthralling' vindication of Gluck's (at the time) underrated opera: '[The singing and orchestral execution] were both in eloquent partnership, for the supple shaping, springy rhythms and poised balance of the instrumental parts supported the voices, drew the drama directly out of the notes. The beauty of sound was a constant delight.'[8] José van Dam was at his considerable best as Agamemnon. The other principals also shone: John Aler, as Achille, Lynne Dawson, singing Iphigénie at very short notice, and Anne-Sofie von Otter as Clitemnestre.

The revelation of the concert programme in the cathedral was the little-known *Membra Jesu Nostri* by Dieterich Buxtehude (1680), a mourning cycle of seven sacred cantatas lifted from near obscurity by Gardiner at the head of the English Baroque Soloists and the Monteverdi Choir, with lutes and viols prominent. In all, there were nine concerts in the cathedral and eighteen recitals in the cloître Saint-Sauveur.

Contemporary music didn't feature. The organisers of the Centre Acanthes had decided to move their training programme to the Chartreuse de Villeneuve-lès-Avignon during the Avignon theatre festival. At Aix, the Centre's work had never felt integral to the Festival, and perhaps was not valued enough, despite Erlo's best intentions. The decision to move was never fully publicly explained, but the view of *Le Monde* was that opera audiences were not interested in the music of their own time. The Centre Acanthe's programme at Avignon in 1987 was one of the most impressive in years. The resident composer was Olivier Messiaen, while Patrice Chéreau gave lessons based on the creation of a new production of Chekhov's *Platonov* for Avignon.

Despite the predominance of co-productions, and new relationships with sponsors, the Festival's outgoings far exceeded its income. Every year the cost of mounting an opera production went up. Government funding hadn't increased since 1983. The extensive 1987 season had been particularly expensive to mount. Ticket prices, if lower than at Salzburg, were high for France. Erlo didn't believe they could be raised any higher. Hervé Grillet, secretary general of the Festival, told the press: 'The reality is this: we cannot make people pay the actual price of the show they've come to see.' So, if a season was ambitious, the next had to be less so.

The 1988 edition of the Festival consisted of three productions, and they were relatively safe choices: Mozart's *La clemenza di Tito* and *Così fan tutte*, and Rossini's *Armida*, sponsored, respectively, by Air France, the Lyonnaise de Banque and Seita, and co-produced by the opera houses of Lyon, Orléans and Nice. For the fourth consecutive year, The Sixteen was the resident chorus at the Théâtre de l'Archevêché.

La clemenza di Tito, in Michaël Cacoyannis's neo-classical production, completed Erlo's cycle of Mozart's major operas. The austere beauty of Mozart's music (Armin Jordan conducted the Ensemble Orchestral de Paris) inspired performances of true feeling from David Rendall as a sympathetic Titus, Jeanne Piland as the tormented Sextus (her fourth trouser role in four consecutive seasons at Aix), and Charlotte Margiono as Vitellia, ably supported by Elzbieta Szmytka and Anne Mason. The score was truncated, presumably to shorten the running time.

Denis Llorca and Jeffrey Tate's new account of *Così fan tutte* was the first at Aix since Jean Mercure and Charles Mackerras's impressive production of 1977. They had in common the English Chamber Orchestra but little else. Llorca's production, set in an 18th century gambling room, was provocatively contrary as well as claustrophobic. The directorial flourishes started during the overture: a young woman, the loser of a game of poker, willingly lifted her skirt while dancing on a table. The justification was that Mozart's fiancé Constance shocked Mozart by lifting her skirt at a party. As the opera progressed, unknown figures silently watched the action, and, at intervals, the room was invaded by sinister revellers in Venetian masks.

It was original and compelling but not entirely successful. The only characters who truly benefitted from the staging were José van Dam's outstanding Alfonso, a saturnine ringmaster who instigated a cruel game and then watched it play out, and his accomplice, Dawn Upshaw's Despina. The young lovers were left to flounder by their actual director, but perhaps that was the point. Olaf Baer and Hans Peter Blochwitz played Guglielmo and Ferrando unambiguously as macho brutes. Brigitte Poschner-Klebel and Eirian James as the young women were hardly more rounded or appealing. Jeffrey Tate and the musicians of the English Chamber Orchestra, master Mozartians all, delivered a scintillating account of the score. David Murray's opinion of the production was favourable: 'Llorca has the essential flair for bringing characters into explosive confrontations, always powered by the music.'[9]

Rossini's rarely-seen *Armida*, an epic melodrama set during the Crusades, places huge demands on its principals. The title role is fiendishly demanding, and the score calls for no fewer than four leading tenors. June Anderson was vocally superb as Armida, and rightly acclaimed by the opening night audience, but couldn't make the character convincing. The playing of Orchestre de Nice, under Gianfranco Masini, was uneven. Jean-Claude Fall's staging provoked laughter at certain moments – the unfortunate members of The Sixteen were required to portray both crusaders and dancing nymphs.

In the cathedral, the acoustics were improved by the suspension of a structure of plastic tubes above the nave and altar. There were performances of Haydn's *La Création* – Christian Thielemann and the English Chamber Orchestra; and Mozart's Mass in C minor – Theodor Guschlbauer and the Ensemble Orchestral de Paris. The choir for both was the London Oriana Choir. In the cloisters, conducted by Leon Lovett, the choir sang Byrd's *Ave verum corpus*, Lotti's *Crucifixus*, Herbert Howells's Requiem, and a sequence of spirituals from Tippett's *Child of Our Time*. The concert given by The Sixteen included Schütz's *Musik Musikaisphe Exequien*.

TEN

Ancient and Modern

1989-1991

i 1989: PURCELL AND SHAKESPEARE

The ambitious 1989 season consisted of five operas: three new creations – Mozart's *Die Zauberflöte*, Purcell's *The Fairy Queen*, unseen (in a complete form) since its premiere in 1692, and Claude Prey's *Le Rouge et le noir* – plus the transfer from Lyon of Erlo's production of Prokofiev's *L'Amour des trois oranges* and a revival of the previous year's *Così fan tutte*. Prey's *Le Rouge et le noir*, after Stendhal, was the first premiere of a new opera at Aix for many years. Prokofiev's *L'Amour des trois oranges* would be followed, during the next few seasons, by two further 20th century masterpieces, Britten's *A Midsummer Night's Dream* and Stravinsky's *The Rake's Progress*.

The success of the concert performance of Purcell's *King Arthur* in 1985 encouraged Erlo to mount a stage production of *The Fairy Queen*. 'Purcell's work, so anticipated, so unclassifiable, is essential to the mission of the Festival, and the Théâtre de l'Archevêché is the right space for such a grand project,' Erlo wrote.[1] Because John Eliot Gardiner had moved on, Erlo turned to William Christie and his ensemble Les Arts Florissants. Christie founded Les Arts Florissants in 1979. His version of Lully's *Atys* at the Opéra-Comique in 1987 confirmed that Les Arts Florissants belonged in the front rank of period instruments ensembles and that William Christie was an important interpreter of stage works as well as choral and instrumental music.

The idea was to stage Purcell's semi-opera in all its madcap, eccentric glory, and shimmering, heartfelt beauty. The original text was a bastardised version of Shakespeare's *A Midsummer Night's Dream*. Purcell wrote short musical preludes to each act and the dance music and songs of the masques. These songs, linked metaphorically to the play, were performed, as was the convention of the time, by either supernatural or pastoral characters. Christie created a new performing edition of the score. 'Nothing – not even the witty allusion to Mendelssohn – offends against the spirit of the piece,' wrote Gerald Larner in *The Guardian*. 'Much of it, like the solo violin counterpoint to "Oh Let Me Ever, Ever Weep" with theorbo and guitar accompaniment, is strikingly beautiful.'[2]

Erlo invited the young director Adrian Noble of the Royal Shakespeare Company to stage the opera. Noble replaced the original's faux-Shakespeare with the real thing and integrated the spoken text, musical interludes, episodes of grotesque buffoonery, songs of sweet melancholy, and sequences of lyrical dance, into a seamless whole. For Hilary Finch, 'It was the fine tuning between Noble's pacing and William Christie's musical direction which fused to propel the drama through its glorious macedoine of styles.'[3]

Most of Noble's players came from the Royal Shakespeare Company – Roger Allam (master Shakespearean but also the creator of Javert in *Les Misérables*), Gemma Jones (who first played Titania in Peter Brook's iconic RSC production), Geoffrey Freshwater, Niamh Cusack (fresh from playing Desdemona and Juliet), Sylvestra Le Touzel, Sean Murray, David Killick, Albie Woodington, and Paul Greenwood. They were joined by Alan Corduner and Christopher Ryan. They performed with tremendous finesse and vitality. Noble ensured that their physical interactions told the story as effectively as the poetry. The singers of Les Arts Florissants included Thomas Randle, Nancy Argenta, Lynne Dawson, and Bernard Deletré. The future stars Véronique Gens and Sandrine Piau were at the beginning of their careers. As part of the integrated concept, some of the actors, including Roger Allam and Gemma Jones, sang during the masques and everyone danced. The lyrical choreography, by Francine Lancelot and Béatrice Massin, was performed by their company Ris et Danceries.

Deirdre Clancy's 17th century-inspired settings of a candle-lit chamber and moon-lit cut-out forest and grotto under a slowly darkening sky were of a stylish simplicity. Because the characters were in the metaphorical domain of a dream, the chequered floor remained after the transition to the forest. Noble's *mise en scène* had a lucidity, an unshowy charisma, that made everything feel right. Olivier Rouvière thought that the production signified a new approach in the staging of an opera of the Baroque era at Aix, which, for this repertoire, had always favoured a spectacular approach: 'Noble's *Fairy Queen*,' he wrote, 'was certainly prodigious in costumes and colours, but was more focused on theatre than on pageantry.'[4] Noble recalled later: 'It was a wonderful mix of nationalities. Artistically, it was joyous to create something with actors, singers, dancers and musicians – in the open air in one of the most romantic settings: the courtyard of the old Archbishop's Palace in Aix. The sun was setting, the light was fading, and the cast lit hundreds of candles on stage. It was a magical time.'[5]

Le Monde admired the production but wasn't convinced by the insertion of so much of Shakespeare's play, untranslated. This view wasn't widely held. Mihaï de Brancovan wrote in the *Revue des deux mondes* of the 'the pleasure of savouring the text (barely modified) of *A Midsummer Night's Dream*, spoken and played by fabulous English actors; of succumbing to the magic of the sets and costumes of Deirdre Clancy'. The production was a 'model of intelligence, taste, refinement'.[6] David Murray viewed the production as the high watermark of English participation in the Festival:

> At Aix each opera begins amid twilight birdsong – and towards the close of Purcell's *The Fairy Queen*, the midsummer stars on the backdrop merge with the real ones. Though it is no opera, Purcell's masque is the undoubted triumph of the Festival. Under Louis Erlo, Aix has had a long tradition of British participation. *This Fairy Queen* caps it superbly; the mad, incorrigible Englishness of it, the veering between knock-about japes and elevated melancholy, the air of fanciful improvisation all have a hugely exotic appeal.[7]

Die Zauberflöte, opening the season, was directed by Jorge Lavelli. This was Lavelli's first production at Aix since his controversial *Le nozze di Figaro* of 1979. There were imaginative individual ideas but no overriding big idea or concept on this occasion. The three boys pedalled across the stage on a white tricycle under a twirling parasol; Sarastro rode a wooden horse on wheels. The main scenic device was a curtain of quivering threads through which characters passed and which perhaps represented a crossing point between worlds. Tamino and Pamina looked like members of the Nazi Youth; the three ladies of the Queen of the Night were fairy tale witches riding broomsticks. Nothing connected the various elements, but perhaps that was the point. The opera was well sung by an ensemble of young singers: Kurt Streit, Luba Orgonasova, Hellen Kwon, Erich Knodt, Anton Scharinger, Edith Schmid-Lienbacher, and Thomas Randle. Armin Jordan conducted the Ensemble Orchestral de Paris.

Prokofiev's surreal comedy *L'Amour des trois oranges*, the first major 20th century opera to be seen at the Festival since Britten's *The Prodigal Son* in 1970, was staged and performed with style and panache by Erlo, his designer Jacques Rapp, his cast, and the musicians of the Orchestre de l'Opéra de Lyon under Kent Nagano. The abstract set, consisting of movable shiny white blocks, allowed quick transitions and sudden apparitions. This was not a dark reading of the work. There was little sign of the truly sinister. Instead, there was a stunning sense of the absurd along with moments of tenderness and poetry. Two quarrelling groups of theatre fans clambered around the auditorium and eventually invaded the stage. No less a figure than Gabriel Bacquier, as the King, began the night as a bothersome latecomer, disturbing audience members in the stalls. He was on majestic form, as was Jules Bastin, as the formidable Cook, and Jean-Luc Viala, as the Prince. Vincent Le Texier, Georges Gautier, Gregory Reinhart, Michele Lagrange, and Catherine Dubosc, all contributed to the success of the show. Gabriel Bacquier was made a Commandeur des Arts et Lettres during the interval.

Claude Prey's *Le Rouge et le noir* was presented at the Grand Théâtre d'Aix by Mireille Laroche's company La Péniche-Opéra and the musicians of Ars Nova conducted by Philippe Nahon. Mireille Laroche's production was handsomely designed by Marc Boisseau. Stendhal's novel was difficult source material, but Prey's interest lay in irony, structuralism, and analyses, not the human condition. The score included endless parodies of both classical and romantic opera.

The concert series was once again centred on sacred works in the cathedral. Charpentier's *David et Jonathas* was given a rare outing by William Christie and Les Arts Florissants. Other concerts were given by Armin Jordan and the Ensemble Orchestral de Paris (Haydn's *Les Sept dernières paroles du Christ en croix*); Jeffrey Tate and the English

Chamber Orchestra (Mendelssohn's *Elijah*); and the Hilliard Ensemble (Pérotin, Ockeghem, Tallis, and Palestrina).

ii 1990: THE RETURN OF RAMEAU

The 1989 edition of the Festival had been one of the most successful since the heyday of Dussurget. Over 50,000 tickets were sold, a record. In August 1989, Erlo announced a similarly ambitious programme for 1990: three Mozart operas, *Die Entführung aus dem Serail*, *Il sogno di Scipione* and *Il re pastore*, Rameau's *Les Indes galantes*, Rossini's *Don Pasquale*, a revival of *Der Rosenkavalier*, and a stage production of Bach's *St Matthew Passion* directed by Adrian Noble. *Les Indes galantes* would initiate a Rameau cycle – *Castor et Pollux* following in 1991 and a revival of *Les Boréades* in 1992.[8]

Presumably, Erlo had asked the government for an increase in funding for 1990. When this didn't materialise, the following projects had to be abandoned: *Il sogno di Scipione*, *Il re pastore*, *St Matthew Passion*, *Les Boréades*, and *Der Rosenkavalier*. Because of Noble's appointment to run the Royal Shakespeare Company, the *St Matthew Passion* project may have been cancelled anyway. *Der Rosenkavalier*, conducted by Semyon Bychkov, was dropped late on – the Festival couldn't afford to pay the Orchestre de Paris to work for three weeks in Aix.

The subsidy from the Ministry of Culture remained capped at 2.8 million francs; all public subsidies combined amounted to 9.8 million francs, which was twenty-eight per cent of the total budget for 1990 of thirty-five million. The festival had to self-finance the other seventy-two per cent. Despite sponsorship, the burden still fell on ticket sales. Even with a reduced programme, Erlo was forced to increase the price of admission. The mayor of Aix acknowledged that this situation couldn't continue. Discussions with the Ministry were ongoing to achieve a significant increase to the budget in 1991, although the signs were that Mitterrand's socialist government was not going to deviate from its current cultural policy of decentralisation by funding the Festival d'Aix above the current level.[9]

Les Indes galantes was Rameau's first opéra-ballet. Each act tells a self-contained story set in either the East or the New World. The work was a notable success at the Palais Garnier during the 1950s, but the music was re-orchestrated. Aix's production, using Rameau's score of 1736, was another act of restoration by the Festival. *Les Indes galantes* conformed to the primary purpose of the opéra-ballet genre by delivering spectacular entertainment in which stage effects and dancing were the most important elements. However, Rameau's music elevated the dramatic content by expressing sadness and longing.

The director of Aix's production, Alfredo Arias, didn't respond to the layers in the music and, curiously, William Christie, whose interpretation of the score, played by Les Arts Florissants, was exemplary, didn't put him right. Arias directed the work as a satirical pantomime, with vibrantly coloured décor and costumes (by Roberto Platé and Françoise Tournafond), and lots of nudging and winking at the audience. All four acts were presented in a circus tent. During the second act, *Les Incas du Pérou*, the high priest Huascar donned sunglasses while praying to the sun. At the end of the final act, *Les Sauvages*, during the 'Dance of the Great Peace Pipe', the Native Americans, dressed as modern-day punks, shared a marijuana joint. Only occasionally did one of Arias's jokes hit its mark: for instance, when the volcano erupted at the end of act two, the décor rotated to reveal the machinist at work. Admittedly, the staging was enjoyable; one just had the feeling that Rameau deserved better. 'The style and substance of Alfredo Arias's production amount to a comprehensive statement of non-belief in the work's intrinsic revivability,' wrote Max Loppert in *The Financial Times*.[10] Ana Yepes's choreography for the dancers of Ris et Danceries lacked substance in this context. Thankfully, the versatile performers – among them François Le Roux, Catherine Dubosc (confirmed as one of Aix's best 'discoveries'), Laurence Dale, Nicolas Rivenq, Isabelle Poulenard, Miriam Ruggeri, and Jean-Paul Fouchécourt – sang beautifully.

The season's second opera, *Die Entführung aus dem Serail*, was directed by Jorge Lavelli. The young conductor Carlos Kalmar was in charge of the music. It was mysterious why Erlo chose to return to the opera so soon after Georges Lavaudant's acclaimed production of 1987. Lavelli set the opera in the 19th century. By taking inspiration from Jules Verne's *Around the World in Eighty Days*, he was responding to the clash of cultures inherent in the opera. But the idea wasn't fully explored. The updating produced some evocative imagery. The deerstalker-wearing Belmont arrived on a steamer. The set's stained-glass panels revealed ghostly images of concubines. The critic of *Le Monde* was not the only reviewer to complain about Kalmar's erratic variations in tempi and the consequent uneven playing of the Warsaw Sinfonietta.[11] The quality of the spoken German was substandard.

The season's final opera, Donizetti's *Don Pasquale*, was an import from the Opéra de Lyon. Patrizia Gracis's charming production, conducted by Gabriele Ferro at the head of the Warsaw Sinfonietta, offered a feast of great singing (and character acting) by Gabriel Bacquier, Barbara Hendrickx, and Gino Quilico.

Despite the reduced budget, the concert programme was very well thought out. Among the artists who, in 1990, gave the 'Une heure avec...' recitals in the cloître Saint-Sauveur were François Le Roux (Schönberg, Strauss and Sibelius), Catherine Dubosc (Schumann, Haydn and Debussy), and Isabelle Vernet (Fauré, Ravel and Satie). Federica von Stade demonstrated her range in a recital in the cour de l'Hôtel de Ville: Respighi, Puccini, Schubert and Mozart in the first half, Messiaen, Honegger, Satie and Schönberg in the second. Alfred Brendel performed Schumann's *Études Symphoniques* and Beethoven's Sonata no. 31 (op. 110) in the Théâtre de l'Archevêché.

William Christie and Les Arts Florissants gave three concerts in the cathédrale Saint-Sauveur centred on the music of the French Baroque that were revelatory. The pieces included Charpentier's *Actéon*, Purcell's *Dido and Aeneas*, Couperin's *Leçons de ténèbres pour le mercredy*, and an extract from Campra's petit motet *Cum invocarum*. Perhaps of most significance was the concert devoted to Rameau: the performances of the one-act operas *Anacréon* and *Pygmalion* served the composer much more faithfully than the production of *Les Indes galantes*. Also in the cathedral, Romano Gandolfi conducted the London Oriana Choir, the Soloists Charlotte Margiono, and the singers Frederica von Stade, Raul Gimenez, and Dimitri Kavrakos, in performances of Rossini's *Petite messe solennelle* and *Stabat Mater*.

Max Loppert wrote of the 1990 edition: 'Artists involved in one event do happy duty in others; it is a small contributory part of the atmosphere that off-duty singers all seem to find time to be in the audience at each other's shows. And the best, most genuinely festive side of the Festival is that even in a short Aix sojourn one makes discoveries, about music and performers out of one's normal run, which the *genius loci* seems to have directly brought about.'[12]

iii 1991: A NEW MANAGEMENT MODEL AND BRITTEN'S DREAM

At the beginning of its review of *Don Pasquale*, *Le Monde* commented that the ticket prices across the 1990 season had been 'intolerable', especially as the operas had been of uneven quality, and took the government to task for expecting the Festival to self-finance seventy per cent of its budget.[13]

The municipality had been the main player in the organisation of the Festival for some years. Jean-François Picheral, Aix's mayor since 1989, headed the Association du Festival d'Aix. He was proactive and committed. He presided over the press conference at which the 1991 programme was revealed in March of that year. The budget for 1991 was fifty-five million francs, a figure that allowed Erlo to mount the kind of season that Aix deserved – four new opera productions in repertory.

This turnaround had been achieved, not through a large increase in government funding (the music department of the Ministry of Culture believed that a change in artistic leadership was the way forward, and wanted Erlo to be replaced by Hugues Gall, director of the Grand Théâtre de Genève), but because the Ville d'Aix – rejecting the call for Erlo's dismissal – responded quickly and positively to Culture Minister Jack Lang's instruction to local authorities that they assume responsibly for the development of arts organisations. The Ville d'Aix changed the management and funding model, closing the Association and establishing a mixed economy semi-public company (Société d'économie mixte or SEMETA), with multiple private firms contributing (twelve did so in 1991).

As well as organising the Festival, SEMETA was charged with clearing the circa six million francs deficit accumulated under the Association, and with managing the Théâtre de l'Archevêché all year round so that it was properly maintained and refurbished. As had been the case with the Association, the executive board of SEMETA was led by the Ville d'Aix, with the mayor as president. His vice-president for finance was Gilles Nancy, a professor of law at the Université d'Aix. The board appointed the artistic director of the Festival but otherwise, at least in principle, did not interfere in artistic matters.

It remained to be seen whether this funding model would work effectively for more than one season, allowing the budget to be expanded without significant top-ups from the public purse. Picheral gave it a positive spin and announced that the building of a new theatre as part of the Sextius-Mirabeau development would go ahead, and that, unrealistically as it turned out, it would be ready by 2000. Edmonde Charles-Roux, who at this time was the personal representative of the Minister of Culture on the board of directors of the Festival, and who supported Lang's policy, responded to *Le Monde*'s criticisms of the Ministry in a letter published in the paper on 21 July. She believed that it was right for the Ville d'Aix to assume responsibility and that the new funding model was an opportunity for the Festival.

'The 1991 edition will be the biggest festival in ten years,' Picheral said. It was certainly one of the biggest, and arguably the most rounded and adventurous, bringing together at the Théâtre de l'Archevêché operas from the Baroque era (Rameau's *Castor et Pollux*), the classical era (Mozart's *Le nozze di Figaro* and *Schuldigkeit des ersten Gebots*, marking the bicentenary of the composer's death), and the underrepresented 20th century (Britten's *A Midsummer Night's Dream*). Technically, the scale of the operation placed huge demands on a mid-sized theatre. As well as a large cast of singers and dancers, *Castor et Pollux* required fourteen stagehands, eight lighting technicians, seven make-up artists, and seven dressers.[14] After the curtain fell, at around one-thirty, the stage crew worked until dawn to build the set and lighting for that night's show. In total, the Festival employed around eighty technicians. Many returned year after year, and, unusually for an opera house, people from various trades worked harmoniously together.

'Happily, Mozart is now done everywhere,' Louis Erlo told the press. 'We have the privilege of watching as other festivals do their bit to catch up.'[15] Unfortunately, *Le nozze di Figaro*, directed by Rudolph Noelte, working for the first time in France, continued the recent run of disappointing Mozart productions at Aix. 'If Noelte found anything interesting in the opera, he kept it to himself,' wrote

Christian Leble in *Liberation*. All the interior scenes took place in the same 18th century oval antechamber, in which the characters stood or sat (on Louis XV chairs) apart, unable to connect. The décor (by Eva Maria Hieber) was stylish, if not original. The show irritated people who wanted Mozart's *Figaro* and not Noelte's.

Friedrich Haider, little known in France, conducted the Ensemble Orchestral de Paris from the harpsichord. Several critics felt that he was too absorbed in playing and didn't keep pit and stage together. The singing of Andreas Schmidt (the Count) and Judith Howarth (Susanna) was admired. Veteran festivalgoers were delighted to discover that Renato Cappechi, Dussurget's first Don Giovanni in 1949, was singing Bartolo. *The New York Times* reported that Erlo 'made no effort to disguise his disappointment' with *Le nozze di Figaro*. He admitted that there were risks associated with his policy of engaging directors 'who were themselves discovering a work'.

There are two versions of *Castor et Pollux*, the original of 1737 and the substantially revised second version of 1754. The first *Castor* had been a relative failure. Influenced by the ideas of Voltaire, with whom he had been working, fractiously, on the unperformed tragedy *Samson*, Rameau placed the moral dilemma faced by Pollux at the centre of the opera, reducing action and the stage time of the actresses. Daringly, he started the opera in the middle, after Castor's death in battle. There was a mythological prologue (as convention dictated until Rameau composed an opera without one), but the opera proper began with Castor's funeral, and the most extraordinary music: it is the finest of all Rameau's opening scenes. Berlioz wrote of the lament of Télaïre over Castor's grave that it was 'one of the most sublime conceptions of dramatic music'.[16] This music was retained in the revised *Castor et Pollux* but moved to the second act where it had less impact. The prologue was dropped, and new music written throughout the acts. Rameau's revisions were designed to make the opera more compelling for the patrons of the Opéra, with more of the action taking place on the stage this time and the female characters more prominent. Both versions are valid, but the first is darker and more concentrated, cerebral, and original.[17] The previous high-profile sighting of this seldom-seen opera, conducted by Roger Norrington for the English Bach Festival at Covent Garden in 1981, used the 1754 version. Christie chose the original version. Nicholas Kenyon thought that this was the wrong choice, too static and mediative, but admired the music and Christie's conducting: 'There is music of suppressed passion, especially in the chromatically inflected choruses and plangent laments, and of classically restrained exuberance, especially in the wonderfully varied and supple dances. The vocal declamation is natural, beautifully shaped, and there are several extraordinary twists in Rameau's highly original harmonic language.'[18]

To direct the production, Erlo invited back Pier-Luigi Pizzi, whose account of Rameau's *Hippolyte et Aricie* in 1983 was fondly remembered. Pizzi chose to adopt, in an updated form, some of the scenic practices of the 18th century, including machine effects. The stage pictures were both spectacular and charmingly naïve – cardboard trees appeared and disappeared; Jupiter descended on a cloud. Some of the images – the broken columns and veiled mourners of the first act; the Poussin-inspired pastoral elegance of the conclusion – were beautiful. 'Pizzi has not tried to be more intelligent than the libretto,' Christie remarked. This may have been an oblique criticism of the director he worked with on *Les Indes galantes*. Pizzi's costumes, though, were ugly and comical. The unfortunate dancers of Ris et Danceries wore golden ankle boots and body stockings; Castor and Pollux wore large helmets and tight costumes in blue Lycra. It is unclear whether Pizzi was parodying the kitsch world of the Folies Bergère deliberately or by accident. The pain of unrequited love (possibly inspired by Rameau's love for the woman who married his brother) was not fully explored. However, the critics responded positively to the production's 18th century aesthetics and Christie's passion for Rameau's music, a passion shared by his singers: Howard Cook as Castor, François Le Roux as Pollux, Agnès Mellon as Télaïre, Véronique Gens as Phebé, Claron McFadden as Vénus, Mark Padmore as l'Amour, and Bernard Deletré as Jupiter.

Mozart composed the sacred singspiel *Schuldigkeit des ersten Gebots* (*Le Devoir du premier commandement*) in 1767, when he was only eleven years old. It was the first part of a three-part work; the remaining music, by Michael Haydn and Anton Adlgasser, is lost. Mozart's manuscript was purchased by Prince Albert in 1841 and placed in the Royal Collections at Windsor.

This allegorical work is more a dramatic cantata for three sopranos and two tenors than an opera. It consists of recitatives and arias but is dramatically inert. A festival like Aix, with a long tradition of devotion to Mozart's music, was better placed than most to resurrect this work from his childhood.

Erlo decided to mount the work as an opera in the Théâtre de l'Archevêché, with a lavish set that, curiously, replicated Venice's Palladio Theatre. Despite the best efforts of Jean-Claude Fall, the work seemed too small and static in this setting. The score was beautifully served by a first-rate cast – Elena Vink, Lorraine Hunt, Valerie Masterson, Bruce Ford and John Daniecki. Tamas Pal conducted the Salieri Chamber Orchestra. Aix's Mozart celebrations were completed by a cycle of his concert arias, performed by Carol Vaness, Hélène Donath, Teresa Berganza, and Margaret Price.

The final show at the Théâtre de l'Archevêché transformed a middling festival into one of the most significant of recent times. In a front-page review of Britten's *A Midsummer Night's Dream*, *Le Monde* declared: 'Here, finally, to everyone's relief, is the *coup d'éclat* that the Festival has been waiting for. It is the most daring opera production we have seen in a long time.'[19]

This was one of those rare occasions when the various elements that constitute the art of opera aligned perfectly. Because Shakespeare's play and Britten's opera take place in a domain of multiple unrealities, the director can let his or her imagination run free. The young Canadian director Robert Carsen, who had learned his craft as an assistant director at Glyndebourne (1980-85) before making his name with productions of Mozart's *La finta giardiniera* at the Camden Festival in London and Boito's *Mefistofele* at the Grand Théâtre de Genève, followed Peter Brook in creating an abstract, poetic, metaphorical mindscape in which longing, pain, desire and playfulness co-existed. Carsen even copied Peter Brook by suspending the sleeping lovers in the air. Michael Levine's elegant design used vivid greens and night blues. Under a crescent moon, the stage floor initially appeared to represent a green field but gradually became recognisable as a huge bed, with two enormous white pillows, over which Oberon and Titania played their game of desire and jealousy.

Although Britten, in writing the libretto with Peter Pears, wanted the naturalistic forest of tradition, faithfully realised by John Gielgud at Covent Garden in 1961 (during the dress rehearsal the great Shakespearean was heard to shout 'Will someone turn off that damn music!'), his score is wonderfully strange and nocturnal in its conjuring of the rhythms of sleep and the disorientation of dreaming.

While Britten gives Puck, the mechanicals, and the lovers their own instrumentation, the connecting night music, dominated by harpsichord, harp, celeste, delicate percussion and gliding strings, is intimate, psychologically astute and a little feverish. The score could have been written for Carsen's production. Carsen thankfully made two changes to the libretto. The changeling boy was not a child, but a baby doll, and the spoken role of Puck was not a ballet dancing youth but a sardonic middle-aged comedian (played by Emil Wolk).

Anne Rey, writing in *Le Monde*, perceptively analysed the production: 'Nothing in this dream is redundant. Shakespeare's all-seeing philosophy, Britten's aristocratic melancholy; the biting, soaring, poetic imagery of the production; the luminous, impalpable sonorities obtained by Steuart Bedford from the Ensemble Orchestral de Paris; the abstraction of Michael Levine's décor; the atonalism mixed with the archaisms of the score, the sensuality of the instrumental harmonies, everything, here, is complete without superfluity.'[20]

Steuart Bedford weighted with subtlety the sophisticated parodies that Britten weaved into the score, hunting horns referencing Weber's *Oberon* and Wagner's *Tristan*, and the multi-layered musical and literary references of the mechanicals' account of the death of Pyramus and Thisbe. He assembled an excellent cast: James Bowman and Lillian Watson as Oberon and Titania; Juliet Booth, Eirian James, John Graham-Hall and Gerald Finley as the lovers; and Roderick Kennedy, Donald Adams and Christopher Gillett as Bottom, Peter Quince and Flute. David Murray concluded: 'In a properly organised world, this production would already be headed for London; but its Aix predecessor just two years ago, an exhilarating version of Purcell's *Fairy Queen* by Les Arts Florissants and a contingent from the RSC – expensive, admittedly – never found the funds to strut at home. That must not be the fate of this *Dream*.'[21]

ELEVEN

Funding Woes Deepen

1992-1996

i 1992/93: STRAVINSKY AND HANDEL

The 1991 edition was, overall, a success, but it quickly emerged that the new funding model, trumpeted with such hope in the run-up to the season, was already in trouble. The large sum of money that allowed Erlo to mount an ambitious programme turned out to be a one-off. The season hadn't broken even, and the deficit had increased. With a large deficit and less sponsorship money coming in than predicted, the budget for 1992 was forty-five million francs, nearly ten million francs lower than the 1991 figure, meaning that Erlo could only programme two new productions and one revival. Not one of Erlo's final five editions would be adequately funded.

Perhaps Erlo reflected later that he should have stepped down after the 1991 season. He had been in charge for ten years and could be rightly proud of his achievements. But letting go of a great festival, opera house or theatre company, is profoundly hard. Like Dussurget before him, Erlo kept going despite the growing difficulties.

Before Gilles Nancy had finalised the accounts, Erlo had planned to follow 1989's *Fairy Queen* with a stage production of Purcell's *King Arthur*. This expensive project was a casualty of the financial crisis. It was fortunate that Erlo had a hit production, Robert Carsen's *A Midsummer Night's Dream*, that he could immediately revive. The 1992 season in the Théâtre de l'Archevêché was completed by new productions of *Don Giovanni* and Stravinsky's *The*

Rake's Progress. This last was the third major 20th century opera mounted by Erlo since 1989, a clear achievement.

Aix's latest failed attempt to emulate the achievement of its renowned *Don Giovanni* of 1949 opened the season. Giorgio Marini's old-fashioned production lacked inspiration. There were broad brushstrokes but few illuminating details. Arduino Cantafora's design consisted of false prosceniums, half-curtains, and huge painted flats (depicting the rooms or gardens of a grand estate) that descended from the flies. The singers, led by Andreas Schmidt's Giovanni, seemed under-rehearsed. The English Chamber Orchestra sounded ordinary under Armin Jordan's direction.

Alfredo Arias's *The Rake's Progress* was vaguely set in the 20th century. Stravinsky wrote the work with Britten's former collaborator W.H. Auden, but *The Rake's Progress* suffered in comparison with the elegant singularity of Britten's *Dream* as directed by Carsen. Arias's main idea was to double the three principals with dancers (which, given the money problems, Erlo probably should have vetoed). The choreographer was Andy Degroat. Certain moments in the opera were underlined by video images, such as a mouse trapped on a wheel. A scene's location was written on a descending flat. Arias began the show at the end, in a Bedlam asylum inhabited by vulnerable young women, and then flashed back. The setting consisted of scaffolding and a grim, graffiti-covered wall. The show's chief asset was its cast, led by Samuel Ramey as Nick Shadow, Dawn Upshaw as Anne, and Jerry Hadley as Tom. Kent Nagano, conducting the Orchestre de l'Opéra de Lyon, expertly handled the music's acidic irony.

During the 1992 season, Gilles Nancy told *Le Monde* that SEMETA 'has already given a lot of money: ten million francs in capital when the Association had none'. An increase for next year exceeding six million francs was being discussed, but it proved unrealistic. *Don Giovanni* and the *Dream* played to eighty-three per cent capacity; but *The Rake's Progress*, despite a significant reduction in the ticket price for local people, struggled at sixty-five per cent. With revenue from sponsorship still down, the deficit grew.[1] Picheral had hoped to raise twenty million francs from sponsors in 1992. Four million francs were pledged by the public works companies constructing the new Sextius-Mirabeau quarter, but the eventual total fell short by three million francs. Picheral and Gilles Nancy hoped that the 1993 budget wouldn't be less than forty-two million francs, but even that would be a reduction on the figure for 1992. Under these circumstances, it was impossible to plan for the longer term, which placed huge pressure on Erlo and his team. *Le Monde* noted that: 'Never has a festival of national interest been so dependent on industrial patronage.'[2]

Therefore, the 1993 season was even more financially stretched than its predecessor. There were two new productions, Weber's *Euryanthe* and Handel's *Orlando*, and an unwanted revival of Giorgio Marini's disliked *Don Giovanni*. Twelve opera performances were scheduled, less than in 1992 and way below the number the Festival wanted and deserved.

The rarely staged *Orlando* was at least eagerly anticipated. The director was Robert Carsen, working for the first time with William Christie and Les Arts Florissants. Erlo wanted the two to produce a body of work at Aix. Carsen's designer, Anthony McDonald, had delivered compelling designs at the RSC during the previous few years, including the 1989 Mark Rylance *Hamlet*. *Orlando* is one of Handel's most daring works (1733). Both the music and the dramatic action are highly concentrated. There are no choruses and few ensembles. Based on Ariosto's *Orlando furioso*, the theme of unrequited love is given a surprisingly modern psychology. This was Carsen's way into the opera. The production was deliberately plain and unmagical. The stage was often dark, and empty. McDonald's décor consisted of triangular panels that opened and closed like the lens of a camera. Felicity Palmer, as Orlando, bravely went for broke in the mad scene, temporarily sacrificing vocal beauty in the process. Carsen downplayed the comedic and pastoral elements and removed the sorcery altogether: Dorinda (Rosa Mannion, outstanding) washed and ironed bedsheets while singing; the magician Zoroastre wore a grey suit and raincoat. An emblem of corporate threat, he was constantly on stage, silently observing. Carsen's reading was often striking, but it lacked the coherence of his *Dream*.

Christie paced the music perfectly, ensuring that the inexorable see-saw of recitatives and arias progressed smoothly without sacrificing tension. An English critic suggested that the string tone was too romantic, something that provoked an understandably prickly response from the conductor. Carsen was booed during the curtain calls: a badge of honour for any young director.

The boos that greeted the director of *Euryanthe*, Hans Peter Cloos, were more virulent, but at least it was a reaction. The critic of *Le Monde* wrote that 'mute indifference' would have been more appropriate. Erlo's decision to stage Weber's neglected proto-Wagnerian opera was admirable, but the lacklustre production did it few favours. The singing and staging were substandard. Perhaps there hadn't been enough time to find a way of interpreting Weber's medieval melodrama for a contemporary audience, but that didn't excuse the amateur blocking. The critic of *Liberation* could not detect any 'dramatic intelligence in the play of the acting'. The orchestral music was well realised by Jeffrey Tate and the English Chamber Orchestra but needed more players. The singers were lumbered with bad historical costumes and seemed to be getting negligible help from the pit. On the plus side, Jean Kalman's lighting design was beautiful. Rodney Milnes didn't mince his words: 'Had I paid £90 for my seat, I would have been round the management offices the next day to demand a refund. What on earth has happened to Aix?'[3]

Back in March, President Mitterrand's Socialist Party had suffered a calamitous defeat in the legislative election, winning only ninety-five seats. Parties of the right were now in the majority. Mitterrand had no choice but to appoint a member of parliament from the Gaullist RPR party – Édouard Balladur – as prime minister. Jack Lang's long reign as Minister of Culture was over. His replacement was the right-wing politician, Jacques Toubon. How would this political change impact the Festival d'Aix and France's other flagship arts organisations? Discussions were expected to start after the 1993 season.

Jacques Toubon attended the opening night of *Euryanthe*. One is tempted to think that this was unfortunate. But perhaps Erlo wanted him to see this production and not *Orlando* because he could argue that underfunding was the underlying cause of the farrago. Perhaps, also, Erlo was happy for him to witness a new phenomenon in the Théâtre de l'Archevêché: some of the flimsy seats had started to spontaneously collapse under their unfortunate occupants. Toubon, though, was using Culture as a stepping stone to Justice and was gone within two years.

With only one opera succeeding, Erlo was grateful that the two high-profile concerts in the Théâtre de l'Archevêché were memorable. Charles Dutoit conducted the Orchestre national de France in two of Ravel's masterpieces – *La Valse* and *Daphnis et Chloé*. Erlo's scrutiny of the French operas of the Baroque continued with Campra's *L'Europe galante* of 1697. The piece was entrusted to a new maestro, Marc Minkowski, conducting his period instruments ensemble Les Musiciens du Louvre.

ii 1994/95/96: ERLO'S LAST SEASONS AND THE APPOINTMENT OF STÉPHANE LISSNER

A little over a month before the beginning of the 1994 edition of the Festival, the stage cage of the Théâtre de l'Archevêché collapsed: the resulting works would cost the Ville d'Aix four million francs. This, along with the collapsing seats, symbolised the financial state of the Festival, which was now dire. The festival had not known a crisis like this since the final years of the Dussurget era. The number of operas, performances (and the length of the Festival) had declined precipitously since 1989. In 1994, there would only be one production – a new *Die Zauberflöte* from William Christie and Robert Carsen – and fifteen concerts. It would all be over in fifteen days.

The Aixois wondered whether the Festival would even survive. Veteran attendees yearned for the splendour of the old days, the glamour of festival nights, of white tuxes and diamonds, of dining post-show on the Cours Mirabeau, conveniently forgetting that Dussurget's way of coping with too little money was to revive certain productions year after year. Many editions consisted of one new production and two revivals, others of two new productions and one revival. The productions needed to be relatively cheap to mount and were. Dussurget engaged talented but inexperienced singers even in leading roles, made them stars, and then benefited from their loyalty for years. Most of his sets were made from canvas. It was cheaper to engage a great artist to paint a picture on a backcloth than a professional theatre designer to design a three-dimensional set that needed to be built, dismantled, and stored. In other words, Dussurget made a virtue out of limited means. His Aix was unique, unrepeatable.

The festival's relationship with the citizens of the town had rarely been as poor. While shop owners and restaurateurs were angered by the decline, the general view oscillated between indifference and resentment. With thirteen per cent unemployment in the town, the Ville d'Aix's financial support of a festival which ordinary people didn't attend needed to be justified. The festival's attempt (demanded by the government) to democratise the Festival had achieved limited results. In truth, democratisation was near impossible to achieve without changing the nature of the Festival so that it presented only the most commercially popular operas and musicals, with big name singers. Picheral admitted that few local people went to the Festival but said: 'Lyrical art is a showcase.'

With government subsidies rising only slightly, the Festival had been forced to be rather reckless in its pursuit of sponsors. It had budgeted on promises of money that never materialised. *Le Monde* reported that the Festival had suffered losses of twenty-two million francs since 1991. During this time, the budget had risen to unsustainable levels before crashing: thirty-eight million francs in 1990 (sixteen opera performances); fifty-five million francs in 1991 (twenty performances); forty-five million francs in 1992 (sixteen performances). In 1994, the budget was twenty-seven million francs, a sum that only allowed eight evenings. The budget would have been less if SEMETA hadn't provided capital to pay off some of the deficit. This capital was now gone.

There was no doubting the passion of Erlo and his team, nor of the mayor. Erlo began each planning phase more in hope than expectation. As well as *Die Zauberflöte*, he had hoped to mount a new production of Handel's *Semele* and a revival of *Orlando* in 1994, but by January the last two had been scrapped. Some of Picheral's political opponents naturally blamed the crisis on the way the Festival was managed, believing that a budget of nearly thirty million francs was enough. 'This festival is badly managed,' declared the RPR party's Jean-Bernard Raimond, a candidate in the upcoming mayoral elections.[4] Erlo replied that the cost of mounting opera had increased drastically in recent years. Even with high ticket prices, the eight performances of *Die Zauberflöte* were expected to make a loss of 4.8 million francs. This was because each performance would cost around 1.5 million francs but only bring in 900,000 at the box office. Erlo reiterated that the Théâtre de l'Archevêché was still too small (1,650 places compared to 8,000 at Orange). Picheral didn't expect the second theatre to be built for many years.

Picheral and Erlo requested more money from the government. They made the case that the Paris Opéra and the Paris orchestras received subsidies that were prodigiously higher. Picheral was bullish: 'State aid is a masquerade,' he said. 'Aix receives twelve and a half million francs in public subsidies: four million francs from the city, three million from the department and one and a half million from the Region. Against four million francs from the State.'[5] The Opéra received five hundred million francs. But this wasn't a reasonable comparison given the size of the Opéra's operation, its permanent orchestra and ballet company, etc. The government allocated more money to Aix than any other festival.

The dispute had become political after the coming to power of the right-wing government. Picheral, the socialist mayor of Aix, would surely not have attacked the Ministry of Culture so directly if the socialist Lang was still in office. Some within the Ville d'Aix believed that the Ministry wanted to 'kill the Festival in a city run by socialists'. The festival's financial woes had started under Lang (who had refused to increase funding) so the claim was not wholly convincing. However, Picheral and Erlo were right to believe that a significant increase in the contribution from the government was the only solution. The festival was in limbo. In an interview, Erlo challenged the government:

> The responsible authorities haven't made the necessary decisions that would determine the existence or non-existence of the Festival. If it is to exist, they have to adopt the proper financial measures, to give us a chance for long-term planning. If they can't provide the funds, then they should have the courage to say that we can't continue. Nobody is taking the lead.[6]

Erlo's Administrative Director, Herve Grillet, chipped in with: 'We want to stay in the club of international festivals, renowned for quality and innovation, but the government doesn't want to acknowledge this. Provence is far from Paris, and in a centralised state, that's not good for us.'[7]

Any decision on the Festival's future was placed on hold until after the presidential and local elections of 1995. It had become clear that Erlo's contract would not be extended when it came up for renewal. The music department of the Ministry believed that poor management was a factor, that the operating budget of eight million francs was extravagant. They asked Erlo to accept a significant drop in salary. Stephane Martin, the Ministry's director of music, made the old arguments: 'If we give more money, we want to know the Festival will reach a wider range of people. In its present form, Aix is expensive and elitist.' So far, so familiar. What he said next was extraordinary, for it suggested that he had no appreciation for the Festival's history and no interest in its future as a festival of opera of the calibre of Salzburg or Glyndebourne: 'Aix doesn't have a public funding problem – we've actually increased the subsidy. The problem is the artistic side. The festival needs to reduce its dependence on opera, raise its volume of activity and develop ideas which will interest the public.'[8] Perhaps Erlo's public utterances were the cause of this bizarre statement. Despite this public jostling, the expectation was that in the end the government wouldn't allow the Festival to fail and didn't want it to change its mission. Why? Because of its international reputation and prestige. There was a sense in which Erlo and Picheral were engaging in brinkmanship: spending more money than they had in the belief that the government would eventually increase its subsidy. But the government wasn't going to act until Erlo was removed.

Christie and Carsen's *Die Zauberflöte* was a success. It was a product of Erlo's refusal to dumb down. It was elegant, brilliantly crafted and, after several recent failures, thankfully worthy of the Festival's Mozartian heritage. The stage, pit and proscenium were painted blue. Carsen and his designer Patrick Kinmouth's abstract setting (dominated by a cyclorama that changed colour, from blue to blood red and finally to white), stylish modern costumes and emblematic imagery, such as a gnarled winter tree of wisdom, freed a work that too often had been over-burdened by scenic devices as well as ponderous allegorical meanings. There was no heavy concept. Carsen directed the opera as a simple morality tale that concluded in a celebration of fraternity and joy (the cast removed their costumes to reveal white trousers and shirts before invading the auditorium). 'It is no power struggle between the forces of good and evil,' wrote John Higgins in *The Times*, 'but a fairy-tale in which the sins of the malefactors are quickly forgiven. The snake's attempt on the life of Tamino and Monostatos's foiled rape of Pamina are but shreds of nightmares blown away by light of day.'[9] Under Christie, the music sounded vibrantly fresh. As was typical of Erlo's Aix, big name stars were absent, but not missed. The talented cast included Rosa Mannion as Pamina, Anton Scharinger as Papageno, Natalie Dessay as the Queen of the Night, Hans Peter Blochwitz as Tamino, and Reinhard Hagen as Sarastro.

The short 1994 edition at least didn't add to the deficit. The Ville d'Aix gave the Festival a new one-off payment of nine million francs, as well as increasing its annual subsidy by one million francs. This meant that the budget for 1995 was thirty-eight million francs. Erlo was able to programme three operas – two revivals (Carsen and Christie's *Die Zauberflöte* with the same cast, and Denis Llorca's *Così fan tutte*, conducted by Jeffrey Tate) and one creation (Rossini's *Le Comte Ory*, directed by Marcel Maréchal and conducted by Evelino Pido). Better but still not good enough.

Erlo announced some positive news. The festival had created a resident orchestra, made up of young musicians who were mostly graduates of Claudio Abbado's European Community Youth Orchestra. The idea came from Jeffrey Tate. These musicians, most of whom were employees of major orchestras, agreed to use their five weeks of leave each summer to work together in Aix as the Orchestre européen du Festival d'Aix. This was much cheaper than bringing in an established ensemble. It was a return to the kind of arrangement that Dussurget had made with the Orchestre des concerts du Conservatoire. The musicians were contracted for two seasons. The future was uncertain because Erlo would not be in post after 1996. Also, the unions were unhappy.

Rossini's *Le Comte Ory* concerns the satanic Ory's unsuccessful attempts to seduce the chaste Adèle while her husband is away at the Crusades. Marcel Maréchal staged it as a farce. Ory and his followers are meant to disguise themselves as female pilgrims during the second act. Maréchal dressed them as nuns, presumably for comic effect.

The critics admired Sumi Jo's performance as Adèle (John Higgins: '[There is] meat in the voice, coupled with distinct hauteur in the eyes').[10] Unfortunately, the veteran tenor William Matteuzi was in poor voice. Booed at the end, he smiled graciously and applauded back. Evelino Pido, making his debut at the Festival, pitched the music perfectly. The Orchestre européen du Festival d'Aix was praised for the quality of its playing. As well as being in the pit for *Le Comte Ory* and *Così fan tutte*, it gave a scintillating concert, under

Tate, of works by Mozart, Britten, and Mahler. In the cathedral, Christie conducted Les Arts Florissants in performances of Handel's *The Messiah* and Beethoven's *Missa Solemnis*.

Jacques Chirac of the RPR won the presidential election in April 1995. Picheral was re-elected as mayor of Aix that June. The Minister of Culture, Philippe Douste-Blazy, wanted Aix's next artistic director to be Stéphane Lissner, at that time Director General of the Théâtre du Châtelet and the Orchestre de Paris. In his plan, the Orchestre de Paris would resume its former role as the Festival's resident orchestra. The new president wanted this too. As mayor of Paris, Chirac had used Lissner's Théâtre du Châtelet, run by the Ville de Paris, to score points over the Paris Opéra, run by Mitterrand's socialist government. The appointment, though, was the responsibility of the mayor of Aix and the Festival's conseil d'administration. Had the RPR's Jean-Bernard Raimond been elected mayor it was believed that Lissner would have been appointed immediately. Picheral wanted to take time and consider other applications as well. He stated clearly that prospective candidates would need to submit a detailed artistic and financial plan.

Picheral told *Le Monde* that he would make up his own mind: 'I don't know Stéphane Lissner. I haven't offered him the direction of the Festival d'Aix, but you inform me that he is "going to come". I'm used to these announcements. Barely had M. Erlo been appointed than rumours circulated about the identity of his successor. You see, he is still there. All the music directors in the ministry tried to put someone in charge of the Festival. Everyone has their own idea.'[11]

A recruitment process was initiated in November 1995. To the chagrin of the Ministry, Picheral extended Erlo's contract by one year so that he would oversee the 1997 edition. *Le Monde* reported that the other candidates included Alain Lombard (former director of the Grand Théâtre de Bordeaux), William Christie, Jeffrey Tate together with Jean-Marie Blanchard (general administrator of the Opéra Bastille), Nicolas Joël (director of the Théâtre du Capitole de Toulouse), and Henri Maïer (head of the Opéra de Montpellier).

President Chirac and the Ministry's support of Lissner had to be taken into account. It was expected that the annual subsidy allocated to the Festival by the Ministry would be increased from five to fifteen million francs to launch the new era. This increase was crucial.

It wasn't clear that the increase would be forthcoming if Lissner wasn't appointed.

Lissner's provisional appointment was announced by Douste-Blazy and Picheral at a press conference held at the Ministry on 23 November. If he produced a detailed financial plan by the end of January, the appointment would be confirmed. His tenure would begin with the 1998 edition. His appointment wasn't only connected to the unfortunate way partisan politics had seeped into the domain of the arts. He had an outstanding track record and his vision for the future of the Festival included the creation of a European Academy of Music. There would be four operas per season, and his plan for the repertoire included one 20th century opera every year, alongside one by Mozart and one from the period 1600 to 1899. Artists appearing at the Festival would give masterclasses. The Ministry confirmed that the subsidy would be increased to fifteen million francs. Erlo was understandably aggrieved. Doubly so when he was told, in February, that the 1997 anniversary season, which he was to have organised, had been cancelled: it would happen under Lissner in 1998.

A report by the Chambre régionale des comptes de Provence-Alpes-Côte d'Azur (Regional Chamber of Accounts) on the management of the Festival, published in February, was damning. The report questioned why such a large deficit had been allowed to grow. It questioned the allowances and 'excessive' salaries paid to the organisers, and condemned the inaction of the State, shareholders and especially the Ville d'Aix. The report noted the establishment of SEMETA in 1992 but found that it had failed because no one took responsibility for the securing of sponsors. At the same time, no action had been taken to reduce costs. The festival was living beyond its means. In particular, the report condemned the unnecessarily large sums of money given to a leading communications company. The increase in Erlo's salary was condemned, as were the expenses necessitated by his travel arrangements. The report also criticised the renting of a villa for Erlo during the Festival. If these last points seemed churlish, the fact that Erlo was running the Opéra de Lyon at the same time as the Festival was clearly not ideal. He had hired an 'artistic adviser' despite the reluctance of the Ville d'Aix and the director of music at the Ministry. In his defence, Erlo claimed that his salary was half that paid to the directors of other international festivals. It was agreed from the start that he could continue to run the Opéra de Lyon. 'How could I have been lax or overpaid when the State implicitly recognises, by going from five million francs to fifteen million francs in aid, that this festival lacked funds?'

How much of this was politically orchestrated by the Ministry of Culture and Picheral's opponents in the RPR? The report was ordered by Jacques Toubon when he was the minister in 1993. Both Toubon and his successor Philippe Douste-Blazy expected the findings to be highly critical of Erlo and Picheral. The Ministry, although criticised, gets off very lightly, while Erlo and Picheral are given no quarter. The report did not take into account the particular pressures and paradoxes faced by the manager of an underfunded opera theatre at a time of recession, an opera theatre expected to meet the highest international standards of excellence and innovation. However, as mentioned above, Erlo and Picheral had lived beyond their means in the expectation of an increased subsidy from the government.

The festival was left hanging during the two years before its rebirth under Lissner in 1998. There was one opera and a few concerts in 1996. The edition only lasted for twelve days. The festival didn't take place in 1997. Lissner, in post from November 1996, had over a year to prepare for 1998 and beyond.

The 1996 programme was only approved by the Festival's conseil d'administration at the end of March. Erlo ended his era at Aix with a masterpiece of the Baroque never before staged in France, Handel's *Semele*. Christie and Carsen came together at Aix for the fourth time. Carsen set the opera in the England of Elizabeth II. The partnership of Carsen and Kinmouth delivered another imaginative production, with emblematic décor and uncluttered scenography. Juno was dressed like the Queen (green wellies; headscarf); Rosemary Joshua's provocative Semele wore a silk negligee for much of the show. The theme of William Congreve's libretto – the folly of greed, lust and ambition – was vividly presented in this setting. Rockwell Blake's Jupiter was an ageing, off-duty, playboy in a denim shirt. Willard White, as Somnus, God of Sleep, emerged from a pile of sleeping bodies. The finale was a toff's Champagne party celebrating Bacchus.

The Orchestre européen du Festival d'Aix gave four concerts in the Théâtre de l'Archevêché. Symphonies by Mozart and Schubert and Schumann's Piano Concerto (Christopher Hogwood and pianist

Hélène Grimaud); a 'bel canto romantique' programme (Evelino Pido and Sumi Jo); Mozart's Concerto for Piano no. 12 (Evelino Pido and pianist Mari Kodama); and Wagner's *Siegfried Idyll* and Strauss's *Bretano Lieder* (Armin Jordan and Natalie Dessay). Les Arts Florissants performed grands motets by Mondonville at the Théâtre de l'Archevêché, and Couperin's *Leçons de ténèbres* (1713) in the cathedral.

Despite its brevity, the 1996 edition was recognisably by, and of, Aix. Erlo signed off in the programme:

> I would like to tell you how happy these fifteen years in Aix have been. Obviously, as always in the field of creation, there are some regrets and disappointments, but also achievements of audacity and originality, which I share with my team and with great artists. *Les Boréades, La finta giardiniera, The Fairy Queen, Les Indes galantes, A Midsummer Night's Dream, Die Zauberflöte,* among many others, are wonderful memories.[12]

Few, I think, would disagree with Erlo's choice of his era's finest productions. It was an era that served the music of the Baroque, especially the French Baroque, splendidly and with a pioneering and innovative spirit that should be applauded. To create this work, he chose outstanding collaborators – John Eliot Gardiner and William Christie. But Erlo also programmed 20th century operas at the Théâtre de l'Archevêché.

Edmonde Charles-Roux, interviewed in 2008, said: 'I think that the treatment of Louis Erlo was a little ungrateful. He brought in extraordinary singers. He persuaded Jessye Norman to sing Rameau with the period instruments of John Eliot Gardiner in 1983. He has retired from musical life and now lives in Corsica. I think of him with affection and admiration.' Gabriel Dussurget, who died during the 2006 edition, also admired Erlo.

Part Four

The NIGHTS of STÉPHANE LISSNER

TWELVE

Renaissance

1998-2002

i LAYING NEW FOUNDATIONS

Details of the Festival d'Aix's new era were announced by Philippe Douste-Blazy and François Picheral at a press conference held on 27 January 1997 at the Hôtel de Ville in Aix. Also present were Jean-Marie Messier, chief executive of the Compagnie générale des eaux (soon to merge with Canal+ to form the media conglomerate Vivendi), and the Festival's new director, Stéphane Lissner. The organising structure of the Erlo era had been dismantled. Once again, the 1901 law was used to create an Association. The new conseil d'administration (board of directors) consisted of three representatives of the government and four representatives of the local authorities (town, department, region), plus five qualified individuals and three 'active members' appointed by the general assembly. Jean-Marie Messier was the first president of the Association.

The Ville d'Aix, for so many years left to preserve the Festival on its own, had finally been joined by the government. Douste-Blazy stated that the Festival was as important as the Paris Opéra. There would be no festival in 1997. This would allow the deficit to be cleared and give the time needed to prepare for the new era. Douste-Blazy outlined the details of the new financial structure. The budget was fifty-eight million francs, of which twenty-nine million were allocated to cover artistic expenses. Fifteen million francs came from the government, seven from the city, three from the department, two from the region, and three from the Casino. This still left a substantial amount to be generated from revenue and sponsorship. The financial structure was designed to reduce fixed costs. All the stakeholders signed an agreement to maintain the level of funding for six years in the first instance.

Stéphane Lissner's contract allowed him to work simultaneously elsewhere. He had planned to run the Teatro Real in Madrid as well as the Festival d'Aix, but withdrew when the Spanish authorities wouldn't accept his plans. In May 1997, he accepted an invitation from Peter Brook to co-direct the Centre international de créations théâtrales at the Bouffes du Nord in Paris. He took up the post in January 1998. The idea was to create a close relationship between Aix and the Bouffes du Nord.

Unsurprisingly, given the financial straits and creative limbo of the previous few years, Lissner discovered that the infrastructure of the Festival had almost disappeared. It almost certainly helped him that he was able to start again. He had a vision for Aix's future; and, since fifty per cent of the Festival's budget was now covered by public subsidies, he had the means to make it real. Released from the need to go from hand to mouth, he was able to plan ahead, and had the backing to change the nature and the scope of the Festival.

He began with the Festival's buildings and organisation. He recognised that the Festival needed a production centre. This would not only facilitate the production process; it would also save money. On the outskirts of the village of Venelles, seven kilometres north of Aix on the road to Pertuis, Lissner found an abandoned warehouse, a large two-storey modern building on an industrial estate that was suitable for conversion. As a working environment it was not picturesque, but it had the size to accommodate three workshops for the creation of décor and costumes and two large rehearsal rooms in which the stage of the Théâtre de l'Archevêché could be replicated. The twelve permanent members of staff were joined by two hundred additional employees during the runup to the Festival. Administration and production staff, costume makers, artists, musicians, directors, and conductors could now work together in the same building.

Equally important was the remodelling and renovation of the Théâtre de l'Archevêché. The theatre created in 1985 hadn't aged well. The auditorium was ugly, with cheap seating; the decorative proscenium belonged to a different age; the stage machinery needed modernisation; and there was no interior front of house space where spectators could gather in the intervals or escape a rain shower. The new theatre looked as if it belonged in the courtyard. The seating, reduced to two levels, complemented the high stone walls. Before, the seats had been attached to a metal structure that could be quickly dismantled. Now, the architects Jean-Loup Roubert and Jean-Michel Battesti created a solid structure with elegant lines. To create more space, there were fewer places (1,305). The seats were made from teak, a yellowish wood that chimed with the ochre stone of the courtyard. As the wood weathered it would become silver-grey. The new stage frame was also made of wood. To aid sightlines, the stage was lowered by one metre. Rooms in the palace alongside the courtyard were merged and converted to create a vaulted room where audience members could mingle and enter the auditorium in comfort.

Lissner created a second theatre in the courtyard of the Hôtel Maynier d'Oppède. This space, opposite the Théâtre de l'Archevêché, had been used frequently for recitals during the Dussurget era. Lissner realised it would work well for chamber-sized operas performed by the students of the new Académie européenne de musique, the most important of his innovations. This postgraduate academy would make Aix unique among Europe's opera festivals.

In a nutshell, the purpose of the Académie was to introduce talented young singers, musicians, composers, conductors, and directors to the professional world during two months of intensive training conducted by leading figures in the various fields. The students would be involved in the creation and performance of productions as part of the Festival. This was the crucial part of Lissner's plan. It wasn't an entirely new concept, since the Centre Acanthes, albeit on a smaller scale and with a syllabus restricted to the work of composers of the avant-garde, had run a training course every year between 1977 and 1986, but Lissner's academy was fully integrated into the life and *raison d'être* of the Festival in a way that the Centre Acanthes never had been. (We should also record that Louis Erlo had wanted to establish a workshop studio for young opera composers, but the Ministry of Culture turned down his request for funding.)

In the first year, fifty-four candidates from sixteen countries were given places in the Académie (auditions were held in Paris, London and New York). Lissner invited Eva Wagner-Pasquier, director of programming at the Opéra Bastille and the future co-director of the Bayreuth Festival, to lead the recruitment of the singers. Béatrice de Laage, Lissner's colleague in the directorship, also played a crucial role. A wing of the collège Mignet, Zola and Cézanne's old school in the Mazarin quarter, became the Académie's base. Lissner appointed the young American conductor David Stern as the Académie's music director. The students assembled in Aix at the end of May. There were three main components: song, chamber music and composition. The aim was to create a community of artists. The Académie prompted Lissner to dream of a future that would see Aix become a European centre of music: 'That could be the future of the Festival: an extraordinary academy where singers, musicians and composers work and make music together during Christmas, Easter, and the summer, almost throughout the year. In five years, I'll have twenty-five productions, so we could even do winter reprises. That, in a sense, is the Utopia.'[1]

Lissner wanted glamour and prestige and looked to engage the finest directors and conductors, both established and up-and-coming. Where singers were concerned, like his predecessors Dussurget and Erlo, he wanted to discover and nurture new talent. Big name stars went against the ethos of the Festival. Young singers brought their own kind of glamour. Lissner introduced lengthy (for the opera world) rehearsal periods of five weeks or more. Peter Brook began work on the 1998 edition's most anticipated production, *Don Giovanni*, in April.

Another innovation concerned the issue of broadening the Festival's audience and reconnecting with the town. Lissner's solution was (one) to offer, for one hundred francs, a pass giving access to all the recitals and public rehearsals of the 1998 edition, and (two) to programme four preview performances of *Don Giovanni*, reserved for local people, with tickets at half-price. Lissner hoped that his policies would bring to Aix 'a new public, more curious than the traditional conservative opera-going public, enabling us to strike a balance between the well-known and the less known'.[2]

To share costs, Lissner continued the practice of co-producing work with other opera companies. However, for by far the majority of these co-productions, he made sure that they were created in Aix and were therefore products of the Festival.

ii 1998: THE FIFTIETH EDITION, YEAR ONE OF THE ACADÉMIE

To open his era, and to celebrate the fifty years of the Festival, Lissner programmed five operas by composers who represented markers in the history of opera. Two of the five were from the 20th century. In the Théâtre de l'Archevêché, alternating with *Don Giovanni*, were Monteverdi's *Orfeo* and Bartók's *Le Château de Barbe-Bleue*. In the courtyard of the Hôtel Maynier d'Oppède, Purcell's *Dido and Aeneas* alternated with Britten's *Curlew River*.

To create the productions in the Théâtre de l'Archevêché, Lissner invited to Aix four of the greatest figures of post-war theatre and music: Peter Brook, Claudio Abbado, Pierre Boulez, and Pina Bausch. Lissner was making a statement not only about the quality of his address book, but about Aix's renaissance.

The two productions in the Hôtel Maynier d'Oppède were creations of the Académie: students formed the casts and the orchestra; David Stern conducted. These were festival productions, not fringe events and had to be of the same professional standard as the operas in the Théâtre de l'Archevêché. Lissner was taking a calculated risk: it paid off. A second group of students formed the chorus in Brook's *Don Giovanni*, while a third worked under David Stern, Stéphane Braunschweig, and the soprano Regine Crespin, on a production of Mozart's *Die Zauberflöte* to be presented in 1999. Significantly, the students' journey would continue after the Festival with major tours of *Don Giovanni* and *Dido and Aeneas* and *Curlew River*.

It immediately became apparent that the influx of so many enthusiastic young people invigorated the Festival for its participants and its attendees. The students gave impromptu concerts in care homes and hospitals as well as planned performances. They attended the rehearsals of their colleagues and asked Lissner to schedule an additional performance of *Dido* starting at midnight. The creators/teachers responsible for the productions of *Dido* and *Curlew River* included Stern, the actor and director Marcel Bozonnet of the

Comédie-Française, who directed the Purcell, the actor Yoshi Oida, from Brook's troupe, who directed the Britten, the tenor Robert Tear, the violinist and conductor Augustin Dumay, and the gambist Jay Bernfeld.

Part of the Académie's mission was to support and mentor young composers and to commission new work from them for their fellow students to premiere. In 1998, Pierre Boulez directed the composition residency, supported by the composers Philippe Manoury and Marc-Andre Dalbavie, the conductor Pierre-André Valade, the director Pierre Strosser, and the singer Hanna Schaer. In the autumn of 1997, they selected five young composers – Vsevolod Chmoulevitch, Juan Jose Eslava, Jonathan Golove, Juha T. Kostinen, and Alexandraos Markeas – who each created either a short opera or dance work that was performed during the Festival. Ballet Preljocaj provided the dancers. Commissioning has remained a vital part of the Académie's work (for a full list of pieces, see the appendices).

Youth was the theme of the Festival, because of the Académie, but also because of the young musicians of Abbado's Mahler Chamber Orchestra and Mahler Youth Chamber Orchestra. The former was in the pit for *Don Giovanni*, conducted by either Abbado or twenty-two-year-old Daniel Harding; the latter for *Le Château de Barbe-Bleue*, conducted by Boulez. Harding, while still in his teens, pre-Cambridge, had been Simon Rattle's assistant at Birmingham before working with Abbado in Berlin. He met Lissner when he stepped in for Rattle at the Châtelet. This led to the invitation to conduct at Aix.

Dido and Aeneas inaugurated the courtyard of the Hôtel Maynier d'Oppède as an opera theatre. The stage, constructed across the centre of the courtyard, beneath a mighty tree, incorporated the circular fountain. The instrumentalists sat at the rear to one side. The spectators sat on risers on three sides. Because of the rustling of the leaves and the wonderous canopy of the night sky, there was little more for the designer to do. The costumes were Grecian or north African in character. Eighteen-year-old Rinat Shaham, who shared the role of Dido with Silvia Hablowetz, was the revelation of the show. Her dark-eyed presence was complemented by the glowing timbre of her mezzo-soprano voice. The other singers moved and reacted to each other elegantly under Bozonnet's direction, but some of the non-English speakers among them struggled with the English text. There was sensitive yet spirited playing from the instrumentalists. Because of the youthfulness of the performers – their natural, unactorish style of playing – and the intimacy of the setting, this *Dido* felt like a rediscovery. The lament had rarely sounded as beautiful or forlorn.

Britten's deeply humane parable *Curlew River* shared the same configuration as *Dido*, but the stage surrounding the fountain was a wooden platform. Yoshi Oida's production, referencing the libretto's Noh drama origins, was austere and stylised. The platform became the river ferry. The space was bare save for two lighted braziers. Britten's sonorities, rooted by suspended notes on the organ, and watery arpeggios for harp and woodwind, sometimes pulsating, sometimes glittering and percussive, sounded mysterious and primal under the night sky. Because the score is written for solo instruments, the musicians needed to be outstanding and were. Michael Bennett as the Madwoman and Andrew Rupp as the Traveller stood out in an excellent all-male cast. *Curlew River* is shorter than most operas, but more profound and more haunting than most too. This noteworthy performance completed the cycle of Britten's church parables at Aix started by Dussurget in 1969.

A lot was resting on Peter Brook's *Don Giovanni*, the symbolic key event of Aix's renaissance under Lissner. Entering the theatre, one was confronted by Tom Pye's neutral setting – an orange-coloured stage floor; a few coloured benches and poles. The wall of the courtyard formed the backdrop. The players wore chic modern clothes (by Chloë Obolensky). The opera's dark themes were unmitigated in this setting.

Brook followed the method he used when directing a classical play. Rub the slate clean. Ignore everything that had gone before. All the comforting, pleasurable, trappings of the opera form were removed to leave only the words and music. The staging was lapidary, deceptively simple. Brook presented Mozart's characters as people, not operatic archetypes. Giovanni, for all his impetuosity, predatory charm, and callous temper, had a tragic dimension, driven by a compulsion he couldn't control. Despite being in his prime, the Panama hat and cream linen suit he wore suggested he was halfway to becoming an old roué. At the end, Brook brought Giovanni back to stare forlornly and enviously at the two couples.

Leporello's catalogue aria is, of course, a dazzling showpiece; but what is really being said? Brook directed the scene so that it became clear that the controlling Leporello was using the aria as a very effective means of hurting and humiliating Elvira. The production was full of such insights. The opera was shared by two casts, performing alternately: Peter Mattei or Roberto Scaltriti as Don Giovanni, Gilles Cachemaille or Nicola Ulivieri as Leporello, Melanie Diener or Veronique Gens as Elvira, Carmela Remigio or Monica Colonna as Donna Anna, Lisa Larsson or Catrin Wyn Davies as Zerlina, and John Mark Ainsley or Kenneth Tarver as Don Ottavio.

The most important consequence of Brook's approach was that it made one listen intently to the music, something that rarely happens in the opera house. Mozart's music sounded more ambiguous and more poignant than is usually the case. Abbado decided that Daniel Harding should conduct the opening night performance. 'I leave the baton to my little genius,' he said.[3] Harding's spirited, unsentimental reading of the score was crucial to the production's success. 'Harding whipped up a fury while uncovering the tenderness behind it,' wrote Andrew Clark in *The Financial Times*.[4]

While the production was a great success, it alienated the purists and there were some dissenting critical voices. Rodney Milnes wrote: 'There was an inescapable whiff of suburbia to a show that seemed to be happening in a Surbiton bar.' However, Milne greatly admired the playing of the Mahler Chamber Orchestra. 'The young players [...], many smiling seraphically, watching the conductor (this doesn't always happen), watching the stage when not otherwise occupied, were doing far more than accompanying. They were leading an act of inspired communal music-making. [...] Transitions between recitative and aria were handled with thrilling theatrical know-how; the action sped along.'[5] Lissner decided to make Harding and the Mahler Chamber Orchestra the Festival's resident conductor and orchestra, a role they would fulfil for the next ten years. Not since the days of Rosbaud had a conductor been so crucial at Aix.

Pierre Boulez and Pina Bausch's production of Bartók's *Le Château de Barbe-Bleue* was less successful. Bausch was revisiting a work she had created in 1984. Bartók's short opera for two singers became a dance work which only Bausch could have created. Female dancers in silk dresses and male dancers in designer suits ran frantically across a white stage backed by white panels or mirrors. Bausch used her dancers to express the characters' thoughts and feelings. While the two singers, Violetta Urmana and Laszlo Polgar, were, at moments, skilfully integrated into the choreography, they were mostly swamped by it. The concept would have worked more powerfully, and intimately, had there been only two dancers. Boulez coaxed wonderful playing from the precocious musicians of the Mahler Youth Chamber Orchestra.

The final production in the Théâtre de l'Archevêché was also the work of a choreographer. Trisha Brown's version of Monteverdi's *Orfeo* was brought in from La Monnaie, Brussels. René Jacobs conducted his ensemble Collegium Vocale. The white set turned black when Orfeo entered the Underworld. The choreography was elegant, and Robert Aeschlimann's minimalist sets and symbolic use of colour produced striking effects. Simon Keenlyside was formidable as Orfeo. The production offered visual commentary on the opera, but not the opera itself. Tom Sutcliffe, reviewing the production on its visit to the Barbican Centre, summed up the issue: 'The trouble with getting a choreographer to stage opera is that dance, or at least most modern dance, is expressive only of itself. But operatic music is expressive of words and situations, which need a telling context if they are to add up.'[6]

Artistically, the season flattered to deceive a little. There were five productions, but two of the five were short pieces performed in a very small venue, a third was also short, and presented as a dance work, and a fourth, also dance-dominated, originated elsewhere. Only Brook's *Don Giovanni* was extraordinary. Lissner was clearly being fiscally careful, as he was expected to be. Crucially, though, the 1998 season caught the imagination of the public. The Théâtre de l'Archevêché was over ninety-eight per cent full across the season while 3,000 people bought the pass giving access to the work of the Académie. In all, 22,000 people, many of them from Aix, attended the rehearsals, workshops and performances. This produced box office revenue of seventeen million francs, significantly more than hoped for. The tours would bring in more revenue; and from sponsorship, the Festival earned ten million francs in 1998.[7] Local businesses supported the Festival like never before. It remained to be seen whether this level of interest was largely due to the significance of 1998 as a new beginning for the Festival, and therefore unsustainable.

iii 1999: LE DOMAINE DU GRAND SAINT-JEAN

In 1999 there were indications of cost-cutting, which, given the increase in subsidy guaranteed for six years, and the box office success of 1998, was perplexing. But Lissner had big plans for the years ahead.

For the second year, the concert programme was mostly left to the students of the Académie. The opera programme consisted of new productions of Monteverdi's *L'incoronazione di Poppea* and Mozart's *Die Zauberflöte* (workshopped in 1998); the return of Brook and Harding's *Don Giovanni* (Peter Mattei, Gilles Cachemaille and Lisa Larsson were joined by new cast members Mireille Delunsch as Dona Elvira, Alexandra Deshorties as Donna Anna, and Mark Padmore as Don Ottavio); and a revival of an old production of Offenbach's *La Belle Hélène* co-produced with the Salzburg Festival.

Lissner's policy of engaging the big beasts of European theatre continued with the arrival of Klaus Michael Grüber to stage *L'incoronazione di Poppea*, an opera not seen at Aix since 1961. Grüber created an enigmatically personal version of Monteverdi's masterpiece in his meticulous style of theatre, a style characterised by gravitas. The production was handsome and languorous, better suited perhaps to the Wagner of *Tristan und Isolde* than to Monteverdi. The fine cast was led by Anne Sofie von Otter as Nero, Mireille Delunsch as Poppea, and Lorraine Hunt as Ottavia. This difficult assignment – for Grüber expected the music to bend to his will – was handed to Marc Minkowski, who realised the score beautifully.

The second opera in the Théâtre de l'Archevêché, Offenbach's *La Belle Hélène*, was the first work by the composer to be performed at Aix. Stéphane Petitjean conducted the Solistes de l'Orchestre de Paris. Herbert Wernicke's production dated from 1991. The set represented a semi-circular reception room, with red chairs and a large dining table. Into this space arrived a motorcycle, a toy train, and can-can dancers. Nora Gubisch sang beautifully as Hélène.

A performance of Monteverdi's madrigals, conducted by Marc Minkowski in the courtyard of the Hôtel Maynier d'Oppède, was semi-staged by Ingrid von Wantoch Rekowski. Actors wearing ruffs and carrying plastic lobsters walked between the musicians. The dumb show went on for fifteen minutes without a note of music being played. The soloist was Paul Agnew.

The inauguration of a new theatre at the Domain du Grand Saint-Jean, a 16th century semi-derelict château and estate owned by the Ville d'Aix and located some thirteen kilometres northwest of the town on the sun-baked plateau de Puyricard, was the event of the 1999 edition. Here the Festival could offer the Glyndebourne experience – al fresco dining and opera – but in good weather. The eight hundred and seventy-seat theatre was constructed in the château's courtyard so that the building's facade formed the backdrop. 'It doesn't yet have the splendour of Glyndebourne,' wrote Renaud Machart in *Le Monde*, 'but it comes close: a park, a superb country house, woods all around. We climb a few steps and discover the open-air theatre, grand yet intimate, austerely chic.'[8]

Lissner chose to mount the Académie's production of *Die Zauberflöte* here. The students involved in the previous year's workshop sang the principal roles. They included the excellent Stéphane Degout as Papageno, Christine Rigaud as Papagena, Christoph Genz as Tamino, Hélène le Corre as Pamina, and Irina Ionesco as the Queen of the Night. Stéphane Braunschweig presented *Die Zauberflöte* as Tamino's dream. This allowed him to stage this over-familiar opera as a peculiar tale that needed no explanation. The stage floor was black. A bank of TV screens provided a sense of magic since characters would exit the stage and suddenly appear on the screens running across the fields of the domain. Otherwise, the only large prop was a bed in which Tamino began the evening alone and ended it with Pamina. Simple, youthful, engaging, poignant: four elements that made this a noteworthy *Die Zauberflöte*.

David Stern conducted the Orchestra of the Académie. Unsurprisingly, the acoustics were problematic, and the inexperienced musicians struggled to produce a sweet, homogenous, sound in the open-air. While Renaud Machart put this down in part to Stern's decision to ask some of the musicians to play period instruments, as well as their inexperience as orchestral musicians, he concluded that the Académie would have to do better in future, whatever the circumstances.[9] The young singers were stretched vocally, but their youth and naturalness won out.

The Grand Saint-Jean experience and the revival of Brook's *Don Giovanni* prevented the 1999 season from being, artistically, an embarrassing damp squib. Thankfully, the financial figures were good. The edition came in within budget. Revenue from ticket sales (nineteen million francs) and sponsorship (just over ten million francs) met Lissner's targets. The overall attendance figure was ninety-two per cent, compared to ninety-eight per cent in 1998. While *Die Zauberflöte* sold out, and *Poppea* and *Don Giovanni* achieved figures in the high nineties, *La Belle Hélène* only sold seventy-eight per cent of its tickets.

Ninety-one young musicians were accepted by the Académie européenne de musique. The pass ticket scheme was again successful. Some 30,000 people attended the Académie's public rehearsals, masterclasses, and performances, which were dedicated to either percussion or the voice. A new piece for percussion by Yan Meresz was premiered.

iv 2000: ULYSSES

The 2000 edition saw the arrival of Simon Rattle, the return of Adrian Noble and William Christie, and the opening of the restored Théâtre du Jeu de Paume. The festival celebrated Pierre Boulez's seventy-fifth birthday in the presence of the composer. Boulez taught at the Académie européenne de musique. The other professors included William Christie, Laurence Equilbey, Adrian Noble, Claude Buchvald, Claudio Desderi, Jean-François Bellèvre, Christine Mollvik, Christophe Desjardins, Alain Planès, and soloists of the Ensemble Intercontemporain.

Lissner mounted a rich and varied feast of music that included a concert series of remarkable depth and appeal – Boulez, Rattle, Harding, Minkowski, Christie, and René Jacobs, conducted works by Monteverdi, Bach, Handel, Haydn, Schubert, Brahms, Dvořák, Scriabin, Mahler, Debussy, Ravel, Schönberg, Stravinsky, Webern, Berg, Varèse, and Boulez. For the first time in the history of the Festival, an opera by Janáček was produced – *L'Affaire Makropoulos*.

Janáček's penultimate opera, written in 1925, opened the season in the Théâtre de l'Archevêché. Janáček based his libretto on Karel Čapek's play, a strange, philosophical tale about an immortal woman who, because she can't die, is ultimately unable to obtain any positive meaning or pleasure from life. Simon Rattle, a long-time advocate for Janáček's operas, conducted his City of Birmingham

Symphony Orchestra. Stéphane Braunschweig directed and designed. His décor, economical and emblematic, included a bookcase of large archive volumes stretching the length of the stage, a bare platform, and a scarlet curtain. The great German soprano Anja Silja was darkly majestic as Emilia, and there was fine support from Willard White as Prus, Goran Eliasson as Gregor, Peter Hoare as Vitek, and Graham Clark as Hauk-Sendorf. Janáček's very distinctive sound world needed time to beguile the audience but did so by the end. David Murray reported that a man sitting near to him at the opening night grumbled that the music was 'Trop tchèque pour moi!' during the interval. 'But Silja's full-voiced eloquence at the end, bleak and very beautiful, moved him to awe and vociferous gratitude like everybody else.'[10]

A new production of *Così fan tutte*, directed by Chen Shi-Zheng with Chinese-influenced décor by Peter Pabst, was charming but insubstantial. René Jacobs conducted the Concerto Köln and a chorus made up of students of the Académie. The French-Canadian soprano Alexandra Deshorties, playing Fiordiligi, stood out in an inexperienced cast. Unfortunately, the opening night in the Théâtre de l'Archevêché was plagued by gales. The third production at this venue was a revival of the previous year's *L'incoronazione di Poppea*.

At the Grand Saint-Jean, Lissner mounted an Académie production of Rossini's *Cenerentola*. The score was arranged for chamber orchestra by Jonathan Dove and conducted by Laurence Equilbey, the first woman to take charge of an opera at Aix. Claude Buchvald's unpretentious production unfolded on a bare stage with a border of coloured lights. The opening night was cancelled because of persistent rain, something that had rarely happened in the history of the Festival. The next night was still unseasonably cold, and the thirteen young instrumentalists of the Académie were too few to make Rossini's music sparkle in the open-air. The young cast struggled too, but, having been coached for some weeks at the Académie by the great Rossini master Claudio Desderi, they were robust and came through in the end. The baritone Stéphane Degout, in his second year at Aix, impressed as Dandini, and was well matched by Anna Agathonos as Cinderella, Christine Gerbaud and Jennifer Tani as the sisters, Maurizio Lo Piccolo as Don Magnifico, and Wojciech Gierlach as Alidoro.

The Théâtre du Jeu de Paume is located on the rue de l'Opéra, a narrow street that begins at the eastern end of the Cours Mirabeau and gently climbs to place Miollis. Cézanne was born in a house sixty metres further up the road. As was common in the 17th and 18th centuries, Aix's *théâtre à l'italienne* was created by converting a *jeu de paume* court, hence its modern name. It was built in 1756. During the Dussurget era, the Théâtre du Jeu de Paume was where festival recordings were made. Pre-restoration, it was never used by the Festival as a performance venue. In 1996, the Ville d'Aix appointed Dominique Bluzet as director of the theatre. It was renovated and modernised between 1998 and 2000, with the agreement that every July it would be used by the Festival.

The restored Théâtre du Jeu de Paume provided the Festival with its first indoor theatre. The building next door was converted into dressing rooms and offices, and, with incredible adroitness and imagination, the theatre's tiny backstage was modernised to provide space for sets, people, and modern machinery. The exquisite horseshoe-shaped galleried auditorium was lovingly renovated in warm shades of red; and Louis Gautier's azure and gold *coupole* was returned to its original splendour. Four hundred and eighty-nine air-conditioned seats in velvet and wood provided elbow room and comfort. Dominique Bluzet and Stéphane Lissner took great care over the acoustics. A leading specialist was engaged during the design process to ensure that the materials used, and the arrangement of the boxes, would enhance and not dampen the quality of the sound. Clarity and warmth were achieved.

This gem of a theatre deserved a remarkable production. Monteverdi's late masterpiece *Il ritorno d'Ulisse in patria* completed the cycle of his operas that Lissner had launched in 1998. It reunited William Christie and Adrian Noble ten years after their *Fairy Queen* of 1989. The setting, designed by Anthony Ward, consisted of an ochre-coloured wall at either side of the stage, and, in between, a bare expanse of sand. A few Greek clay pots were the only objects on the stage. An azure backdrop represented both sea and sky. The production began with a bare flame emerging out of pitch blackness, finally revealing in its fragile light a naked man (Human Frailty, played by Ben Abdeslam) pursued by a young woman (Fortune, played by Stéphanie d'Oustrac). Effects and images were conjured from very little, with sleight of hand, and seamless fluidity. They looked ravishing. Jove descended from the flies on a magic carpet.

Because a curtain of narrow metal strands, each ending in a dot of light, descended at the same time, the wires holding up the carpet were invisible. Minerva (Gaëlle Méchaly) and Telemaco (Cyril Auvity), journeying to Ithaca, were suspended in the air above a billowing sheet of blue-green silk, beautifully lit by Jean Kalman. Other images were created from the basic elements of space, light, and a single figure. Renaud Machart, writing in *Le Monde*, described the 'beauty of Minerva, leaning against the wall in a steel-grey half-light'.[11]

Noble's staging revealed the philosophical and creative points of contact between Monteverdi and Shakespeare, two contemporaries living at opposite ends of Western Europe, almost certainly with no knowledge of each other, but connected by their humanism, compassion, humour, and melancholy, as well as by an extraordinary instinct for the theatrical. Noble directed the singers as if they were performing a Shakespeare play, with a sense of the poetic; but he directed them to move and sing naturally, to watch each other intently when they weren't singing and to express nuances of feeling. Krešimir Špicer, as Ulisse, had the presence and stature of a young Albert Finney; the statuesque Marijana Mijanovic, as Penelope, was regal and austere, but troubled by pain and longing. The Shakespeare factor was best represented by the recognition scene between Ulisse and his son Telemaco, a moment of profound feeling beautifully realised by Krešimir Špicer and Cyril Auvity. Noble made Minerva Ulisse's silent guardian: ever-present, and often disguised as a shepherd, she guided him towards his reunion with Penelope. The other roles were played by Martin Robson, Éric Raffard, Rebecca Ockenden, Bertrand Bontoux, Marcio Soares-Holanda, Andreas Gisler, Zachary Stains, Joseph Cornwell, Robert Burt, Geneviève Kaemmerlen, Christophe Laporte, and Bertrand Chuberre.

Christie and Noble worked with these young artists for weeks, and the result was a tremendous vindication of Lissner's decision to establish the Académie. As for the playing of Les Arts Florissants, Alex Ross wrote: '[They] gave a sense of what it must have been like to witness a Monteverdi masterpiece amid the chaos of a Venice carnival. The freedom of the playing was thrilling: Les Arts seemed to be making up the score as it went along.' Ross wrote that the show 'blazed with life'.[12]

Renaud Machart found the staging subtle, ethereal and of a 'fluid beauty'. Michel Parouty, in *Les Echos*, wrote: 'This show, which constantly surprises, is pure magic.'[13] The production must have been blessed by the muse of opera for it beguiled even the hardened British press pack. Hugh Canning's review was typical: 'It is an unequivocal triumph: a realisation that presents Monteverdi's moving masterpiece with a ravishingly beautiful simplicity that is simultaneously historic and utterly modern.'[14]

The production went on a long tour of Europe and America (including a residency at the Brooklyn Academy of Music in New York) and returned to Aix in 2002.

Boulez gave conducting classes on his own music and on the music of Harrison Birtwistle. His work with the violists and other instrumentalists of the Académie concluded with two concerts. They were joined by soloists of the Ensemble Intercontemporain in a powerful account of *Éclat-Multiples* at the Théâtre du Jeu de Paume. The evening began with Boulez guiding the three student-conductors through sections of the work. Then, at the Cité du Livre, he conducted the Orchestra of the Académie in a performance of *Rituel in memoriam Bruno Maderna*. The evening began with a performance by the Orchestre de gamelan du village de Sebatu, Bali.

The members of the Académie gave their own concerts under the supervision of Boulez, Christophe Desjardins and others.

At the Grand Saint-Jean, Boulez gave two remarkable concerts of 20th century music with the Mahler Youth Chamber Orchestra, the first consisting of Stravinsky's *Le Chant du Rossignol*, Scriabin's *Le Poème de l'extase*, Webern's *Six pièces* for orchestra, op. 6, Berg's *Trois pièces* for orchestra, op. 6, and Edgar Varèse's *Amériques*, and the second of the adagio from Mahler's Symphony no. 10, Schönberg's *Le Chant du Rossignol* from *Gurre-Lieder*, Debussy's *Jeux*, Ravel's *Shéhérazade*, and Bartók's *Le Mandarin merveilleux*. The soloist was the mezzo-soprano Petra Lang.

All of the symphony orchestra concerts took place at the Grand Saint-Jean: Brahms's Violin Concerto and Schubert's Symphony no. 9 were performed by Simon Rattle and the CBSO (with violinist Tasmin Little); Haydn's Symphony no. 83, Dvořák's Symphony no. 8, Handel's *Apollo e Dafne* and Igor Stravinsky's *Apollo* by Daniel Harding and the Mahler Chamber Orchestra (with soloists Mireille Delunsch, Stephan Genz and Emmanuelle Haïm); Haydn's Symphony no. 92 and Mozart's *Bella mia fiamma, addio* and Symphony no. 40 by René Jacobs and Concerto Köln (with soloist Véronique Gens); and Bach's Suites for Orchestra by Marc Minkowski and Les Musiciens du Louvre.

At the Théâtre du Jeu de Paume, William Christie and Les Arts Florissants performed madrigals by Monteverdi. Lissner invited distinguished artists from Central Asia, the Middle East and West Africa to perform music from Ouzbekistan, Azerbaidjan, Iran and Guinea at the Jeu de Paume: Monâjât Yultchieva and the Ensemble Shewkat Mirzaëv, the Ensemble Alim Qassimov, Châhrâm Nâzeri and the Ensemble Dastan, and the balafon player El Hadj Djeli Sory Kouyate.

The season was a success with the public. *Ulisse*, *Così* and *Cenerentola* sold out and *L'Affaire Makropoulos* achieved an attendance figure of ninety per cent.

v 2001/02: JANÁČEK, BRITTEN, TCHAIKOVSKY AND EÖTVÖS

Interviewed in June 2001, Stéphane Lissner reflected on the achievements of his first three years.[15] His core aims had been achieved. The festival had re-found its identity and purpose. Once the new indoor theatre was ready the Festival would have five venues. International artists of the front rank were eager to work at Aix. The workshops at Venelles meant that Aix could provide the excellent working conditions and technical support that these artists required. And the Académie was here to stay. As Lissner had hoped, the influx of young people helped the Festival to reconnect with the town, since the public workshops and performances of the Académie gave the Festival a public face that was welcoming and inclusive. Each year, Lissner revealed, the number of local people attending the Festival had doubled. 'Fighting the elitism of the opera world without falling into demagoguery is a challenge, but I am working on it,' he said. Because productions by the Académie went out on national and international tours, the Festival had a life beyond the weeks of July. Lissner recounted the figures. Within three years he had tripled the budget (it was eighty-five million francs in 2001), secured significant revenue from sponsors, and broken even. In 2000, 50,000 people attended the opera performances, and 30,000 the events of the Académie. Lissner could also point to Aix's high international reputation. 'With Salzburg so preachily pompous and Bayreuth so dreary,' wrote Rupert Christiansen in *The Daily Telegraph*, 'it is Aix-en-Provence that, at least in my book, currently ranks as the most alluring of the European opera festivals.'[16]

When Lissner began his directorship, as well as maintaining the importance of Mozart at Aix, he had two immediate aims: to give prominence to Monteverdi; and to programme the work of two of the greatest opera composers of the 20th century, Leoš Janáček and Benjamin Britten. In 2001, Britten's *The Turn of the Screw* and Janáček's operatic song cycle *Carnet d'un disparu* followed the recent productions of *Curlew River* and *L'Affaire Makropoulos*. Lissner would next turn his attention to Alban Berg, and then to the two big goals of the second phase of his directorship. The first concerned new work. A new opera by Peter Eötvös based on Genet's *Le Balcon* would be staged in 2002, and it was hoped that a new work by Kaija Saariaho would be ready by 2005. The second target was to produce Wagner's *Der Ring des Nibelungen* in the new theatre. This idea came from Simon Rattle, who offered to mount the cycle with his new orchestra the Berliner Philharmoniker.

The last of the Mozart/Da Ponte operas to be mounted by Lissner opened the season in the Théâtre de l'Archevêché. *Le nozze di Figaro* hadn't been staged since 1991. The production was a success, not because Richard Eyre, making his debut in France, relocated and updated the action to the over-familiar (at least for British spectators) upstairs-downstairs world of a great house between the wars, which robbed the opera of its pre-French Revolution social and political context without provided something compelling in its place (designer Tim Hatley added a huge staircase and heavy black doors to the old back wall), but because, under his direction, the acting embraced ambiguity and irony. In Eyre's staging the opera belonged to Susanna and the comtesse Almaviva, who, as played by Camilla Tilling and Véronique Gens, suffered in small and large ways from the pride and egotism of their men but who knew how to outwit them. Also in the outstanding cast were Magdalena Kozena (Cherubino), Jennifer Smith (Marcellina), Laurent Naouri (Almaviva), and Jean-Paul Fouchécourt (Don Basilio). The playing of the Mahler Chamber Orchestra under Marc Minkowski was sublime. Previous productions of *Figaro* at Aix, by Lavelli in 1979 and Noelte in 1991, had failed partly because the public (and some critics) disliked the idea that the characters were troubled and unable to connect. Eyre also favoured melancholy misalliances but got the balance right.

Esa-Pekka Salonen was under commission to write an opera for Aix, but the work wasn't ready. Lissner invited him to conduct a production of Verdi's *Falstaff*, but ill health meant that he was unable to travel from the US to Aix. Enrique Mazzola stepped in to conduct the Orchestre de Paris. Herbert Wernicke directed Willard White as Falstaff. Wernicke didn't want the bloated, booze-debauched, old roué of tradition. He wanted a different beast, scheming, yes, but solitary, dangerous and forlorn. The reading was fine for Shakespeare's *Henry IV* plays because in these masterpieces Falstaff is solitary, dangerous and forlorn, but for Verdi's version of *The Merry Wives* it was somewhat of a stretch – compelling but hard to make work once the production reached the great final scene. White was golden-voiced and the women – Nora Gubisch as Mistress Quickly, Charlotte Hellekant as Mistress Page, Geraldine McGreevy as Mistress Ford, and the young Miah Persson as Nanetta – were a seductive pleasure from first note to last.

Lissner's Janáček's cycle continued with *Carnet d'un disparu* at the Hôtel Maynier d'Oppède. The production was brought in from the Kunstenfestival des arts, Bruxelles, where it had opened in May 2001. Janáček's poetic, mysterious, Kamila Stösslova-inspired, forty-minute masterpiece for two soloists (Adrian Thompson and Hana Minutillo), piano (Alain Planès) and a trio of female voices, was performed, as indicated by the composer, in near darkness, with the singers' shadows looming against a softly lit backcloth. Claude Régy's production was designed by Daniel Jeanneteau.

Lissner chose the beautiful Théâtre du Jeu de Paume as the venue for Luc Bondy's production of *The Turn of the Screw*. It was the perfect size, spatially and acoustically, for Britten's intimate, hauntingly enigmatic and disturbing chamber opera, the most distilled product of his sickly obsession with the seductiveness and corruptibility of innocence. Presented as a ghost story, the opera is really about the abuse of two children. Most directors water this down, but not Bondy.

Richard Peduzzi's grey-blue décor, atmospherically lit by Dominique Bruguière, consisted of tall blocks that opened out the space or contracted it to create small, claustrophobic rooms. A square-shaped cutting in a wall represented a window. The minimal props included a white rocking horse. Such was the cold, intense grip exerted by both Bondy's staging and Daniel Harding's pacing of the tightly controlled score's variations on a twelve-note theme, that the pretty auditorium seemed to disappear. Rupert Christiansen described Peduzzi's poetic abstractions and Bondy's forensic probing thus: 'Walls move silently together, turning Miles's bedroom into a prison cell; Quint stands at an open window, behind a fluttering curtain, like Peter Pan in search of his shadow; Miss Jessel seems to emerge out of the lake in which she may have drowned herself. These simple but stunning visual effects are complemented by the revelatory psychological touches of Bondy's interpretation – the hostility with which the children greet the Governess, for example; or Miss Jessel's attempt to teach Flora a thing or two about her burgeoning womanhood.'[17] More than this, the Governess's relationship with Miles had a sexual dimension. Bondy's direction of the final scene – Mireille Delunsch's sensual Governess's interrogation of Miles became an attempt at seduction, and Marlin Miller's long-haired, white frock-coated Peter Quint executed a sinister parody of a courtly dance around their bodies – was provocative and unforgettable.

The instrumentalists of the Mahler Chamber Orchestra were acutely sensitive to the score's sonorities and ironic nursery rhymes. Bondy drew remarkable performances from the children playing Miles and Flora (Pablo Strong and Pipa Woodrow alternating with Gregory Monk and Nazan Fikret), and the adults were all exceptional: Marie McLaughlin as Miss Jessel, Hanna Schaer as Mrs Grose, and Olivier Dumait as the Narrator. The production was preceded by a masterly essay on Britten's art by Renaud Machart in *Le Monde* ('Benjamin Britten et les fantômes de l'innocence bafouée').[18]

The opera programme ended with a revival of Braunschweig's *Die Zauberflöte*, produced on this occasion not as an Académie production at the Grand Saint-Jean, but at the Théâtre de l'Archevêché with the Orchestre de l'Opéra national de Lyon conducted by Philippe Jordan. Stéphane Degout, Hélène le Corre and Christine Rigaud reprised their roles. Natalie Dessay played the Queen of the Night.

The concert series was disappointing if compared to the many splendours of 2000. There were two concerts in the Théâtre de l'Archevêché. Pierre Boulez (replacing Esa-Pekka Salonen) led the Orchestre de Paris in performances of Bartók's *Le Prince de bois* and the Concerto for Orchestra; and Laurence Equilbey conducted the Chœur de chambre Accentus, the pianists Brigitte Engerer and Josèphe Jude, and the singers Cécile Perrin and Stéphane Degout, in a chamber version of Brahms's *Un Requiem allemande*.

Soloists of the Mahler Chamber Orchestra gave two concerts of music by Roussel, Ravel, Tchaikovsky, Nielsen, and Prokofiev. Under the title *D'Alep à Séville*, works by Georges Aperghis, Ivan Fedele, Pascal Dusapin, Claudio Monteverdi, Isaac Albeniz and Enrique Granados were performed by the cellist Sonia Wieder-Atherton with Marc Marder (contrebasse), Françoise Rivalland (zarb and cymbalom), and the Quatuor Parisii.

As a celebration of song, the concert series contained many pleasures. The recitals – by Nora Gubisch and Alain Altinoglu, Yann Beuron and David Zobel, Miah Persson and Roger Vignoles, Mireille Delunsch and François Kerdoncuff, Geraldine McGreevy and Christopher Gould, Camilla Tilling and Roger Vignoles, and Laurent Naouri and Stéphane Petitjean – included obvious choices by Schubert, Schumann, Wolf, Strauss, Fauré, Debussy, and Ravel, but also relative rarities by Grieg, Rachmaninoff, Manuel de Falla, Roussel, Korngold, Stenhamar, and Sibelius. These concerts took place either at the Théâtre du Jeu de Paume or the Hôtel Maynier d'Oppède.

The revenue from ticket sales in 2001 was much the same as in previous years despite fewer performances resulting from the temporary closure of the Grand Saint-Jean. The operas achieved an attendance rate of over ninety-nine per cent. Over 55,000 people attended the Festival, an increase of twelve per cent on the 2000 figure. The festival's good financial position was enhanced by the decision of the regional authority, PACA, to increase its level of support.

On the eve of the 2002 edition, the Festival's president Jean-Marie Messier was forced to resign as the head of multi-media conglomerate Vivendi when it was revealed that the company had lost billions of dollars during the previous year. At a meeting of the board of directors of the Festival, the Minister of Culture, Jean-Jacques Aillagon, proposed that Messier, who wasn't present, should be replaced as president by Edmonde Charles-Roux. The board agreed. Lissner let it be known (in *Le Monde*) that Messier was a friend, and that he had been an excellent president of the Festival. Asked about the Festival's sponsorship deal with Vivendi, he revealed that a three-year contract, guaranteeing 380,000 euros annually, had been signed. The key event on paper of the 2002 season was the premiere of a new opera commissioned by Lissner – Peter Eötvös's *Le Balcon*, based on the play by Jean Genet. *Le Balcon* was joined in the Théâtre de l'Archevêché by Tchaikovsky's *Eugène Onéguine* and a revival of Brook's *Don Giovanni*. In the Théâtre du Jeu de Paume, Janáček's *La Petite renarde rusée* was presented by the Académie. Having toured the world, Noble and Christie's *Il ritorno d'Ulisse in patria* returned to its theatre of origin.

The success story of Daniel Harding and the Mahler Chamber Orchestra continued with *Eugène Onéguine*. Harding's interpretation of Tchaikovsky's score was unsentimental, finely detailed, and sensitive to the needs of the singers who, under Irina Brook's direction, performed with a naturalness that was Chekhovian. The production was the work of two young maestros – Harding was twenty-six and Brook thirty-eight – and it told: the period was conveyed by the costumes, but they were simplified and cut to look modern. The setting, minimalist and poetic, combined literary sophistication with a dreamlike sense of disorientation. During the dual scene, instead of the usual snow, a shower of red petals fell onto the desolate stage, a symbol of the young life so recklessly sacrificed. The designer was Noëlle Ginefri.

Irina Brook was inevitably asked about her famous father, who was also in Aix – and working with Harding – to revive *Don Giovanni*. She politely explained that she was her own person and director. The two productions shared the baritone Peter Mattei, who was mercurial and unpredictable as both Don Giovanni and Onéguine. Mattei's Onéguine and Olga Guryakova's Tatiana reached the tragic heights imagined by Tchaikovsky. Olga Guryakova and Ekaterina Semenchuk, as Olga, brought to these characters youth, sensuality, and an authenticity that non-Russian singers struggled to achieve. However, it was Daniil Shtoda's Lenski who, in Irina Brook's staging, made the lasting impression. On the night before the dual, he stood before a brazier into which he dropped Olga's letters. Facing Onéguine the next morning, he lowered his pistol and walked forward to meet the fatal bullet.

The season had opened with Peter Eötvös's *Le Balcon*. Coincidentally, it was Peter Brook who directed the first production of Genet's play in France, at the Théâtre Gymnase in 1960. Eötvös condensed Genet's text into ten tableaux and expressed its sardonic contempt in music written for eighteen musicians, brilliantly played by members of Ensemble Intercontemporain under his direction. Stanislas Nordey's staging served the piece well. Rupert Christiansen commented on the static nature of the work, and the sizeable walkout that marred the opening performance. However, he admired the opera: 'The music creates an alluring sound world, drawing on various 1950s idioms, from sexy, savvy cocktail jazz to strident serialism. Witty and cool, its precision is immaculate – not a note seems rhetorical or excessive. Every word is audible through the vocal line, every character is vividly painted.'[19]

La Petite renarde rusée was stylishly staged by another talented young director, Julie Brochen, and performed, with the fearlessness of youth, by members of the Académie. The simple décor, consisting of sheets of paper with black and white drawings, referenced the story's origin as a picture book. The director's approach was to present the animals as people. Yvette Bonner's charismatic vixen wore baggy trousers, braces, and a little vest top; the hens wore little dresses and red stilettos. Yvette Bonner was outstanding, as was Ronan Nédélec, playing the gamekeeper, and Olivier Dumait (who, in 2001, had played the Narrator in *The Turn of the Screw*). It was a shame that the small size of the venue meant that Janáček's full orchestration wasn't used. Jonathan Dove's skilful adaptation exposed the technique of some members of the Orchestra of the Académie.

THIRTEEN

Lissner Part Two

2003-2006

i 2003: STRIKES WRECK THE FESTIVAL

The programme devised by Lissner for 2003 juxtaposed Berg and Schönberg with Mozart and Verdi: *Wozzeck, Pierrot lunaire, La Traviata,* and *Die Entführung aus dem Serail.* The directors and conductors were Stéphane Braunschweig and Daniel Harding, Klaus Michael Grüber and Pierre Boulez, Peter Mussbach and Yutaka Sado, and Jérôme Deschamps and Marc Minkowski.

French theatre and film workers benefited from a system of protection backed by the government that was the envy of their counterparts in other countries. It was designed to support French culture by giving temporary theatre workers (*les intermittents*) sufficient unemployment benefits. The system was called the 'Régime des salariés intermittents du spectacle'. If theatre employees worked for five hundred and seven hours during a year, they were entitled to twelve months of unemployment benefits.

The scheme had been abused by some employees and employers for years and was running a huge deficit. Managements accused some theatre workers of working while claiming unemployment benefits; unions accused managements of paying workers inferior wages because they were entitled to benefits. Following Chirac's re-election as president in April 2002, the conservative government decided to reform the system. The Minister of Culture, Jean-Jacques Aillagon, announced the change in June 2003. An agreement was struck with the three centrist unions at the end of June; it preserved the system but decreased the number of months from twelve to eight. The left-wing Confédération générale du travail (CGT), outraged that the socialist candidate in the presidential election had been squeezed out of contention because of the National Front factor, resulting in the re-election of the unpopular Chirac, rejected the offer and began to organise strike action. Aillagon was not prepared to back down. The summer festivals, dependent upon *les intermittents*, were the CGT's main target.

The opening of the Festival, on 4 July, was postponed, meaning that the first nights of *Wozzeck* and *La Traviata* were cancelled. Lissner's staff were divided, but such was their loyalty that they agreed to resist pressure from the unions and work. As a result, Lissner was determined to go ahead, on 7 July, with the premiere at the Théâtre du Jeu de Paume of a triptych created by Pierre Boulez and Klaus Michael Grüber: the works were Manuel de Falla's *Les Tréteaux de maître Pierre*, Stravinsky's *Renard* and Schönberg's *Pierrot lunaire*. Boulez and Grüber were collaborating for the first time. Grüber placed Boulez and his musicians on the stage. The set was a box, lit sickly green or blue, and separated from the auditorium by the bars of a cage. Part prison cell, part monkey cage (indeed, a monkey sat on a pedestal below an oval window, close to the musicians of the Ensemble Intercontemporain), the setting was surreal, sinister and alienating. The legendary German singer Anja Silja performed Pierrot. Lissner was close to both Boulez and Grüber and the production meant a lot to all three of them. They agreed that if protestors charged up the narrow rue de l'Opéra they would lock the doors.

A few hundred protestors, having somehow been seen off by Lissner at the public entrance, massed at the other side of the building in the rue de la Mule Noire, where they pummelled the metal doors that gave access to the backstage area of the theatre. The banging could be heard inside the theatre, but Boulez rallied his troops and the audience and continued to the end of the performance.

Two nights later, Lissner decided to open *La Traviata* in the Théâtre de l'Archevêché. However, the militant unions trucked in workers from Marseille and Montpellier and organised a protest outside the Théâtre de l'Archevêché. Armed with drums, trumpets and fireworks, the strikers ruined the performance; as people left the venue, they were verbally harassed and some of the protesters threw leaflets in their faces. Lissner was outraged that his artists, trying to do their best in a deplorable situation, and audience members, who had bought their tickets in good faith, were intimidated in this way.

Lissner cancelled the rest of the season. He estimated that the losses would bankrupt the Festival. Only the government could save it. Jean-Jacques Aillagon announced that he wouldn't allow Aix or the other festivals to fail going forward. Negotiations between the concerned parties began to ease the tension. If the crisis point had passed, the issue of finding an equitable solution for *les intermittents* that also cleared the deficit and made the system workable, had not been settled. The issue would rumble on.

The festival's board of directors met on July 16. Aillagon announced that a special subsidy of five million euros would be granted to the Festival to recompense ticket holders and pay the salaries of the artists and staff. The 2004 edition would have a full programme. Lissner had already decided the repertoire: two of the cancelled 2003 shows, *La Traviata* and *Die Entführung aus dem Serail*, would be joined by a William Christie/Luc Bondy staging of Handel's *Hercules*, Prokofiev's *L'Amour des trois oranges*, and the premiere of Toshio Hosokawa's *Hanjo*, directed by Anne Teresa De Keersmaeker. Regarding the other cancelled shows, it was announced that the Braunschweig/Harding *Wozzeck* would be produced in 2005 in place of a planned *Lulu*, and the Boulez/Grüber Falla-Stravinsky-Schönberg triple bill would be produced in 2006.

In September 2003, Lissner added the position of Director of Music of the Wiener Festwochen (joining Luc Bondy who was the Festival's Intendant) to his portfolio of jobs (the others being Aix, the Bouffes du Nord, and the Théâtre de la Madeleine, Paris).

ii 2004: HANDEL, PROKOFIEV, AND HOSOKAWA

In July 2004, just before the start of the Festival's comeback edition, Lissner announced that ticket sales were down, at eighty per cent, a consequence of the uncertainty caused by the crisis of 2003. However, he remained confident about the future. The artists he admired were still eager to come, and the new indoor theatre would finally be ready in 2007. In the six years since he took over, the local population had embraced the Festival: in 2004, fifty per cent of the attendees came from the Aix region.

The 2004 edition had no mainstream concert programme to speak of. In 2003 there had only been three. Lissner had decided to place the programme on hold until the new theatre became available. The forty-odd concerts given by the Académie began in June and felt less integrated than before. There were no Académie opera productions.

The opening of *La Traviata* in the Théâtre de l'Archevêché, a year after the traumatic events of 2003, should have been a moment of celebration for the Festival, and especially for Mireille Delunsch, who had bravely performed as protestors partied outside the theatre. But since 2003, there had been cast changes, Daniel Harding and the Mahler Chamber Orchestra had replaced Yutaka Sado and the Orchestre de Paris, and the production – which wasn't a creation of the Festival d'Aix but of the Berlin Staatsoper – had been seen in Rouen. Mireille Delunsch conveyed Violetta's vulnerability and despair but was vocally a little off-colour. Director Peter Mussbach took inspiration from the tragedies of Marilyn Monroe and Princess Diana. It wasn't subtle – Delunsch wore a blonde wig and a white dress, and the black set alluded to a road and underpass in the rain – but it worked. A new star tenor, Rolando Villazon, sang Alfredo.

The season opened at the Grand Saint-Jean with Philippe Calvario's production of Prokofiev's *L'Amour des trois oranges*. It was Aix's second production of the work in ten years. The staging, a riot of silent movie slapstick and outrageous costumes, was stylish and vivacious. Tugan Sokhiev, music director of Welsh National Opera, conducted the Mahler Chamber Orchestra with an innate understanding of Prokofiev's style. The singers, led by Alexei Tanovitsky, Kirill Dusechkin and Ekaterina Shimanovitch, were graduates of the Mariinsky Academy.

Luc Bondy's *Hercules* wasn't conceived for the traditionalists. The walls of Peduzzi's abstract set overlooked a sand-covered stage, reminding one a little of Aix's *Il ritorno d'Ulisse in patria*. The few props were emblematic, such as the huge torso and decapitated head of Hercules, in black stone. The singers wore jeans or khaki jackets, which prompted one critic to describe the production as 'Gulf War meets Benetton'. This, though, was an elegant staging, deceptively simple, and paced with precision as the tension grew (Bondy worked with the playwright Martin Crimp to ensure that the drama was compellingly concentrated). *Hercules* was the first collaboration between Bondy and William Christie, whose interpretation of the score brought out the dramatic tension contained in Handel's music. Joyce DiDonato sang powerfully as the obsessive Dejanira. Camilla Tilling was outstanding as Iole. William Shimell's Hercules was too dumb to be formidable, but, because of Handel's genius, his end was tragic.

The second world premiere of the Lissner era, *Hanjo* by Toshio Hosokawa, was mounted in the Jeu de Paume. The libretto, in English, was adapted from a story by Yukio Mishima, based on a classic tale: a former geisha, abandoned by her male lover, is held captive by a woman who is in love with her. It was unclear why the great choreographer Anne Teresa De Keersmaeker chose to direct such a static piece for three characters. Kazushi Ono conducted the Orchestre de chambre de la Monnaie.

Die Entführung aus dem Serail, at the Grand Saint-Jean, closed the season. Jérôme Deschamps and Macha Makeïeff's production, conducted by Marc Minkowski, wasn't a creation of Aix, but of Baden-Baden (June 2003).

iii 2005: MOZART'S COSÌ

Lissner's policy of bringing the greatest figures of the contemporary Francophone theatre to Aix reached its zenith in 2005 with the arrival of Patrice Chéreau to join Luc Bondy and Richard Peduzzi. Chéreau was returning to opera for the first time since 1994.

In the lead-up to the 2005 edition, in April, it was announced that Lissner had accepted the positions of superintendent and artistic director at La Scala Milan, Europe's grandest opera house, a house that had been dysfunctional for some time. Staff unrest had resulted in strikes and, finally, the resignation of La Scala's long serving music director Riccardo Muti. It was a brave man who walked willingly into the snake pit of La Scala. Lissner intended to remain in charge of Aix until the end of his contract in 2009. He told *Le Monde* that he would remain hands-on at Aix until the conclusion of the 2007 season, after which there would be a period of transition. He wouldn't seek a renewal of his contract at Vienna on its expiration in 2007, and he would step down as Brook's co-director of the Bouffes du Nord. He would retain the Madeleine, a private theatre. However, it seemed unlikely that even someone who had never failed, and who had an endless capacity for work, could run Aix and drama-stricken Milan at the same time with full effectiveness, even for a relatively short period. His critics, particularly in Austria, resented his supposed empire-building, the fact that he wasn't an artist or a musician, and his practice of working remotely, but not one of them could deny the artistic strength of his programmes.

In November, the situation was clarified. Lissner let it be known that, while the French Minister of Culture, Renaud Donnedieu de Vabres, wanted him to stay on at Aix, his new masters in Milan demanded that he work there full-time. Lissner still hoped to continue at Aix until after the 2007 edition, but subsequently had to accept that the 2006 edition would be his last.

Lissner's financial management of the Festival was as assured as ever, with a significant amount of money coming from sources other than the central government. The budget for 2005 was 16.3 million euros, of which artists and production costs (operas, concerts, the Académie) amounted to 9.3 million euros (fifty-six per cent); permanent staff and structural costs, 3.5 million (twenty-two per cent); and temporary technical staff, 3.5 million (twenty-two per cent). The break-down of revenue and funding was as follows: 3.5 million euros came from ticket sales (twenty-two per cent – of the 50,000 places, 21,600 were priced under fifty euros); 2.8 million from the government (seventeen per cent); 940,000 from the Ville d'Aix (six per cent); 1.4 million from the Casino d'Aix (nine per cent); 750,000 from the Bouches-du-Rhône general council (five per cent); 370,000 from the PACA regional council (two per cent); 330,000 from the community of the Pays d'Aix (two per cent); 2.3 million from sponsorship (eleven per cent); and 950,000 from co-productions (six per cent). These figures must have helped Lissner secure the Milan job.

Chéreau was never going to deliver the comic *Così fan tutte* of tradition that most festivalgoers, and some critics, craved; neither, though, was he going to impose modern attitudes on an 18th century work, or judge the characters. Chéreau examined Mozart's music to discover the meaning of the story and the soul of the characters: 'In opera,' he said, 'there are two texts: the libretto and the score.'[1]

One senses that he hoped to find something unexpected in the opera but concluded that to be true to *Così fan tutte* one had to play it straight, while allowing the staging to be guided by the melancholy and ambiguity that existed, not in the libretto, but in Mozart's music. In his production notes, he wrote: 'I don't see what's funny in all this. All this – including the cynicism of Don Alfonso – is composed with such truth and sincerity, all this looks crazy, the girls are heroic, we can't do anything about their pain, that they want to die, it's not comical, the boys are scared and manipulate dangerous feelings, explosive situations (to verify that one is loved...) and there is such beauty in so many farewells.'[2] The production's conductor, Daniel Harding, strongly believed that Mozart's tempi represented the beating of the characters' hearts, that the accelerations and augmentations were better indicators of their thoughts and feelings than Da Ponte's words.

In Chéreau's production, Alfonso's cruel experiment provoked in the two young women a nagging ache of confusion and doubt: they were clearly trying to process what had happened as the opera reached its deceptively harmonious conclusion. Chéreau staged the opera with choreographic elegance in an environment by Peduzzi (lit by Bertrand Couderc) that represented the dusty backstage of a *théâtre italienne* with flaking faded blue walls, a plethora of leaning ladders, a fire extinguisher, and 'Vietato fumare' painted in red on the rear wall. The cast wore beautiful 18th century clothes by Caroline de Vivaise. The setting introduced its own sense of alienation and irony.

The casting wasn't wholly successful: the veteran Ruggero Raimondi was unnerving as Don Alfonso, but his voice was in decline. Erin Wall as Fiordiligi and Elīna Garanča as Dorabella acted beautifully and looked wonderful. Wall's voice was a little vulnerable. It is by making these characters enigmatic that performers lift them from the page, and Wall and Garanča did just that. Stéphane Degout, now confirmed as one of the great finds of the Académie, was impressive as Guglielmo.

Chéreau's production was wise, humane, and poetic, but it wasn't startlingly original or generous to its audiences. Expectations demanded something extraordinary à la Chéreau's *Der Ring des Nibelungen*, but whereas Wagner's huge Germanic feast requires a striking concept to make it digestible, Mozart's *Così* does not. The critical consensus was that Chéreau's *Così* was a failure. 'Patrice Chéreau doesn't have much to say about *Così*,' declared Christian Merlin in *Le Figaro*. Daniel Harding and the Mahler Chamber Orchestra were criticised because the music didn't 'caress'. Harding analysed the score as forensically as Chéreau and brought out an almost Beethoven-like darkness. There were some positive and perceptive reviews. Rupert Christiansen found the interpretation of the music 'ravishing'. He wrote of Chéreau's production that it was 'dark, dour, downbeat and subtle'. 'The six solo characters seem to have walked out of a painting by Chardin. They are not guyed or patronised, and their emotions are painfully keen and real throughout. [...] In the final moments, the lights gradually dwindle to complete darkness: the legacy of Alfonso's trickery is confusion rather than resolution.'[3]

The season's second Mozart opera, *La clemenza di Tito*, directed by Lukas Hemleb, was an abject failure, lacking personality or heat, despite sensitive playing by the Mahler Chamber Orchestra under Paul Daniel, who was working at Aix for the first time. Krešimir Špicer, the wonderful Ulysses in Adrian Noble's production of 2000, was left floundering here. Stéphanie d'Oustrac impressed as Annio.

Julie, a new opera by Philippe Boesmans, written and directed by Luc Bondy, played alongside a revival of Bondy's acclaimed account of Britten's *The Turn of the Screw* in the Théâtre du Jeu de Paume. Kazushi Ono conducted the Orchestre de chambre de la Monnaie. *Julie*, a creation of La Monnaie, opened in Brussels in March. Boesmans and Bondy created a compellingly tense and claustrophobic chamber opera from August Strindberg's play, powerfully performed by Malena Ernman or Tove Dahlberg as Julie, Garry Magee or Davide Damiani as Jean, and Kerstin Avemo or Hendrickje Van Kerckhove as Kristin.

David Radok's production of *Le Barbier de Séville*, at the Grand Saint-Jean, was enlivened by Camilla Tilling's delightful Rosina and Peter Mattei's Figaro. Daniele Gatti conducted the Orchestre du Teatro comunale di Bologna.

There were only a handful of orchestral concerts. At the Théâtre de l'Archevêché, the Orchestre du Teatro comunale di Bologna, under Daniele Gatti, performed works by Donadini, Petroni, Abdrazakov, Stravinsky, and Wagner; while Daniel Harding's concert with the Mahler Chamber Orchestra consisted of Mahler's

Symphony no. 4. In the cathedral, Laurence Equilbey conducted her Chœur Accentus in music by Rachmaninoff and Scriabin.

The recital series, at the Hôtel Maynier d'Oppède, consisted of chamber and piano music. Over several nights, Alain Planès performed all of Debussy's solo piano music. Pierre-Laurent Aimard's recital juxtaposed Boulez with Chopin and Ravel. Pieter Wispelwey performed Britten's music for solo cello. Quartets by Ravel and Schubert were performed by the Quatuor Tokyo; trios by Beethoven and Haydn by the Wiener Klaviertrio. The Ensemble Musicatreize, directed by Roland Hayrabedian, presented contemporary music by Ligeti, Martinu, Messiaen, and Xenakis. Once again, Lissner invited musicians from beyond Europe: 'Music from the Pamir mountains' was performed by artists from Tajikistan and Afghanistan; and 'Music of the steppes' by artists from Mongolia and Kyrgyzstan.

At the Théâtre du Jeu de Paume, there were several concerts devoted to electronic music, featuring world premieres by Bardi Johannsson and Ulf Langheinrich. As was the case the previous year, the Académie was not involved in the creation of the operas. Its programme was centred on music for string quartet and the piano, under the supervision of Alain Planès and Pierre-Laurent Aimard. Fifteen concerts were given in the cour de l'Hôtel de Ville.

iv 2006: LISSNER'S FINAL SEASON

In March 2006, it was announced that Bernard Foccroulle, director general of La Monnaie de Bruxelles, had been appointed to succeed Lissner as head of the Festival d'Aix from January 2007. Lissner's final innovation was the 'Laureates of the Académie' scheme, financially supported by HSBC. Each year, nine or ten of the most promising members of the Académie, selected by the artistic director of the Festival, are given this recognition and the guarantee of concert engagements in France and abroad. The 2006 laureates were the mezzo-sopranos Anastasia Boldyreva (Russia) and Anna Stéphany (France-United Kingdom); the baritone Daniel Schmutzhard (Austria); the bass Tomasz Slawinski (Poland); and the members of the Minetti Quartet (Austria) – Maria Ehmer (violin), Anna Knopp (violin), Markus Huber (viola), and Leonhard Roczek (cello).

Lissner set a number of projects in motion, including Aix's first *Der Ring des Nibelungen* cycle, masterminded by Simon Rattle, which would play in the new theatre in the Sextius-Mirabeau quarter, the Grand Théâtre de Provence. Lissner had managed to get the decades-old scheme to build this theatre (initiated by Bernard Lefort in 1974) over the line, but it wasn't ready in 2006. The cycle's first opera, *Das Rheingold*, played in the Théâtre de l'Archevêché. This was only possible because *Rheingold* required a smaller orchestra than its successors.

Joining *Das Rheingold*, were productions of *Die Zauberflöte*, Offenbach's *Histoire vraie de la Périchole*, Rossini's *L'Italiana in Algeri*, Purcell's *Dido and Aeneas*, and a revival of Pierre Boulez and Klaus Michael Grüber's triptych (Falla's *Les Tréteaux de maître Pierre*, Stravinsky's *Renard* and Schönberg's *Pierrot lunaire*), performed once in 2003 before the season was cancelled.

Rattle's director was Stéphane Braunschweig. The opening night began well. It was ten o'clock and darkness had fallen. The bass rumble that begins *Das Rheingold* sounded even more ominous than usual in the night air. Braunschweig made no attempt to realise the libretto as written (no one blamed him), but neither – as yet – could one detect an original interpretation of his own, unless one agreed that it was enough to be vaguely psychological and metaphorical. The *Ring des Nibelungen* as a dream or a study in delusion. But whose dream, whose delusion? The attractively austere set was white and clean; images of water, fire and clouds were projected against it. Braunschweig's solution to the challenge posed by mythological or historical subjects was to dress nearly all the characters – gods, giants, Rhine maidens – in modern suits or dresses. Rattle paced the music beautifully. Willard White had the necessary authority and presence as Wotan. Lilli Paasikivi and Anna Larsson sang well as Fricka and Erda, but, fatally, Dale Duesing was vocally stretched in the pivotal role of Alberich. Robert Gambill's cross-dressing Loge wore a shimmering evening gown but his face, unmade up, was mean and masculine.

Die Zauberflöte was created in Vienna. Krystian Lupa's production was widely disliked. Daniel Harding was blamed for the lacklustre singing. For the first time at Aix, he was booed at the curtain call.

A chamber piece called the *Histoire vraie de la Périchole*, created by Julie Brochen from Micaëla Villegas's novel and Offenbach's comic opera, played in the courtyard of the Hôtel Maynier d'Oppède. The cast of actors, led by Jeanne Balibar, sang well enough. Vincent Laterme directed a small chamber ensemble from the piano. It was no more than a curiosity.

At the Grand Saint-Jean, the opening of a pleasant but unremarkable production of Rossini's *L'Italiana in Algeri* by Toni Servillio (Riccardo Frizza conducted the Mahler Chamber Orchestra) was disrupted by repeated flyovers by a squadron of the French Air Force.

The residency of the Berliner Philharmoniker cost the Festival 150,000 euros a day. Lissner decided to maximise their impact, while celebrating the centenary of Cézanne's death, by organising a free concert at the quarry site beneath Sainte-Victoire (essentially a field of worn grass and red dust, but spectacular nevertheless) during which the Berliners performed Mahler's Symphony no. 5. Unfortunately, the amplified sound was murky and distorted.

A theatre was created in one of the rehearsal rooms at the Festival's facility at Venelles for an Académie performance of *Dido and Aeneas* conducted by Kenneth Weiss, who had tutored the young musicians and singers for some weeks. The outstanding mezzo-soprano Jennifer Johnston made her international debut as Dido.

Part Five

The NIGHTS of BERNARD FOCCROULLE

FOURTEEN

In Lissner's Shadow

2007-2011

i 2007: JANÁČEK'S DE LA MAISON DES MORTS

The high cost of committing to the four Wagner operas and the residency of the Berliner Philharmoniker placed a heavy strain on the Festival's finances. Having managed the accounts admirably until his final year, Lissner left a problem for his successor. Going forward, Bernard Foccroulle would need to make savings to prevent the growth of a large deficit. However, the new theatre meant that the Festival could sell more tickets and make some gains as a result.

An organist and composer as well as a director, Foccroulle had run La Monnaie for fifteen high-achieving years. He had a proven track record and was admired by his peers. His appointment as director of the Festival d'Aix was therefore uncontroversial and welcomed. Foccroulle didn't make any grand statements. He said that the Festival would remain true to its founder's vision – Mozart, early music and contemporary music were essential and would remain ever-present. However, works by Wagner were not a perversion of that tradition in his view. The festival needed to evolve. Like Lissner, Foccroulle was committed to innovation and new works – George Benjamin was among the composers under commission – and he reaffirmed the vital importance of the Académie.

Foccroulle placed emphasis on engaging with young people from all backgrounds, which meant increasing the Festival's education, community and social work (outreach). To this end, he created a service called Passerelles (gateways) run by the Festival's Education Department. Artistically, he wanted more involvement from Eastern Europe; and he wanted the Festival to engage more with the musical cultures of its own part of the world, the Mediterranean.

Foccroulle's first edition, 2007, included revivals of the 2003 Basil *Die Entführung aus dem Serail* (Deschamps and Minkowski) and the 1998 Brussels *Orfeo* (Trisha Brown and René Jacobs), and part two – *Die Walkerie* – of the Rattle/Braunschweig *Der Ring des Nibelungen*. *Die Walkerie* inaugurated the Grand Théâtre de Provence. The theatre was designed by the Italian architects Vittorio Gregotti and Paolo Colao. Inspired by the colours of Sainte-Victoire and matching the other new buildings and squares of the Sextius-Mirabeau quarter, the exterior of the building was unrecognisable as a theatre at first sight, a curious design choice. Inside, the scarlet auditorium consisted of 1,370 seats. *Die Walkerie* added little to the previous year's *Das Rheingold*, but Eva-Maria Westbroek was rightly acclaimed for her interpretation of Sieglinde. It was clear that Braunschweig wanted to imbue Wagner's characters with normal human feelings, such as pain, longing, and doubt. It remained to be seen whether this would be enough to make the cycle memorable. Simon Rattle was disappointed by the acoustics, as was Pierre Boulez. After the Festival, Foccroulle engaged the acoustician Daniel Commins to make the necessary improvements.

Much rested on new productions of *Le nozze di Figaro*, in the Théâtre de l'Archevêché, and Janáček's *De la maison des morts*, in the Grand Théâtre de Provence. Daniel Harding and the Mahler Chamber Orchestra were celebrating ten consecutive years at Aix. Harding conducted *Le nozze di Figaro*, Vincent Boussard directed. The first night had to be postponed because of heavy rain. The opera's farcical elements were highlighted. The *haute couture* fashion designer Christian Lacroix was commissioned to create statement costumes. The cast included Kate Royal and Nathan Gunn. For the third year running Harding was criticised in the French papers by reviewers who thought his Mozart style was too idiosyncratic. The tone of the criticism was peculiar. The critic of *Le Monde* blamed Harding for the 'failure' of Chéreau's *Così fan tutte* and expressed his relief that to create *De la maison des morts* Chéreau was working with Pierre Boulez, a 'true conductor'. Harding was sanguine, at least in public, and robust, telling Michael Henderson: 'People think that because I'm young, I set out to be different, but I simply try to do what is put in front of me. As for arbitrary tempi, if you look at any Mozart opera, you can find forty tempo markings. He was very specific, and you have little room for manoeuvre if you intend to observe them all. Some are slower than people expect, others are faster. Nobody likes to be publicly flagellated for doing their job but, as fellow conductor Nikolaus Harnoncourt has said, you can listen to what people have to say, but you can't change the order of days in a week, and you can't let anybody come between you and the score.'[1] Nevertheless, Harding decided to end his relationship with Aix.

De la maison des morts, a co-production, was instigated by Lissner. It was created in Vienna and seen in Amsterdam before transferring to Aix. Boulez and Chéreau's account of Janáček's final opera, after Dostoevsky, was bleak and brutal but poignantly compassionate. Its musical power and scenic lucidity were remarkable. The arc of the music and the arc of the drama were aligned to perfection. 'Patrice Chéreau's staging has the simplicity and humility of genius,' wrote Rupert Christiansen in *The Telegraph*. 'His lifelong collaborator Richard Peduzzi has designed a set consisting of nothing except massive concrete walls, sections of which move to allow entrances and exits. The end of the first act contains a *coup de théâtre* of stunning, shocking beauty, as a massive burst of detritus drops like a hailstorm from the flies, but elsewhere Chéreau's matchless power as a director manifests itself in the intensive work he has done with the cast: every person on stage has a vivid and credible personality.'[2] This was all the more remarkable because of the size of the ensemble: there were fifteen actors as well as the singers led by John Mark Ainsley as Skuratov, Olaf Bär as Goriantchikov, Eric Stoklossa as Alyeya, and Stefan Margita as Filka. The musicians of the Mahler Chamber Orchestra were inspired by the broken majesty of Janáček's difficult score under Boulez's direction.

Foccroulle re-instated the practice of allocating a festival production to the Académie européenne de musique. At the Théâtre du Jeu de Paume, members of the Académie performed a theatre piece created from some of Monteverdi's madrigals by Willy Decker and Kenneth Weiss. As usual, the Académie presented concerts and *activités pédagogiques*. Members of the Berliner Philharmoniker gave chamber concerts and masterclasses. The Berliner Philharmoniker's education department worked with local schools to create a show based on *Die Walküre*.

It was a memorable year, but only because of *De la maison des morts*, a production not created in Aix. Foccroulle was able to publish some good figures at the end of the edition. Eighty thousand tickets were sold. The free activities organised by Foccroulle during the opening weekend attracted 13,000 people.

ii 2008/09: DUSAPIN'S PASSION, THE RING CONCLUDES

The budget for 2008 was 18.8 million euros. Public funding remained at about thirty-three per cent of the total, the same as in 2005, but significantly lower than the fifty per cent provided at the beginning of Lissner's tenure. Bruno Roger, who had succeeded Edmonde Charles-Roux as president of the Festival in 2005, made the point.

Foccroulle's programme for 2008 included another project inherited from Lissner, a new opera by Pascal Dusapin, *Passion*, written to be staged in the Théâtre du Jeu de Paume. Mozart's early opera *Zaïde* (1779) played alongside *Così fan tutte* in the Théâtre de l'Archevêché; while Handel's *Belshazzar* was staged in the Grand Théâtre de Provence, and Haydn's *L'infedeltà delusa* in the courtyard of the Hôtel Maynier d'Oppède. The *Ring des Nibelungen* continued with *Siegfried*.

Zaïde entered the repertoire. Peter Sellars, working at Aix for the first time, directed the opera as if Mozart had predicted the Western world's 20th century relationship with the Middle East when he was simply adopting one of the most popular entertainment tropes of his own time. The largely unknown cast struggled to sing well. Louis Langrée conducted the Camerata Salzburg.

To direct *Così fan tutte*, Foccroulle engaged the renowned Iranian filmmaker Abbas Kiarostami. This generated good pre-publicity, and the hope that an important artist new to opera would produce something extraordinary. The production had an elegant simplicity, but Kiarostami's interpretation of the libretto was criticised. Rupert Christiansen's verdict was fair: 'It doesn't suggest,' he wrote, 'that the four lovers are anything other than ordinary young people in a muddle. [...] The net effect was just a bit too nice.'³ Kiarostami's use of film was memorable, but the singers seemed undirected. Other than William Shimell, as Alfonso, they were inexperienced: Sofia Soloviy's Fiordiligi stood out. Christophe Rousset's account of the score, played by the Camerata Salzburg, was refined.

Forty-nine years after the Festival's production of *Le Monde de la lune*, Haydn's rarely seen comic opera *L'infedeltà delusa* was performed, in modern dress, by members of the Académie in the intimate setting of the Hôtel Maynier d'Oppède. Richard Brunel directed; Jérémie Rhorer conducted Le Cercle de l'Harmonie.

The highlight of the season was Pascal Dusapin's *Passion*. A chamber opera for a man and a woman, with a libretto in Italian by the composer based on Orpheus and Eurydice, it was – musically, dramatically, and scenically (the director was Giuseppe Frigeni) – refined but sensuous, languid but tense. Dusapin's love for the operas and madrigals of Monteverdi informed the work. 'J'ai une relation très profonde avec cette période de l'histoire de la musique qui ressemble beaucoup à la nôtre par son goût de la recherche expérimentale,' he told Jean-Louis Validire of *Le Figaro*.⁴ Dusapin's score included parts for harpsichord, Arabic lute, synthesiser, organ, woodwind, brass, harp and strings. The musicians of the Ensemble Modern, under Franck Ollu, skilfully delivered Dusapin's layered harmonies and complex counterpoint. The soprano Barbara Hannigan and the tenor Georg Nigl were remarkable. Musical lines embraced and separated like the bodies of the singers.

In 2009, the Rattle-Braunschweig *Der Ring des Nibelungen* reached its conclusion with *Götterdämmerung*. While Braunschweig's tastefully minimalistic approach worked better here than in the earlier operas, the project was an honourable failure. Wagner's libretto could not sustain Braunschweig's decision to treat it as if it explored the human condition with the profundity of Shakespeare. Visually, the staging was often wonderful – spare, elegant, and masterly in its use of film, light, and space. There were longueurs: Gunther's vassals were dressed like country club tennis players. The singers, led by Ben Heppner (Siegfried), Katerina Dalayman (Brünnhilde), Gerd Grochowski (Gunther), and Anne-Sofie von Otter (Waltraute), were admirable.

Because of the high cost of *Der Ring des Nibelungen*, Foccroulle only programmed three other productions – *Die Zauberflöte* at the

Grand Théâtre de Provence and Mozart's *Idomeneo* and Offenbach's *Orphée aux enfers* at the Théâtre de l'Archevêché. *Die Zauberflöte* had been created during Foccroulle's tenure at La Monnaie (2005). The revival was deserved – William Kentridge's unique visual language was startlingly imaginative, and René Jacobs conducted the excellent Akademie für alte Musik – but Aix couldn't really claim any of the credit. There was no malaise, however.

The most eagerly anticipated production of the 2009 edition was Olivier Py's version of *Idomeneo*, conducted by Marc Minkowski. Py's inventive, high-concept form of theatre, had been tried and tested at the Odéon (where Py was director) and elsewhere. The multi-level metallic set, dazzling neon lighting in red and white, and cloudy perspex front screen, were recognisably the work of Py and his designer Pierre-André Weitz. Each level represented a different domain. Py set *Idomeneo* in our modern world of terrorism, fear and alienation. Unlike Peter Sellars, Py avoided direct references to geo-politics and produced some striking images. His direction of the singers was exemplary. Because Marc Minkowski, conducting Les Musiciens du Louvre, chose the Viennese version of the opera (1786), Idamante was played by a tenor, Yann Beuron. The first-rate cast also included Richard Croft as Idomeneo, Sophie Karthäuser as Ilia and Mireille Delunsch as Elettra.

iii 2010/11: THE ACADÉMIE RETURNS TO THE GRAND SAINT-JEAN

The slightly disappointing beginning to the Foccroulle era continued in 2010. There was solid work, but the Festival had become over-reliant on productions created elsewhere. The excellent period instruments ensemble Freiburger Barockorchester was in the pit for both productions at the Théâtre de l'Archevêché, Mozart's *Don Giovanni* and Gluck's *Alceste*. It was the beginning of an important relationship, for the orchestra would return in 2014, 2015 and 2016.

Aix's first production of *Giovanni* since Peter Brook's celebrated version of 1998 was directed by Dmitri Tcherniakov. The contrast with Brook's minimalism and maturity could not have been greater. Tcherniakov authored his own theatre work. He changed the characters and their relationships to create a middle-class satire that referenced European art cinema. The concept made Mozart's music redundant despite the faithful playing of the Freiburger Barockorchester under Louis Langrée. The cast members, led by Bo Skovhus's ropey, angst-ridden Don, were clearly committed to their director's vision: Kyle Ketelsen as Leporello, Marlis Petersen as Donna Anna, Kristine Opolais as Elvira, and Kerstin Avemo as Zerlina.

Gluck's *Alceste* (in the Paris version of 1776) was staged by Christof Loy and conducted by Ivor Bolton. The vocal ensemble English Voices formed the chorus. The production was notable for the fine performance of Véronique Gens in the title role. Gens wore a governess's plain black dress for some of the scenes and the white-walled setting suggested both a school and a large home. The members of the chorus – Alceste's subjects – were dressed as her children. Loy's enigmatic concept for *Alceste* felt like a genuine response to Gluck's music and was aesthetically related to the libretto. The Canadian tenor Joseph Kaiser played Admète.

The festival returned to the Grand Saint-Jean for the first time since 2006. Foccroulle had not used the venue during his first seasons because of security and safety concerns. He ensured that the Grand Saint-Jean's reopening was noteworthy by mounting the premiere of a new opera by the Argentine composer Oscar Strasnoy called *Un Retour*, performed by members of the Académie. He enhanced the domain's pastoral charm by organising pre-show performances at different locations – a solo dance work by Michèle Noiret (performed to Purcell's song 'Music for a While'), madrigals by Monteverdi and Strozzi, and spoken texts by Virgil, Homer and Dante. Once darkness had fallen, the spectators took their seats in the courtyard theatre. Strasnoy based his chamber opera on the novel by Alberto Manguel: a man, Nestor, returns to his ruined homeland after long years of exile and is unable to find the woman he loves (Marta). The ghosts of Argentina's *desaparacidos* haunt this poignant work partly inspired by Virgil's *Aeneid*. Thierry Thieû Niang's staging was elegantly simple. Roland Hayrabedian conducted an onstage ensemble consisting of two pianos, brass and percussion. The role of Nestor was alternated by Job Tomé and Hugo Oliveira; and that of Marta by Mariana Rewerski and Amaya Dominguez. The percussive score, dominated by spirals of counterpoint, was skilfully performed by the young musicians and singers.

The edition was completed by two productions brought in from elsewhere. *Le Rossignol et autres fables*, by Stravinsky, was a creation of the Canadian Opera Company, Toronto (2009). Robert Lepage's watery production was a magical, if too colourfully costumed, celebration of Japanese and Chinese classical theatre. Kazushi Ono conducted the Orchestre de l'Opéra national de Lyon. William Christie and Trisha Brown's pretty Rameau evening – extracts from *Hippolyte et Aricie* preceded the one-act ballet *Pygmalion* – was a transfer from the Royal Theater Carré of Amsterdam. Ed Lyon and Karolina Blixt were the singers.

The London Symphony Orchestra gave two concerts of music by Berlioz, Beethoven and Sibelius. Because ill health forced the withdrawal of Sir Colin Davis, the concerts were conducted by Stéphane Denève and Kazushi Ono. This was the beginning of one of Aix's most significant partnerships with an orchestra, for the LSO would act as the Festival's main ensemble for many of the subsequent editions. In 2011, it was the resident orchestra in the Théâtre de l'Archevêché. Verdi's *La Traviata* and Mozart's *La clemenza di Tito* were the two operas.

Verdi's Violetta was shared by Natalie Dessay and Irina Lungu. The fact that the role was a slight stretch for Natalie Dessay's light soprano voice only increased the poignancy of her performance. Irina Lungu's young and achingly vulnerable Violetta was unforgettable too. Charles Castronovo and Ludovic Tézier found complexity in the roles of Alfredo and Giorgio Germont. Jean-François Sivadier took the opera out of its opulent, melodramatic, 19th century comfort zone. The tragedy unfolded on a stage of white boards, which, for the final scene, was bare and forlorn, scattered with dead leaves. Earlier, painted panels depicted cloud-dappled skies and fecund gardens in a stylised and symbolic manner: beautiful but superficial, like the milieu of the opera. The performance ended with Violetta walking towards the audience, into glaring light. At the moment she reached the edge of the stage: blackout. The production was a poetic *tour de force*. *Le Monde* felt that the musicians of the LSO, unused to opera work, were ill at ease in the Verdi (the conductor was Louis Langrée) but much better playing Mozart's *La clemenza di Tito* under Colin Davis. The great conductor was making his debut in the pit at Aix. David McVicar's production used monumental sets but seemed uninspired when compared to his best work. Gregory Kunde replaced John Mark Ainsley at short notice to sing Tito. Sarah Connolly excelled as Sesto.

One of the positives of the new era was the commitment to new work. The 2011 edition opened with the premiere of Oscar Bianchi's compelling opera *Thanks to My Eyes*. Joël Pommerat created an atmospheric show in the Jeu de Paume; Frank Ollu conducted the virtuosic Ensemble Modern. At the Grand Saint-Jean, the Académie presented Handel's *Acis and Galatea*, in a production by Saburo Teshigawara. Leonardo García Alarcón conducted the Orchestre baroque de l'Académie. The young soprano Julie Fuchs sang Galatea.

The highlight of the 2011 edition was William Kentridge's acclaimed production of Shostakovich's *Le Nez*, brought in from New York. Kazushi Ono conducted the Orchestre de l'Opéra de Lyon.

FIFTEEN

A Festival of New Operas

2012-2018

i 2012: BENJAMIN'S WRITTEN ON SKIN

The 2012 season began at the Théâtre de l'Archevêché with a new staging, by Richard Brunel, of *Le nozze di Figaro*. Brunel set the opera in the offices of a legal firm, represented by glass doors and bookcases. It was hard to detect any deep meaning or insight. The work was reduced to the level of a farce. Jérémie Rhorer, conducting Le Cercle de l'Harmonie, seldom slowed down the pace of the music. The members of the good cast, directed to overact, were unsurprisingly vocally shrill: Paulo Szot, Kyle Ketelsen, Patricia Petibon, and Malin Byström.

The following night, Charpentier's rarely performed *David et Jonathas* was presented by the composer's most passionate contemporary interpreters, William Christie and Les Arts Florissants. It was a notable occasion, musically sublime and sensitively staged by Andreas Homoki on an uncluttered stage enclosed by décor in pale wood. The designer was Paul Zoller. The central roles of David, Jonathas, and Saul were beautifully sung by, respectively, Pascal Charbonneau, Ana Quintans and Neal Davies.

It was because of Foccroulle's new work policy that his era was suddenly transformed. The premiere of George Benjamin's *Written on Skin* at the Grand Théâtre de Provence was a landmark in the history of the Festival: a new opera, arguably the most important in more than a generation, by a major living composer that caught the imagination of the opera-going public. Benjamin conducted the

Mahler Chamber Orchestra, returning to the Festival for the first time since 2007. Katie Mitchell directed. Foccroulle had first spoken to George Benjamin about writing an opera in 1992. The composer told Foccroulle that he wasn't ready to write for the stage. It wasn't until 2006, after the success of his short one-act opera *Into the Little Hill*, that Benjamin agreed to write a full-scale piece for Aix. Foccroulle suggested to Benjamin and Martin Crimp that they consider a Provençal subject. He waited patiently, offering support and advice, during the opera's long period of gestation. Finally, in 2012, it was ready.

Crimp's spare libretto was based on a 12th century *vida* of the Occitan troubadour Guillem de Cabestany. According to the legend, when Raimon de Castell Rosselló discovered that his wife had slept with Guillem, he murdered the troubadour and tricked his wife into eating his heart. Crimp reimagined these characters as 'The Protector' (baritone); Agnès, his young wife (soprano); and 'The Boy' (countertenor). The Protector, a powerful landowner who treats his wife as a chattel, engages the Boy to create an illuminated manuscript to immortalise his family and his wealth. The Boy desires Agnès and she reciprocates, risking everything. Her love for the boy is an act of rebellion.

Crimp used a framing device in the form of three 'angels' acting as modern-day narrators and commentators, a method somewhat reminiscent of Britten's *Rape of Lucretia*. It negated the tale's melodramatic tendencies. Katie Mitchell added an extra layer of meta-theatrical commentary by making the angels modern-day conservators/archivists(?) working in the left-side laboratory rooms of Vicki Mortimer's two-level, multi-room set, while, on the right, the medieval drama enfolded in period-specific 12th century rooms. Mitchell's direction of the exceptional cast – Christopher Purves, Barbara Hannigan and Bejun Mehta as the tragic trio; Rebecca Jo Loeb and Allan Clayton as the angels – was sensitive and nuanced.

Benjamin gave the Boy the other-worldly voice of a countertenor and his orchestration included a part for a viola da gamba, meaning that accents of early music lingered within his distinctive vocabulary. There wasn't a single superfluous note. The sonorities were at turns chilling and glowing. The music generated an inexorable tension. 'Using a large orchestra sparingly and unleashing it only in the interludes, [Benjamin] conjures up glistening, mysterious sounds,' John

Allison wrote in *The Telegraph*.[1] *Written on Skin* was conceived, made, and premiered in Aix, but as a co-production it travelled to the great opera houses of Paris, London, Amsterdam, Munich, Vienna, and New York, and everywhere it went it garnered critical acclaim and adulation. *Le Monde* proclaimed unequivocally that *Written on Skin* was the first operatic masterpiece of the 21st century.

The edition's other new work could not have been more different. Foccroulle's desire to extend the reach of the Festival, structurally and thematically, into new artistic and cultural territories led him to mount the premiere of a performance art piece about the founder of the Black Panther Party – *Une Situation Huey P. Newton*, conceived by Jean-Michel Bruyère. In a first for the Festival, the work was presented in and around the Théâtre du Bois de l'Aune, a multidisciplinary venue built in the Jas de Bouffan residential quarter in 2010.

The season was completed by enjoyable Académie productions of Ravel's *L'Enfant et les sortilèges* (a perfect fit in the Jeu de Paume), and Mozart's *La finta giardiniera* (at the Grand Saint-Jean). Vincent Boussard directed the Mozart; Andreas Spering conducted Le Cercle de l'Harmonie. Performed on a reflective stage surface, surrounded by the trees and fields of the domain, the production was notable for the emergence of a new star, Sabine Devieilhe, whose pure but glowingly expressive voice was complemented by the charm of her acting.

ii 2013: CAVALLI, VERDI, STRAUSS, MENDONÇA

The revival of Dmitri Tcherniakov's 2010 *Don Giovanni*, this time with Marc Minkowski and the LSO in the pit, was the only disappointment in 2013, a season enlivened by the return of Patrice Chéreau to direct Richard Strauss's *Elektra* and the rediscovery of a masterpiece by Francesco Cavalli. It was a season which juxtaposed masterpieces from the early Baroque, the middle of the 19th century and the early 20th century.

Verdi's *Rigoletto* made its debut in the Théâtre de l'Archevêché. Robert Carsen, working at Aix for the first time since 1996, created, with designer Radu Boruzescu, a circus setting for the production, a sickly red, menacing milieu of sexual predators in dinner jackets that referenced the decadence of Paris in the 19th century, when brothels, can-can nightclubs and the Opéra provided male patrons with a theatrical demi-monde in which to hunt and exploit young women and girls. Carsen's voyeuristic staging risked being exploitative too, with naked dancing girls and acrobats, but it was a truthful interpretation of Verdi's dark melodrama, a daring, dazzlingly theatrical, *tour de force*.

George Gagnidze's Rigoletto began the evening in front of the curtain, dressed as a sinister white-faced clown and dragging a blow-up doll in a sack. Here was Carsen's *Rigoletto* encapsulated in a single image. However, devoid of his clown's costume and theatrical makeup, in the scenes with Irina Lungu's tender Gilda, Gagnidze achieved a tragic status. Gianandrea Noseda conducted a dark-toned London Symphony Orchestra.

The rediscovery of Cavalli's *Elena* (1659) was Aix at its adventurous best. While Jean-Yves Ruf's production in the Jeu de Paume was messily designed with too many wigs and cheap-looking costumes, the music was exquisite. Leonardo García Alarcón conducted the Cappella Mediterranea and singers from the Académie. The young Hungarian soprano Emöke Baráth was charismatic in the title role.

The edition's new opera was *The House Taken Over* by Vasco Mendonça. The libretto, by Sam Holcroft, was based on Julio Cortázar's story *Casa Tomada* (1946). Part psychological chiller, part political allegory, in which a brother and sister are terrorised by unseen assailants, real or imagined, in their family home, it was elegantly staged by Katie Mitchell at the Grand Saint-Jean. Mendonça's chamber score was played by the Asko Schönberg Ensemble under the direction of Etienne Siebens. The siblings were played by the Académie members Oliver Dunn and Kitty Whately. Regrettably, *The House Taken Over* was the final production at the Grand Saint-Jean. Because of the poor condition of the château, health and safety declared the venue unsafe. (The Festival wanted to retain the Grand Saint-Jean and planned to make the necessary repairs and improvements, should funding be acquired, but Foccroulle's successor, Pierre Audi, would abandon the plan in 2022 when he identified a cheaper, and very different, new performance venue at Vitrolles.)

All eyes were on Strauss's *Elektra* at the Grand Théâtre de Provence. As expected from a director as great as Chéreau, there was no show-off concept. An acute sensitivity to Strauss's score (in tandem with Esa-Pekka Salonen, conducting the Orchestre de Paris), and a love of the craft of theatre and the art of acting, created a production that was musically and visually lyrical but unflinching in its depiction of suffering. One of the great interpreters of Strauss's music, Evelyn Herlitzius, had never been more inspired as Elektra. Waltraud Meier as Clytemnestra and Mikhail Petrenko as Orestes struggled to match her.

The season included a large-scale education project, organised by the Service éducatif du Festival d'Aix, that resulted in a performance of Prokofiev's ballet *Roméo et Juliette* in the Grand Théâtre de Provence by the Orchestre des jeunes de la Méditerranée, Groupe Grenade, and pupils from two of Aix's *écoles élémentaires* – Marcel Pagnol and Alphonse Daudet. Josette Baïz created the choreography. The conductor was Gianandrea Noseda.

iii 2014: AIX EN JUIN, LES INTERMITTENTS

In 2014, Foccroulle, whose view of the importance of culture was utopian, made a new attempt to open up the work of the Festival to a younger, wider and more diverse audience by initiating Aix en Juin, a pre-Festival *fête* of free performances that was successful enough to become a permanent fixture. Aix en Juin was more than a return to the ethos of 'Musique dans la rue' embraced by Bernard Lefort during the 1970s, for it was the creation of the artists, backstage staff (particularly the unit responsible for the Passerelles service) and Académie members of the Festival. It was created by moving most of the Académie's public work from the July weeks of the Festival to June.

Aix en Juin acts as a celebratory prelude to the July programme by offering concerts (in the courtyard of the Hôtel Maynier d'Oppède and elsewhere), workshops, masterclasses, films, and participatory projects. Western classical music rubs shoulders with other genres, including jazz and world music. Each edition of Aix en Juin ends with a free concert in the Cours Mirabeau under the moniker 'Parade(s)'.

The creation of Aix en Juin followed changes to the aims and structure of the Académie introduced in 2013, changes driven by its leaders' mission to make the opera world multi-cultural and diverse. At this time, the Académie's name was changed from the Académie européenne de musique to the Académie du Festival d'Aix. A welcome part of the innovations was the integration of the Orchestre des jeunes de la Méditerranée into the life of the Académie.

The issue of *les intermittents* and unemployment benefits was back on the agenda. In January 2014, eleven years on from the crisis of 2003, the government decided that further action was needed to make the scheme affordable and sustainable. In March, the employers and some of the unions agreed to the review body's recommendations for reform. In June, the government accepted the recommendations but initiated a period of consultation. The consultation process failed to fend off a protest campaign targeting the summer festivals. The anger people felt was compounded by the fact that this reduction to their benefits was being implemented by a socialist government.

In an article published in *Le Monde*, the Minister of Culture, Aurélie Filippetti, wrote about the importance of France's festivals and the essential role played by *les intermittents*. She wrote that the benefits scheme would not be abandoned, but reform was essential. The ongoing consultation would be fair and thorough.[2] The article didn't impress the leaders of the protest, who let it be known that Aurélie Filippetti would not be welcomed if she dared to show her face in Avignon. They particularly didn't like the final paragraph of her article in which she implied that if strikes forced the cancellation of Avignon and Aix the outcome would be fatal for these organisations. The expectation was that, unlike in 2003, the government would not provide compensation. The new director of the Avignon Festival, Olivier Py, was told this by President Hollande's chief of staff.

Aix employed over nine hundred people to run the Festival. Seventy-two per cent of them were *intermittents*. The majority voted against striking, preferring instead to get their message across without disrupting the shows. This was a huge relief for Foccroulle. It was agreed that, before each performance, they would address the audience from the stage. Before the opening night performance of *Die Zauberflöte* at the Grand Théâtre de Provence, director Simon

McBurney spoke in support of *les intermittents*, and then brought all fifty members of the backstage team onto the stage. They wore on the back of their black T-shirts the letter X, emblem of the protests.

However, the people who favoured confrontation and disruption were simply waiting until the following night and the opening of Handel's *Ariodante* at the Theatre de l'Archevêché. A performance in the open-air venue would be easier to disrupt as well as more likely to be attended by members of the government. They massed in the place de l'Archevêché outside the theatre with the usual pots and pans and klaxons. Some members of the technical team decided to strike at the last minute, forcing Foccroulle to tell the audience that the production's lighting design would be rudimentary. Next, the technical team took to the stage and expected the audience to listen willingly to the relay of a very long speech by the Marxist journalist Edwy Plenel. Some audience members, already on edge because of the relentless noise coming from the square, started to boo and shout.

After a long delay, the performance finally began, but some of the protesters managed to invade the backstage areas of the theatre, including the artists' dressing rooms and green room in the Jardin Campra. Sarah Connolly, attempting to reach the stage to make her first entrance as Ariodante, was mistaken for a protestor (it was a modern dress show) by a security man and shoved roughly in the neck. Rarely had the phrase the 'show must go on' been more apposite, for Connolly, Patricia Petibon, Sandrine Piau and their colleagues soldiered on despite the racket generated by the protesters. The police evicted the protestors from the theatre, but one of them had hidden two sirens in the auditorium which went off during the second act. Andrea Marcon, conducting the Freiburger Barockorchester, halted the performance and the curtain was lowered while staff found the sirens and removed them. At the end of the performance, in heavy rain, the audience rewarded the singers and musicians with a standing ovation despite Richard Jones's idiosyncratic staging, which relocated and updated the action to an inward-looking fishing village on a remote Scottish island in modern times, as if the opera was *Peter Grimes*.

The eagerness with which a minority, egged on by outsiders, tried to wreck the festival that gave them their living, was paradoxical as well as upsetting. It didn't need to be this way, as the previous night's dignified protest before the performance of *Die Zauberflöte* had shown. Sarah Connolly later revealed that private belongings had been stolen from the green room and artists' garden.³ The issue of *les intermittents* was complicated and tricky to manage for theatre managers and leading artists, who instinctively wanted to support their colleagues, and wanted them to have secure incomes. Even with the unreformed unemployment benefits system, they struggled to get by. Olivier Py stated publicly that the deficit had grown because of rising unemployment across the sector and not because the payments were too generous. Foccroulle showed his solidarity by joining his workers as they took to the streets to explain to people why they were protesting. They argued that the change to their unemployment rights was an attack on culture: their slogan was La Culture en Danger.

The season continued. Katie Mitchell used extracts from Bach's cantatas to create a work called *Trauernacht* in the Jeu de Paume. The singers and musicians of the Académie performed adeptly under the direction of Raphaël Pichon. William Kentridge's theatrical response to Schubert's *Winterreise*, performed by Matthias Goerne and Markus Hinterhäuser at the Conservatoire Darius-Milhaud, was hauntingly imaginative. The second show at the Théâtre de l'Archevêché was Rossini's *Il Turco in Italia*, conducted by Marc Minkowski. Christopher Alden delivered a decent production in his usual, modern dress style. The Musiciens du Louvre were more at home performing Rameau's *Les Boréades* in concert at the Grand Théâtre de Provence. Minkowski's young singers were Julie Fuchs (Alphise), Chloé Briot (Sémire), Samuel Boden (Abaris), Manuel Nuñez-Camelino (Calisis), Jean-Gabriel Saint-Martin (Borilée), Damien Pass (Borée), and Mathieu Gardon (Adamas). All but Boden were former members of the Académie. The other highlight of the concert programme was Alexandre Tharaud's performance of Bach's *Variations Goldberg* at the Théâtre de l'Archevêché.

The edition would have been artistically a little flat without Simon McBurney's acclaimed *Die Zauberflöte*, created for Pierre Audi in Amsterdam, in which a rough theatre aesthetic (the default setting, as bare and dark as an empty warehouse, consisted of a large moveable platform suspended on cables) was magically transformed by ancient and modern theatrical devices, including live video projections combined with chalk drawings, aerial acrobatics, shadow puppetry (paper birds), and live sound effects that dared to compete with Mozart's music.

Like the other successful interpreters of this elusive work, McBurney told the story simply enough as a dark fable in which the characters were forced to suffer and struggle as they journeyed towards the light. It was the visual flair that set the production apart. McBurney combined the empty stage philosophy of Peter Brook with a masterly manipulation of meta-theatrical effects. To realise his vision, McBurney collaborated with some remarkable designers: Michael Levine (sets), Jean Kalman (lighting), Nicky Gillibrand (costumes), Finn Ross (video), and Gareth Fry (sound). Pablo Heras-Casado conducted the Freiburger Barockorchester.

iv 2015: RATTLE AND DOVE

One of the strands of Foccroulle's directorship was a cycle of works by Handel. In 2015, he mounted, in the Grand Théâtre de Provence, the Festival's first production of *Alcina* since Jorge Lavelli's celebrated version of 1978. Katie Mitchell directed; Andrea Marcon conducted the Freiburger Barockorchester. It was an absorbing staging that exploited the sensuality of its young principals, Patricia Petibon, as Alcina, and Anna Prohaska, as Morgana. Philippe Jaroussky, Anthony Gregory and Krzysztof Bączyk played the roles of Ruggiero, Oronte and Melisso.

The theme seemed to be the fallibility of youth, beauty and power, things that must fade and end. An 18th century-style boudoir was bordered on each side by a dark antechamber/dressing room (designer: Chloe Lamford). When Alcina and Morgana moved into one of these, they aged (actors were used to effect this transformation). Alcina's victims were lifted by an overhead contraption and turned into stuffed animals, an idea that was more droll than sinister. The characters were watched and directed by grim-faced attendants dressed, like the stage managers backstage, in black.

The singing, acting and orchestral playing were mostly first-rate, although the astonishing arias would have had a greater impact had the stage business momentarily stopped to allow the singer (and audience members) a few minutes to concentrate on the music.

It is all too tempting to use those operas of Mozart set in the Middle East to make political points about our modern world, but perhaps the temptation should be resisted. Seven years after Peter Sellars's *Zaïde*, Martin Kusej updated *Die Entführung aus dem Serail* to the colonial 1920s and twisted Mozart's comedy into a brutal study of racial hatred, with a re-written text and on-stage beheadings. At least that was his plan until Foccroulle, reacting to a heartbreaking atrocity in Lyon on the eve of the Festival, instructed him to tone it down. Instead of severed heads, Osmin threw bloodstained clothing onto the stage at the end of the opera. The desert setting (sand; Bedouin tents) was visually effective. Osmin was the only character to benefit from Kusej's ideas – Franz-Josef Selig was menacing in the role. Jérémie Rhorer, conducting the Freiburger Barockorchester, often collaborates with politically minded directors, but Kusej's *Die Entführung* and Mozart's *Die Entführung* were separate things and Rhorer wasn't able to bridge the gap.

Peter Sellars's pairing of Tchaikovsky's *Iolanta* and Stravinsky's *Perséphone* was created in Madrid. For this revival at the Grand Théâtre de Provence, Teodor Currentzis conducted the Orchestre de l'Opéra de Lyon. Stravinsky's dramatic cantata/dance work (1934), from a text by André Gide, brought the great actress Dominique Blanc to Aix.

The highlight of the 2015 season – if one discounts a welcome revival of Robert Carsen's production of Britten's *A Midsummer Night's Dream* (Kazushi Ono conducted the Orchestre de l'Opéra de Lyon) – was *Le Monstre du labyrinth* by Jonathan Dove. A community opera written to bring professionals and amateurs, young and old, together, it was the brainchild of Simon Rattle. Separate productions were created, in different languages, in Berlin, London and Aix under the musical direction of Rattle and chorus master Simon Halsey. In Berlin and London the work was semi-staged; in Aix, there was a full production in the Grand Théâtre de Provence, directed by Marie-Eve Signeyrole. Rattle conducted the combined forces of the LSO and the Orchestre des jeunes de la Méditerranée. Dove's opera was based on the ancient story describing how Theseus rescued the youth of Athens from the Minotaur. The Athenians were played by children and teenagers from local schools and amateur choirs. The roles of Theseus, his mother, and Daedalus were performed by members of the Académie. It was a glorious, life-affirming event.

That December, Foccroulle announced that he would step down at the end of his current term in 2018. By then he would have been in post for ten years. The renewal of his contract was in doubt because the Festival's political masters had been angered by his vocal support of *les intermittents* in 2014. He said that he wanted to concentrate on his work as a musician and composer.

v 2016/17/18: THE FOCCROULLE ERA COMES TO AN END

Aix's preference for radical directorial interpretations reached a new level in 2016.

Christophe Honoré's production of *Così fan tutte* at the Théâtre de l'Archevêché used Mozart's opera to create a thoroughly nasty, but brilliantly executed, exploration of racism and feral promiscuity. Set in Eritrea under Italian colonial rule during the late 1930s, a young black girl was exploited on stage during the overture. This set the tone for a production that hoped to shock in every scene. Dorabella willingly engaged with four men in a prelude to gang sex whilst singing one of her arias. The use of blackface was just one of Honoré's controversial ideas. The singers, particularly Kate Lindsey and Lenneke Ruiten as Dorabella and Fiordiligi, sang beautifully and performed with conviction and skill. Aix had come a long way since the sincere and gentle *Così fan tutte* of 1948, but it was hard to deny that Honoré's production was a major work, as compelling and thought-provoking as it was dark and brutal. Louis Langrée conducted the Freiburger Barockorchester.

Il trionfo del tempo e del disingano is one of Handel's most ravishing works, and Emmanuelle Haïm (conducting her Concert d'Astrée) and Sabine Devieilhe (as Bellezza) didn't disappoint. Krzysztof Warlikowski updated and subverted this allegorical work by making Bellezza a 21st century party girl, drugged up, emotionally drowning and heading towards an overdose or suicide.

Stéphane Degout and Barbara Hannigan were the stars of Katie Mitchell's production of *Pelléas et Mélisande* at the Grand Théâtre de Provence, Aix's first account of Debussy's masterpiece since 1966. Esa-Pekka Salonen conducted the Philharmonia Orchestra. Mitchell's *Pelléas* was less audacious than either Honoré's *Così fan tutte* or Warlikowski's *Il trionfo del tempo e del disingano*, but equally disrespectful of its composer's intentions. Conceived as a study in gender politics disguised as a dream, its world consisted of the *haute bourgeois* rooms of a property locked in time and an empty indoor swimming pool pierced by the branches of a tree. By using a double, Mitchell kept a sleeping Mélisande in the central bedroom. Hannigan's remarkable Mélisande was much more provocative and proactive than is usually the case. Her musical phrasing was impeccable. The main programme in the Grand Théâtre de Provence was completed by a revival of Peter Sellars's double-bill of Stravinsky's *Oedipus Rex* and *Symphonie de psaumes*, created in Los Angeles. It completed a very good season for Esa-Pekka Salonen and the Philharmonia Orchestra. Under the baton of Raphaël Pichon, Rameau's *Zoroastre* was performed in concert by the Ensemble Pygmalion and a very strong cast – Reinoud Van Mechelen (Zoroastre), Nicolas Courjal (Abramane), Emmanuelle de Negri (Erinice), and Katherine Watson (Amélite). The young mezzo-soprano Léa Desandre, a member of that year's residency for singers at the Académie, sang the role of Céphie.

The 2017 season was a little calmer. Jean-François Sivadier directed *Don Giovanni* in an eclectic style that blurred the lines between characters and performers, performing and rehearsing. The singers began the evening in their own clothes before gradually adding items of 18th century dress; they sat at the rear of the stage, applying make-up, or observing their colleagues, when not singing. This style of theatre is decades old, but it doesn't tire if done well. Curtains and screens were brought on, coloured lightbulbs suspended, and across the crumbling concrete wall at the rear of the stage the word 'Libertas' was scrawled in red letters. Liberty from what? This wasn't a production that referenced Mozart's own time (the Enlightenment, the origins of the Revolution). Sivadier had some strong ideas, among them his treatment of Elvira's maid (Juliette Allain), who, while never singing, was ever-present. When she succumbed to the Don (thereby betraying Isabel Leonard's compassionate Elvira) it had a greater impact than anything else in the opera. Philippe Sly's Don was a young sociopath playing at being a rockstar. He had no inner life and no capacity for empathy. The production was visually strong and the young singers – Sly, Leonard, Nahuel di Pierro, Julie

Fuchs and Eleonora Buratto – were stylishly good. Jérémy Rhorer conducted Le Cercle de l'Harmonie.

The second show at the Théâtre de l'Archevêché saw the much-anticipated return of Simon McBurney. In staging Stravinsky's *The Rake's Progress*, McBurney began with a white box (or blank page) and then conjured magical visual transformations using video projections. However, despite a strong cast – Paul Appleby as Tom, Julia Bullock as Anne, and Kyle Ketelsen as Shadow – he was only fitfully able to disguise the aridity of Stravinsky's score or the politeness of Auden's libretto. This was no fault of the excellent Orchestre de Paris. The production should have marked the return of Daniel Harding, but he was indisposed. Eivind Gullberg Jensen replaced him.

In Dmitri Tcherniakov's re-imagining of Bizet's *Carmen*, the characters became businesspeople attending, perhaps, a conference in a hotel. A programme note told the audience that Tcherniakov had conceived the opera as the therapy session of a man (Don José) unable to form emotional relationships.

Four years after *Elena*, Foccroulle programmed a second Cavalli rarity, *Erismena*. Jean Bellorini's production in the Jeu de Paume featured former members of the Académie, including Léa Desandre, whose great promise was confirmed, Jonathan Abernethy, and Francesca Aspromonte, excellent in the title role. New to Aix was Susanna Hurrell. These young singers' pleasure at performing together was evident, their radiant singing often miraculous. Leonardo García Alarcón conducted the chamber ensemble Cappella Mediterranea. The opera contained sublime music of a melancholy disposition. Bellorini kept his uncluttered stage moodily dark. A metal platform was lifted to form the wall of a cage. Hanging lightbulbs and colourful contemporary costumes (street chic) prettified this alienating environment.

The season's high point was a new opera by Philippe Boesmans, based on Carlo Collodi's *Pinocchio*. A dark morality tale masquerading as an opera for children, Joël Pommerat's libretto used the framing device of a performance given by a circus troupe. Stéphane Degout played the menacing ringmaster among other roles. Another graduate of the Académie, Chloé Briot, beguiled in the central role, played as an insolent rebel. Pommerat staged his episodic libretto with flair and imagination. Boesmans's score, rich in orchestral colours and stylistic variations, had depth and scale despite being written for only six singers.

The opening production of the 2018 season, Foccroulle's last, was Katie Mitchell's account of Strauss's *Ariadne auf Naxos*, her sixth show at Aix in as many years. The production was less well-received than most of its predecessors, perhaps because of over-familiarity. Mitchell is one of those directors who uses the same style of *mise en scène* and set of ideas whatever the opera. Sabine Devieilhe, Lise Davidsen and Angela Brower sang beautifully. Marc Albrecht conducted the Orchestre de Paris.

Ondřej Adámek's *Seven Stones*, an opera for four solo singers and a chorus of twelve, was premiered in the Jeu de Paume. A collaboration between Adámek and the Icelandic poet Sjón, this meditation on stones was a poem in words and sounds, as strange and primal as Iceland's geology. The performers sang, spoke, whispered, and produced percussive and other sounds on objects as well as instruments. The director was Éric Oberdorff. The singers of Ensemble Accentus were joined by members of the Académie. This hauntingly unconventional work, the last of Foccroulle's commissions, was a reminder that his tenure had been marked by a commitment to new music.

Mariusz Treliński's staging of Prokofiev's *L'Ange de feu* was created in Warsaw. A lurid theatrical imagination was at work here. Treliński's modernising ideas were justified. Aušrinė Stundytė's Renata, a tormented, vulnerable, young woman possessed (or believing herself possessed) by a demonic angel (or abusive lover), spiralled downwards in a *demi-monde* of seedy hotel rooms and neon-lit bars that was both hallucinogenic and disturbingly real. A drug dealer wearing a tracksuit was ever-present, while Krzysztof Bączyk's Faust appeared in several guises, including that of a blind man ruling over a convent of schoolgirls who looked like Renata. This nightmare subversion of religious iconography was a perfect match for Prokofiev's extraordinary score, dazzlingly well played by the Orchestre de Paris under Kazushi Ono.

At the end of the season, Foccroulle departed without fanfare. The baton was passed to Pierre Audi. Because of the work of Lissner and Foccroulle, the Festival's reputation is high and its funding model relatively sound. However, society is changing and the long-term role of arts organisations like Aix is uncertain. State-funded opera requires the continuation of a difficult-to-justify level of public spending and the support of opera-lovers who remain willing, and financially able, to embrace the absurd as much as the sublime. This truth tends to make some contemporary opera administrators and government ministers uncomfortable, which partly explains the introduction of policies designed to make opera relevant, and which justify its funding.

This subject is beyond the scope of the present history, but it is worth noting that, more than any other opera organisation in France, the Festival d'Aix actively pursues such policies and is passionate about them. Under Audi they formed a central part of Aix's national mission, for in the press release announcing Audi's appointment, the Ministry of Culture stated: 'The Aix-en-Provence Festival is a leading artistic event and a vehicle for cultural innovation and education, bringing openness to a diversity of works, forms, and audiences.' It remains to be seen what impact the prioritising of these policies will have on the delivery of operas in the Théâtre de l'Archevêché, where the box office still relies on what one might call a traditional opera-going public.

Appendices

Directors

1948-1972
Gabriel Dussurget, Directeur artistique
Roger Bigonnet, Administrateur général (1948-64)

1974-1981
Bernard Lefort, Directeur général

1982-1996
Louis Erlo, Directeur général

1997-2006
Stéphane Lissner, Directeur général

2007-2018
Bernard Foccroulle, Directeur général

2019-2025
Pierre Audi, Directeur général

2026-
Ted Huffman, Directeur général

DIRECTORS OF THE ACADÉMIE EUROPÉENNE DE MUSIQUE/ACADÉMIE DU FESTIVAL D'AIX

Stéphane Lissner, founder. David Stern (1997-2000); Antoine Manceau (2001-2008); Émile Delorme (2009-2019)

Festival Venues

Festival performance venues with year first used. Venues used regularly over a long period marked with *. Venues still used in the 2020s in capital letters.

1948
*THÉÂTRE DE L'ARCHEVÊCHÉ
Musée des Tapisseries (grand salon)
*Place des Quatre-Dauphins
Jas de Bouffan (park)
Cour de l'Hôtel Boyer d'Eguilles

1949
Château de la Mignarde (park)

1951
Jardin Campra
Lourmarin: Château de Lourmarin
Ansouis: Château d'Ansouis

1952
*Cathédrale Saint-Sauveur
Cour de l'Hôtel de Ville
Place de Saint-Jean-de-Malte

1953
*COUR DE L'HÔTEL DE MAYNIER D'OPPÈDE
Les Baux-de-Provence (Val d'Enfer)

1957
*Le Tholonet (park)

Le Puy-Sainte-Réparade: Château de Fonscolombe

1958
*Cloître Saint-Louis, Lycée Vauvenargues

1959
*Parc Rambot

1965
Saint-Maximin-la-Sainte-Baume: Couvent Royal

1969
La Roque-d'Anthéron: Abbaye de Silvacane
Saint-Maximin-la-Sainte-Baume: Basilique Sainte-Marie-Madeleine

1974
Place des Cardeurs
Église du Saint-Esprit

1975
Arles: Théâtre antique
Église de la Madeleine
*Cloître Saint-Sauveur
Saint-Cannat: Commanderie de la Bargemone

1979
Hôtel de Caumont, Conservatoire Darius-Milhaud

1980
Cour de l'Hôtel de Valbelle

1982
Parc Jourdan

1983
Pavillon Vendôme (garden)

1989
Grand Théâtre d'Aix

1999
*Domaine du Grand Saint-Jean

2000
*THÉÂTRE DU JEU DE PAUME
Cité du Livre

2007
*GRAND THÉÂTRE DE PROVENCE

2012
Théâtre du Bois de l'Aune, Jas de Bouffan

2014
*CONSERVATOIRE MILHAUD, AUDITORIUM CAMPRA

2021
Arles: Grande Halle, Parc des Ateliers

2022
PAVILLON NOIR
VITROLLES: STADIUM DE VITROLLES

Opera Productions 1948-2023

GABRIEL DUSSURGET

1948

COSÌ FAN TUTTE
by Mozart
director Marisa Morel
designer Georges Wakhevitch
conductor Hans Rosbaud
Orchestre des cadets du conservatoire
Théâtre de l'Archevêché

1949

DON GIOVANNI
by Mozart
director Jean Meyer
designer Cassandre
conductor Hans Rosbaud
Orchestre des concerts du Conservatoire
Théâtre de l'Archevêché

1950

COSÌ FAN TUTTE
by Mozart
director Jean Meyer/Marcello Cortis
designer Balthus
conductor Hans Rosbaud
Orchestre des concerts du Conservatoire
Théâtre de l'Archevêché

DON GIOVANNI
Revival of 1949

ORFEO
By Monteverdi

conductor Ernest Bour
Orchestre des concerts du Conservatoire
Théâtre de l'Archevêché
[Concert version]

1951

DIE ENTFÜHRUNG AUS DEM SERAIL
by Mozart
director Pierre Bertin
conductor Hans Rosbaud
Orchestre des concerts du Conservatoire
Théâtre de l'Archevêché

LE TÉLÉPHONE
by Gian Carlo Menotti
director Pierre Bertin
conductor Jean Gitton

Followed by

LE MARIAGE SECRET
by Domenico Cimarosa
director Pierre Bertin
conductor Gian Andrea Gavazzeni
Orchestre des concerts du Conservatoire
Théâtre de l'Archevêché

1952

LE NOZZE DI FIGARO
by Mozart
director Maurice Sarrazin
conductor Hans Rosbaud
Orchestre des concerts du Conservatoire
Théâtre de l'Archevêché

DON GIOVANNI
Revival of 1949

IPHIGÉNIE EN TAURIDE
by Gluck
director Jan Doat
conductor Carlo Mario Giulini
Orchestre des concerts du Conservatoire
Théâtre de l'Archevêché

1953

LE BARBIER DE SÉVILLE
by Rossini

director Maurice Sarrazin
conductor Carlo Mario Giulini
Orchestre des concerts du Conservatoire
Théâtre de l'Archevêché

COSÌ FAN TUTTE
Revival of 1950
director Marcello Cortis

LE NOZZE DI FIGARO
Revival of 1952

1954

DIE ENTFÜHRUNG AUS DEM SERAIL
Revival of 1951
director Jean-Pierre Grenier

DON GIOVANNI
Revival of 1949

LES CAPRICES DE MARIANNE
by Henri Sauguet
[World premiere]
director Jean Meyer
Orchestre des concerts du Conservatoire
Théâtre de l'Archevêché

MIREILLE
by Gounod
director Jean Meyer
conductor André Cluytens
Orchestre des concerts du Conservatoire
Les Baux-de-Provence

1955

ORPHÉE
by Gluck
director Jean Meyer
conductor Karl Ristenpart
Orchestre des concerts du Conservatoire
Théâtre de l'Archevêché

LE NOZZE DI FIGARO
Revival of 1952

COSÌ FAN TUTTE
Revival of 1950
director Marcello Cortis

1956

LE TÉLÉPHONE
Revival of 1951

Followed by

ZÉMIRE ET AZOR
by Grétry
director Maurice Sarrazin
Orchestre des concerts du Conservatoire
Théâtre de l'Archevêché

DON GIOVANNI
Revival of 1949

PLATÉE
by Rameau
director Jean-Pierre Grenier
conductor Hans Rosbaud
Orchestre des concerts du Conservatoire
Théâtre de l'Archevêché

LE BARBIER DE SÉVILLE
Revival of 1953

1957

CARMEN
by Bizet
director Jean-Pierre Grenier
conductor Pierre Dervaux
Orchestre de l'Association des Concerts Pasdeloup
Théâtre de l'Archevêché

LE NOZZE DI FIGARO
Revival of 1952

COSÌ FAN TUTTE
Revival of 1950

1958

DIE ZAUBERFLÖTE
by Mozart
director Jean-Pierre Grenier
conductor Georg Solti
Orchestre des concerts du Conservatoire
Théâtre de l'Archevêché

DON GIOVANNI
Revival of 1949

LE BARBIER DE SÉVILLE
Revival of 1953

1959

LE MONDE DE LA LUNE
by Haydn
director Maurice Sarrazin
conductor Carlo Mario Giulini
Orchestre de la chambre de Hollande
Théâtre de l'Archevêché

DIE ZAUBERFLÖTE
Revival of 1958
conductors Alberto Erede/Serge Baudo

COSÌ FAN TUTTE
Revival of 1950
conductor Alberto Erede

1960

LA VOIX HUMAINE
by Poulenc
director Jean Cocteau
conductor George Prêtre

Followed by

LE MÉDECIN MALGRÉ LUI
by Gounod
director Jean Meyer
conductor Serge Baudo
Orchestre des concerts du Conservatoire
Théâtre de l'Archevêché

LA SENNA FESTEGGIANTE
by Vivaldi
conductor Guido Turchi

Followed by

DIDO AND AENEAS
by Purcell (realisation: Britten)
director Michel Crochot
conductor Pierre Dervaux
Orchestre des concerts du Conservatoire
Théâtre de l'Archevêché

DON GIOVANNI
Revival of 1949
conductor Alberto Erede

LE NOZZE DI FIGARO
Revival of 1952
conductor Michael Gielen

1961

L'INCORONAZIONE DI POPPEA
by Monteverdi
director Michel Crochot
conductor Bartoletti
Orchestre de la chambre de Hollande
Théâtre de l'Archevêché

LAVINIA
by Henry Berraud
[World premiere]
director Daniel Sorano
conductor Serge Baudo
Orchestre des concerts du Conservatoire
Théâtre de l'Archevêché

COSÌ FAN TUTTE
Revival of 1950
conductor Michael Gielen

COMBATTIMENTO DI TANCREDI E CLORINDA
by Monteverdi
director Jeanine Charrat
conductor Pierre Dervaux
Orchestre des concerts du Conservatoire
Théâtre de l'Archevêché

DIDO AND AENEAS
Revival of 1960

DIE ZAUBERFLÖTE
Revival of 1958
conductor Michael Gielen

1962

LES MALHEURS D'ORPHÉE
by Milhaud
director Michel Crochot
conductor Pierre Dervaux

Followed by

LES NOCES
by Stravinsky
director Georges Skibine

conductor Pierre Dervaux
Orchestre des solistes de l'Association des Concerts Colonne
Théâtre de l'Archevêché

DON GIOVANNI
Revival of 1949
conductor Michael Gielen

LE NOZZE DI FIGARO
Revival of 1952
conductor Michael Gielen

DIE ENTFÜHRUNG AUS DEM SERAIL
Revival of 1951
director Jean Le Poulain
conductor Serge Baudo

1963

ARIADNE AUF NAXOS
by Strauss
director Werner Duggelin
conductor Pierre Dervaux
Orchestre des concerts du Conservatoire
Théâtre de l'Archevêché

IDOMENEO
by Mozart
director Michel Crochot
conductor Peter Maag
Orchestre des concerts du Conservatoire
Théâtre de l'Archevêché

DIE ZAUBERFLÖTE
Revival of 1958
conductor John Pritchard

COSÌ FAN TUTTE
Revival of 1950, but with a new design by François Ganeau
conductor Serge Baudo

THE DAMNATION OF FAUST
by Berlioz
conductor Pierre Dervaux
Orchestre des concerts du Conservatoire
Théâtre de l'Archevêché
[Concert version]

1964

FALSTAFF

by Verdi
director Michel Crochot
conductor Pierre Dervaux
Orchestre des concerts du Conservatoire
Théâtre de l'Archevêché

DON GIOVANNI
Revival of 1949
conductor Peter Maag

LE NOZZE DI FIGARO
Revival of 1952
conductor Peter Maag

L'INCORONAZIONE DI POPPEA
Revival of 1961
conductor Gianfranco Rivoli

1965

ORFEO
by Monteverdi
director Sandro Sequi
conductor Gianfranco Rivoli
Orchestre des concerts du Conservatoire
Théâtre de l'Archevêché

DIE ZAUBERFLÖTE
Revival of 1958
conductor Piero Bellugi

COSÌ FAN TUTTE
Revival of 1950 (1963)
conductor Serge Baudo

L'HISTOIRE DU SOLDAT
by Stravinsky
director Maurice Sarrazin
conductor Louis Auriacome
Orchestre de chambre de Toulouse
Cour de l'École des Arts et Métiers

LE BARBIER DE SÉVILLE
Revival of 1953
conductor Gianfranco Rivoli

1966

PELLÉAS ET MÉLISANDE
by Debussy
director Jacques Dupont

conductor Serge Baudo
Orchestre des concerts du Conservatoire
Théâtre de l'Archevêché

DON GIOVANNI
Revival of 1949
conductor Gianfrano Rivoli

IDOMENEO
Revival of 1963
conductor Peter Maag

ARIADNE AUF NAXOS
Revival of 1963
director Jean-Laurent Cochet
conductor George Sebastian

1967

COSÌ FAN TUTTE
Revival of 1950 (1963)
conductor Michael Gielen

DON GIOVANNI
Revival of 1949
conductor Serge Baudo

DIE ENTFÜHRUNG AUS DEM SERAIL
Revival of 1951
conductor Jerzy Semkow

LE BARBIER DE SÉVILLE
Revival of 1953
conductor Jerzy Semkow

COMBATTIMENTO DI TANCREDI E CLORINDA
Revival of 1961
director Pierre Lacotte
conductor Piero Belugi
Orchestre des concerts du Conservatoire
Château du Tholonet

1968

LE NOZZE DI FIGARO
by Mozart
director Jean-Laurent Cochet
conductor Jerzy Semkow
Orchestre de Paris
Théâtre de l'Archevêché

PELLÉAS ET MÉLISANDE

Revival of 1966
conductor Serge Baudo
Orchestre de Paris

FALSTAFF
Revival of 1964
conductor George Sebastian
Orchestre de Paris

1969

DON GIOVANNI
Revival of 1949
conductor Jerzy Semkow
Orchestre de Paris

COSÌ FAN TUTTE
Revival of 1950 (1963)
director Mauclair
conductor Serge Baudo
Orchestre de Paris

LE BARBIER DE SÉVILLE
Revival of 1953
conductor Gianfranco Rivoli
Orchestre de Paris

1970

LE NOZZE DI FIGARO
Revival of 1968
Orchestre de Paris

L'ITALIANA IN ALGERI
by Rossini
director Jean-Pierre Grenier
conductor Gianfranco Rivoli
Orchestre de Paris
Théâtre de l'Archevêché

IL BALLO DELL'INGRATE
by Monteverdi
conductor Ennio Gerelli
director Sandro Sequi

CURLEW RIVER
by Britten
director Colin Graham
conductor Viola Tunnard
English Opera Group
Basilique Sainte-Marie-Madeleine, Saint-Maximin-la-Sainte-Baume

THE PRODIGAL SON
by Britten
director Colin Graham
conductor Viola Tunnard
English Opera Group
Basilique Sainte-Marie-Madeleine, Saint-Maximin-la-Sainte-Baume

1971

DIE ZAUBERFLÖTE
by Mozart
director Jean-Pierre Grenier
conductor Reynald Giovaninetti
Orchestre de Paris
Théâtre de l'Archevêché

COSÌ FAN TUTTE
by Mozart
director Daniel Leveugle (using Ganeau's 1963 décor and costumes)
conductor Otmar Suitner
Orchestre de Paris
Théâtre de l'Archevêché

FALSTAFF
Revival of 1964
conductor Pierre Dervaux
Orchestre de Paris

BÉATRICE DE PLANISSOLES
by Jacques Charpentier
[World premiere]
director Dominique Delouche
conductor Jacques Charpentier
Orchestre de Paris
Théâtre de l'Archevêché

1972

DON GIOVANNI
Revival of 1949
conductor Wilfried Boettcher
Orchestre de Paris

LE NOZZE DI FIGARO
Revival of 1968
conductor Theodor Guschlbauer
Orchestre de Paris

LES MALHEURS D'ORPHÉE
Revival of 1962

Followed by

LES NOCES
Revival of 1962
Orchestre de Paris
Théâtre de l'Archevêché

PELLÉAS ET MÉLISANDE
Revival of 1966
Orchestre de Paris

BERNARD LEFORT

1973

Festival not held

1974

LE DIRECTEUR DE THÉÂTRE
by Mozart

Followed by

LA SERVA PADRONA
by Pergolesi
director Jean Le Poulain
conductor Jean-Claude Casadesus
Orchestre lyrique de l'ORTF
Place des Quatre-Dauphins

LUISA MILLER
by Verdi
director Nikolaus Lehnhoff
conductor Alain Lombard
Orchestre philharmonique de Strasbourg
Théâtre de l'Archevêché

LA CLEMENZA DI TITO
by Mozart
director Antoine Bourseiller
conductor Alberto Erede
Orchestre lyrique de l'ORTF
Théâtre de l'Archevêché

1975

CARNAVAL DE VENISE
by Campra
director Jorge Lavelli
conductor Michel Plasson

Orchestre du Capitole de Toulouse
Théâtre de l'Archevêché

ELISABETTA REGINA D'INGHILTERRA
by Rossini
director Jean-Claude Auvray
conductor Gianfranco Masini
Orchestre philharmonique de Strasbourg
Arles: Théâtre antique

L'ELISIR D'AMORE
by Donizetti
director Werner Duggelin
conductor Armin Jordan
Orchestre philharmonique de Strasbourg
Théâtre de l'Archevêché

LE DIRECTEUR DE THÉÂTRE
Followed by
LA SERVA PADRONA
Revival of 1974
conductor Michel Gomez Martinez

1976

DON GIOVANNI
by Mozart
director Jean-Pierre Vincent
conductor Jésus Lopez-Cobos
Orchestre du Capitole de Toulouse
Théâtre de l'Archevêché

LA TRAVIATA
by Verdi
director Jorge Lavelli
conductor Michel Plasson
Orchestre du Capitole de Toulouse
Théâtre de l'Archevêché

MEDÉE
by Cherubini
director Dino Yannopoulos
conductor Serge Baudo
Orchestre de Lyon
Arles: Théâtre antique

1977

COSÌ FAN TUTTE

by Mozart
director Jean Mercure
conductor Charles Mackerras
English Chamber Orchestra
Théâtre de l'Archevêché

ROBERTO DEVEREUX
by Donizetti
director Aberto Fassini
conductor Julius Rudel
Orchestre du Capitole de Toulouse
Théâtre de l'Archevêché

IL MAESTRO DI CAPELLA
by Cimarosa

Followed by

IL CAMPANELLO DI NOTTE
by Donizetti
director Jean Le Poulain
conductor Ralph Weikert
Orchestre du Capitole de Toulouse
Place des Quatre-Dauphins

SIRIUS
by Stockhausen
[World premiere]
Cloître Saint-Louis, Lycée Vauvenargues
[Concert]

1978

ALCINA
by Handel
director Jorge Lavelli
conductor Raymond Leppard
Scottish Chamber Orchestra
Théâtre de l'Archevêché

DON PASQUALE
by Donizetti
director Jean-Louis Thamin
conductor Gianfranco Rivoli
Orchestre philharmonique de Radio-France
Place des Quatre-Dauphins

ODE TO SAINT CECILIA
by Purcell

Followed by

DIDO AND AENEAS
by Purcell
director Richard Copley
conductor Charles Mackerras
Scottish Opera
Théâtre de l'Archevêché

1979

LE NOZZE DI FIGARO
by Mozart
director Jorge Lavelli
conductor Neville Marriner
The Academy of St Martin in the Fields
Théâtre de l'Archevêché

WERTHER
by Massenet
director Jean-Claude Fall
conductor Jean-Claude Casadesus
Orchestre de Lille
Théâtre de l'Archevêché

POPORINO
director Patrick Guinand
conductor Ralph Weikert
Orchestre de Lille
Théâtre de l'Archevêché

1980

SÉMIRAMIS
by Rossini
director Pier-Luigi Pizzi
conductor Jésus Lopez-Cobos
Scottish Chamber Orchestra
Théâtre de l'Archevêché

COSÌ FAN TUTTE
Revival of 1977

LES LIAISONS DANGEREUSES
by Claude Prey
director Pierre Barrat
conductor Yves Prin
Hôtel de Valbelle

1981

DON GIOVANNI

Revival of 1976
conductor John Pritchard
Scottish Chamber Orchestra

TANCRÈDE
by Rossini
director Jean-Claude Auvray
conductor Ralph Weikert
Scottish Chamber Orchestra
Théâtre de l'Archevêché

LOUIS ERLO

1982

DIE ZAUBERFLÖTE
by Mozart
director Lucian Pintilié
conductor Theodor Guschlbauer
Nouvel orchestre philharmonique de Radio-France
Théâtre de l'Archevêché

IL TURCO IN ITALIA
by Rossini
director Jean-Louis Thamin
conductor Maurizio Arena
Place des Quatre-Dauphins

LES BORÉADES
by Rameau
director Jean-Louis Martinoty
conductor John Eliot Gardiner
English Baroque Soloists
Théâtre de l'Archevêché

1983

HIPPOLYTE ET ARICIE
by Rameau
director Pier-Luigi Pizzi
conductor John Eliot Gardiner
English Baroque Soloists
Théâtre de l'Archevêché

LA CENERENTOLA
by Rossini
director Nicolas Joel
conductor Ralph Weikert
Pavillon Vendôme

MITHRIDATE
by Mozart
director Jean-Claude Fall
conductor Theodor Guschlbauer
Nouvel orchestre philharmonique de Radio-France
Théâtre de l'Archevêché

PASSAGGIO
by Berio

Followed by

COMBATTIMENTO DI TANCREDI E CLORINDA
by Monteverdi
director Jan Stransfogel
conductor Marcello Panni
Théâtre de l'Archevêché

1984

LE BARBIER DE SÉVILLE
by Rossini
director Roberto de Simone
conductor Gian-Luigi Gelmeti
Nouvel orchestre philharmonique de Radio-France
Théâtre de l'Archevêché

LA FINTA GIARDINIERA
by Mozart
director Gildas Bourdet
conductor Semyon Bychkov
Nouvel orchestre philharmonique de Radio-France
Théâtre de l'Archevêché

1985

LE NOZZE DI FIGARO
by Mozart
director Pier-Luigi Pier'Alli
conductor John Eliot Gardiner
Orchestre de l'Opéra de Lyon
Théâtre de l'Archevêché

ORFEO
by Mondeverdi
director Claude Goretta
conductor Michel Corboz
Orchestre de l'Opéra de Lyon
Théâtre de l'Archevêché

ARIANE À NAXOS

by Strauss
director Götan Järvefelt
conductor Semyon Bychkov
Nouvel orchestre philharmonique de Radio-France
Théâtre de l'Archevêché

KING ARTHUR
by Purcell
conductor John Eliot Gardiner
English Baroque Soloists
Théâtre de l'Archevêché
[Concert version]

1986

DON GIOVANNI
by Mozart
director Gildas Bourdet
conductor Stéphane Soltestz
Orchestre de l'Opéra de Lyon
Théâtre de l'Archevêché

IDOMENEO
by Mozart
director PierreStrosser
conductor Hans Graf
Sinfonia Varsovia
Théâtre de l'Archevêché

TANCREDE
by Campra
director Jean-Claude Penchenat
conductor Jean-Claude Malgoire
La Grande Écurie et la Chambre du Roy
Théâtre de l'Archevêché

ARIANE À NAXOS
Revival of 1985

1987

DER ROSENKAVALIER
by Strauss
director Tobias Richter
conductor Semyon Bychkov
Orchestre philharmonique de Strasbourg
Théâtre de l'Archevêché

DIE ENTFÜHRUNG AUS DEM SERAIL
by Mozart

director Georges Lavaudant
conductor Armin Jordan
Orchestre de l'Opéra de Lyon
Théâtre de l'Archevêché

IPHIGÉNIE EN AULIDE
by Gluck
conductor John Eliot Gardiner
Orchestre de l'Opéra de Lyon
Théâtre de l'Archevêché
[Concert version]

PSYCHÉ
by Lully
director Jean-Claude Penchenat
conductor Jean-Claude Malgoire
La Grande Écurie et la Chambre
du Roy
Théâtre de l'Archevêché

FALSTAFF
by Verdi
director Lluis Pasqual
conductor Sylvain Cambreling
Théâtre de l'Archevêché

1988

LA CLEMENZA DI TITO
by Mozart
director Michaël Cacoyannis
conductor Armin Jordan
Ensemble Orchestral de Paris
Théâtre de l'Archevêché

ARMIDA
by Rossini
director Jean-Claude Fall
conductor Gianfranco Masini
Orchestre de Nice
Théâtre de l'Archevêché

COSÌ FAN TUTTE
by Mozart
director Denis Llorca
conductor Jeffrey Tate
English Chamber Orchestra
Théâtre de l'Archevêché

1989

DIE ZAUBERFLÖTE
by Mozart
director Jorge Lavelli
conductor Armin Jordan
Ensemble Orchestral de Paris
Théâtre de l'Archevêché

THE FAIRY QUEEN
by Purcell (and Shakespeare)
director Adrian Noble
conductor William Christie
Les Arts Florissants
Peter Hall Company
Théâtre de l'Archevêché

COSÌ FAN TUTTE
Revival of 1988

L'AMOUR DES TROIS ORANGES
by Prokofiev
director Louis Erlo
conductor Kent Nagano
Orchestre de l'Opéra de Lyon
Théâtre de l'Archevêché

LE ROUGE ET LE NOIR
by Claude Prey
[World premiere]
director Mireille Laroche
conductor Philippe Nahon
La Péniche-Opéra
Ars Nova
Grand Théâtre d'Aix

1990

LES INDES GALANTES
by Rameau
director Alfredo Arias
conductor William Christie
Les Arts Florissants
Théâtre de l'Archevêché

DIE ENTFÜHRUNG AUS DEM SERAIL
by Mozart
director Jorge Lavelli
conductor Carlos Kalmar
Théâtre de l'Archevêché

DON PASQUALE
by Donizetti
Opéra de Lyon production
director Patrizia Gracis
conductor Gabriele Ferro
Orchestre de l'Opéra de Lyon
Théâtre de l'Archevêché

1991

LE NOZZE DI FIGARO
by Mozart
director Rudolph Noelte
conductor Friedrich Haider
Ensemble Orchestral de Paris
Théâtre de l'Archevêché

CASTOR ET POLLUX
by Rameau
director Pier-Luigi Pizzi
conductor William Christie
Les Arts Florissants
Théâtre de l'Archevêché

DIE SCHULDDIGKEIT DES ERSTEN GEBOTS
by Mozart
director Jean-Claude Fall
conductor Tamas Pal
Salieri Chamber Orchestra
Théâtre de l'Archevêché

A MIDSUMMER NIGHT'S DREAM
by Britten
director Robert Carsen
conductor Steuart Bedford
Ensemble Orchestral de Paris
Théâtre de l'Archevêché

1992

DON GIOVANNI
by Mozart
director Giorgio Marini
conductor Armin Jordan
English Chamber Orchestra
Théâtre de l'Archevêché

A MIDSUMMER NIGHT'S DREAM
Revival of 1991

THE RAKE'S PROGRESS
by Stravinsky
director Alfredo Arias
conductor Kent Nagano
Orchestre de l'Opéra de Lyon
Théâtre de l'Archevêché

1993

EURYANTHE
by Weber
director Hans Peter Cloos
conductor Jeffrey Tate
English Chamber Orchestra
Théâtre de l'Archevêché

DON GIOVANNI
Revival of 1992

ORLANDO
by Handel
director Robert Carsen
conductor William Christie
Les Arrs Florissants
Théâtre de l'Archevêché

L'EUROPE GALANTE
by Campra
conductor Marc Minkowski
Les Musiciens du Louvre
Théâtre de l'Archevêché
[Concert version]

1994

DIE ZAUBERFLÖTE
by Mozart
director Robert Carsen
conductor William Christie
Les Arts Florissants
Théâtre de l'Archevêché

ORFEO ED EURIDICE
by Gluck
conductor Jean-Claude Malgoire
Théâtre de l'Archevêché
[Concert version]

1995

LE COMTE ORY
by Rossini
director Marcel Maréchal
conductor Evelino Pido
Orchestre européen du Festival d'Aix
Théâtre de l'Archevêché

COSÌ FAN TUTTE
Revival of 1998

DIE ZAUBERFLÖTE
Revival of 1994

1996

SEMELE
by Handel
director Robert Carsen
conductor William Christie
Les Arts Florissants
Théâtre de l'Archevêché

STÉPHANE LISSNER

1997

Festival not held

1998

DON GIOVANNI
by Mozart
director Peter Brook
conductor Claudio Abbado/Daniel Harding
Mahler Chamber Orchestra
Théâtre de l'Archevêché

L'ORFEO
by Monteverdi
director Trisha Brown
conductor René Jacobs
Collegium Vocale
Théâtre de l'Archevêché

LE CHÂTEAU DE BARBE-BLEUE
by Bartók
director Pina Bausch
conductor Pierre Boulez
Mahler Youth Chamber Orchestra

Théâtre de l'Archevêché

DIDO AND AENEAS
by Purcell
director Marcel Bozonnet
conductor David Stern

Followed by

CURLEW RIVER
by Britten
director Yoshi Oida
conductor David Stern
Artists of the Académie d'Aix
Hôtel Maynier d'Oppède

1999

L'INCORONAZIONE DI POPPEA
by Monteverdi
director Klaus Michael Grüber
conductor Marc Minkowski
Les Musiciens du Louvre
Théâtre de l'Archevêché

LA BELLE HÉLÈNE
by Offenbach
director Herbert Wernicke
conductor Stéphane Petitjean
Solistes de l'Orchestre de Paris
Théâtre de l'Archevêché

CENA FURIOSA
by Monteverdi
director Ingrid von Wantoch
conductor Marc Minkowski
Les Musiciens du Louvre
Hôtel Maynier d'Oppède

DIE ZAUBERFLÖTE
by Mozart
director Stéphane Braunschweig
conductor David Stern
Artists of the Académie d'Aix
Grand Saint-Jean

DON GIOVANNI
Revival of 1998
Théâtre de l'Archevêché

2000

L'AFFAIRE MAKROPOULOS
by Janáček
director Stéphane Braunschweig
conductor Simon Rattle
City of Birmingham Symphony Orchestra
Théâtre de l'Archevêché

COSÌ FAN TUTTE
by Mozart
director Chen Shi-Zheng
conductor René Jacobs
Concerto Köln
Théâtre de l'Archevêché

L'INCORONAZIONE DI POPPEA
Revival of 1999

CENERENTOLA
by Rossini
director Claude Buchvald
conductor Laurence Equilbey
Symphonie de Chambre de Schönberg
Artists of the Académie d'Aix
Grand Saint-Jean

LE RETOUR D'ULYSSE DANS SA PATRIE
by Monteverdi
director Adrian Noble
conductor William Christie
Les Arts Florissants
Artists of the Académie d'Aix
Théâtre du Jeu de Paume

2001

LE NOZZE DI FIGARO
by Mozart
director Richard Eyre
conductor Marc Minkowski
Mahler Chamber Orchestra
Théâtre de l'Archevêché

FALSTAFF
by Verdi
director Herbert Wernicke
conductor Enrique Mazzola
Orchestre de Paris
Théâtre de l'Archevêché

CARNET D'UN DISPARU
by Janáček
director Claude Régy
conductor Alain Planès
Hôtel Maynier d'Oppède

THE TURN OF THE SCREW
by Britten
director Luc Bondy
conductor Daniel Harding
Mahler Chamber Orchestra
Théâtre du Jeu de Paume

DIE ZAUBERFLÖTE
Revival of 1999
Théâtre de l'Archevêché

2002

LE BALCON
by Peter Eötvös
director Stanislas Nordey
conductor Peter Eötvös
Ensemble Intercontemporain
Théâtre de l'Archevêché

EUGÈNE ONÉGUINE
by Tchaikovsky
director Irina Brook
conductor Daniel Harding
Mahler Chamber Orchestra
Théâtre de l'Archevêché

LA PETITE RENARDE RUSÉE
by Janáček
director Julie Brochen
conductor Alexander Briger
Orchestra of the Académie
Théâtre du Jeu de Paume

A SUMMER NIGHT'S DREAM
by Mozart/Shakespeare
director Franz Wittenbrink
conductor Franz Wittenbrink
Hôtel Maynier d'Oppède

LE RETOUR D'ULYSSE DANS SA PATRIE
Revival of 2000

2003

Season annulled after only a few nights. No performances of most of the productions.

WOZZECK
by Berg
director Stéphane Braunschweig
conductor Daniel Harding
Mahler Chamber Orchestra
Théâtre de l'Archevêché

LA TRAVIATA
by Verdi
director Peter Mussbach
conductor Yutaka Sado
Orchestre de Paris
Théâtre de l'Archevêché

DIE ENTFÜHRUNG AUS DEM SERAIL
by Mozart
director Jérôme Deschamps
conductor Marc Minkowski
Théâtre de l'Archevêché

LES TRÉTEAUX/RENARD/PIERROT LUNAIRE
by Falla/Stravinsky/Schönberg
director Klaus Michael Grüber
conductor Pierre Boulez
Ensemble Intercontemporain
Théâtre du Jeu de Paume

2004

LA TRAVIATA
by Verdi
director Peter Mussbach
conductor Daniel Harding
Mahler Chamber Orchestra
Théâtre de l'Archevêché

L'AMOUR DES TROIS ORANGES
by Prokofiev
director Philippe Calvario
conductor Tugan Sokhiev
Mahler Chamber Orchestra
Grand Saint-Jean

HERCULES
by Handel
director Luc Bondy

conductor William Christie
Les Arts Florissants
Théâtre de l'Archevêché

HANJO
by Hosokawa
director Anne Teresa de Keersmaeker
conductor Kazushi Ono
Orchestre de chambre de la Monnaie
Théâtre du Jeu de Paume

DIE ENTFÜHRUNG AUS DEM SERAIL
by Mozart
director Jérôme Deschamps
conductor Marc Minkowski
Grand Saint-Jean
Théâtre de l'Archevêché

2005

JULIE
by Boesmans
director Luc Bondy
conductor Kazushi Ono
Orchestre de chambre de la Monnaie
Théâtre du Jeu de Paume

COSÌ FAN TUTTE
by Mozart
director Patrice Chéreau
conductor Daniel Harding
Mahler Chamber Orchestra
Théâtre de l'Archevêché

LA CLEMENZA DI TITO
by Mozart
director Lukas Hemleb
conductor Paul Daniel
Mahler Chamber Orchestra
Théâtre de l'Archevêché

LE BARBIER DE SÉVILLE
by Rossini
director David Radok
conductor Daniele Gatti
Orchestre du Teatro comunale di Bologna
Grand Saint-Jean

THE TURN OF THE SCREW
Revival of 2001

2006

DAS RHEINGOLD
by Wagner
director Stéphane Braunschweig
conductor Simon Rattle
Berliner Philharmoniker
Théâtre de l'Archevêché

DIE ZAUBERFLÖTE
by Mozart
director Krystian Lupa
conductor Daniel Harding
Mahler Chamber Orchestra
Théâtre de l'Archevêché

HISTOIRE VRAIE DE LA PÉRICHOLE
after Offenbach
director Julie Brochen
conductor Vincent Leterme
Hôtel Maynier d'Oppède

L'ITALIANA IN ALGERI
by Rossini
director Toni Servillo
conductor Riccardo Frizza
Mahler Chamber Orchestra
Grand Saint-Jean

LES TRÉTEAUX/RENARD/PIERROT LUNAIRE
by Falla/Stravinsky/Schönberg
director Klaus Michael Grüber
conductor Pierre Boulez
Ensemble Intercontemporain
Théâtre du Jeu de Paume

DIDO AND AENEAS
by Purcell
director Jacques Osinski
conductor Kenneth Weiss
Artists of the Académie d'Aix
Festival Production Centre, Venelles

BERNARD FOCCROULLE

2007

DIE WALKÜRE
by Wagner
director Stéphane Braunschweig

conductor Simon Rattle
Berliner Philharmoniker
Grand Théâtre de Provence

LE NOZZE DI FIGARO
by Mozart
director Vincent Boussard
conductor Daniel Harding
Mahler Chamber Orchestra
Théâtre de l'Archevêché

DIE ENTFÜHRUNG AUS DEM SERAIL
by Mozart
director Jérôme Deschamps
conductor Marc Minkowski
Les Musciens du Louvre
Grand Saint-Jean

DE LA MAISON DES MORTS
by Janáček
director Patrice Chéreau
conductor Pierre Boulez
Mahler Chamber Orchestra
Grand Théâtre de Provence

L'ORFEO
Revival of 1998
Théâtre de l'Archevêché

MADRIGAUX
by Monteverdi
director Arco Renz
conductor Kenneth Weiss
Artists of the Académie d'Aix
Théâtre du Jeu de Paume

2008

ZAIDE
by Mozart
director Peter Sellars
conductor Louis Langrée
Camerata Salzburg
Théâtre de l'Archevêché

BELSHAZZAR
by Handel
director Christof Nel
conductor René Jacobs
Akademie für alte Musik, Berlin

Grand Théâtre de Provence
SIEGFRIED
by Wagner
director Stéphane Braunschweig
conductor Simon Rattle
Berliner Philharmoniker
Grand Théâtre de Provence
COSÌ FAN TUTTE
by Mozart
director Abbas Kiarostami
conductor Christophe Rousset
Camerata Salzburg
Théâtre de l'Archevêché
PASSION
by Pascal Dusapin
[World premiere]
director Giuseppe Frigeni
conductor Frack Ollu
Ensemble Modern
Artists of the Académie d'Aix
Théâtre du Jeu de Paume
L'INFEDELTÀ DELUSA
by Haydn
director Richard Brunel
conductor Jérémie Rhorer
Le Cercle de l'Harmonie
Artists of the Académie d'Aix
Hôtel Maynier d'Oppède

2009

GÖTTERDÄMMERUNG
by Wagner
director Stéphane Braunschweig
conductor Simon Rattle
Berliner Philharmoniker
Grand Théâtre de Provence
DIE ZAUBERFLÖTE
by Mozart
director William Kentridge
conductor René Jacobs
Akademie für alte Musik, Berlin
Grand Théâtre de Provence
IDOMENEO, RE DI CRETA

by Mozart
director Olivier Py
conductor Marc Minkowski
Les Musciens du Louvre
Théâtre de l'Archevêché

ORPHÉE AUX ENFERS
by Offenbach
director Yves Beaunesne
conductor Alain Altinoglu
Camerata Salzburg
Théâtre de l'Archevêché

2010

DON GIOVANNI
by Mozart
director Dmitri Tcherniakov
conductor Louis Langré
Freiburger Barockorchester
Théâtre de l'Archevêché

ALCESTE
by Gluck
director Christof Loy
conductor Ivor Bolton
Freiburger Barockorchester
Théâtre de l'Archevêché

HIPPOLYTE ET ARICIE (EXTRACTS)
by Rameau

Followed by

PYGMALION
by Rameau
director Trisha Brown
conductor William Christie
Les Arts Florissants
Grand Théâtre de Provence

UN RETOUR
by Oscar Strasnoy
[World premiere]
director Thierry Thieû Niang
conductor Roland Hayrabedian
Artists of the Académie d'Aix
Grand Saint-Jean

LE ROSSIGNOL
by Stravinsky

director Robert Lepage
conductor Kazushi Ono
Orchestre de l'Opéra de Lyon
Grand Théâtre de Provence

2011

THANKS TO MY EYES
by Oscar Bianchi
[World premiere]
director Joël Pommerat
conductor Franck Ollu
Ensemble Modern
Théâtre du Jeu de Paume

LA TRAVIATA
by Verdi
director Jean-François Sivadier
conductor Louis Langrée
London Symphony Orchestra
Théâtre de l'Archevêché

LA CLEMENZA DI TITO
by Mozart
director David McVicar
conductor Colin Davis
London Symphony Orchestra
Théâtre de l'Archevêché

LE NEZ
by Shostakovich
conductor Kazushi Ono
director William Kentridge
Orchestre de l'Opéra de Lyon
Grand Théâtre de Provence

ACIS AND GALATEA
by Handel
director Saburo Teshigawara
conductor Leonardo García Alarcón
Ensemble baroque de l'Académie
Artists of the Académie d'Aix
Grand Saint-Jean

AUSTERLITZ: EINE KINDHEITSREISE
by Jérôme Combier
[World premiere]
director Jérôme Combier
director Pierre Nouvel

Ensemble Ictus

2012

LE NOZZE DI FIGARO
by Mozart
director Richard Brunel
conductor Jérémie Rhorer
Le Cercle de l'Harmonie
Théâtre de l'Archevêché

DAVID ET JONATHAS
by Charpentier
director Andreas Homoki
conductor William Christie
Les Arts Florissants
Théâtre de l'Archevêché

L'ENFANT ET LES SORTILÈGES
by Ravel
director Arnaud Meunier
conductor Didier Puntos
Artists of the Académie d'Aix
Théâtre du Jeu de Paume

WRITTEN ON SKIN
by George Benjamin
[World premiere]
director Katie Mitchell
conductor George Benjamin
Mahler Chamber Orchestra
Grand Théâtre de Provence

UNE SITUATION HUEY P. NEWTON
Conception by Jean-Michel Bruyère
Le Bois de l'Aune

LA FINTA GIARDINIERA
by Mozart
director Vincent Boussard
conductor Andreas Spering
Le Cercle de l'Harmonie
Artists of the Académie d'Aix
Grand Saint-Jean

2013

RIGOLETTO
by Verdi
director Robert Carsen

conductor Gianandrea Noseda
London Symphony Orchestra
Théâtre de l'Archevêché

DON GIOVANNI
Revival of 2010
conductor Marc Minkowski
London Symphony Orchestra
Théâtre de l'Archevêché

THE HOUSE TAKEN OVER
by Vasco Mendonça
[World premiere]
director Katie Mitchell
conductor Etienne Siebens
Orchestre Asko / Schönberg
Artists of the Académie d'Aix
Grand Saint-Jean

ELENA
by Cavalli
director Jean-Yves Ruf
conductor Leonardo García Alarcón
Cappella Mediterranea
Théâtre du Jeu de Paume

ELEKTRA
by Strauss
director Patrice Chéreau
conductor Esa-Pekka Salonen
Orchestre de Paris
Grand Théâtre de Provence

ROMÉO ET JULIETTE
by Prokofiev
choreographer Josette Baïz
director Josette Baïz
conductor Gianandrea Noseda
Orchestre des jeunes de la Méditerranée
Groupe Grenade
Les enfants des écoles élémentaires Marcel Pagnol et Alphonse Daudet, Aix-en-Provence
Service éducatif du Festival d'Aix
Grand Théâtre de Provence

2014

DIE ZAUBERFLÖTE
by Mozart

director Simon McBurney
conductor Pablo Heras-Casado
Freiburger Barockorchester
Grand Théâtre de Provence

ARIODANTE
by Handel
director Richard Jones
conductor Andrea Marcon
Freiburger Barockorchester
Théâtre de l'Archevêché

IL TURCO IN ITALIA
by Rossini
director Christopher Alden
conductor Marc Minkowski
Les Musiciens du Louvre
Théâtre de l'Archevêché

WINTERREISE
by Schubert
director William Kentridge
baritone Matthias Goerne
piano Markus Hinterhäuser
Conservatoire Darius Milhaud (Auditorium Campra)

TRAUERNACHT
by Johann Sebastian Bach
director Katie Mitchell
conductor Raphaël Pichon
Ensemble baroque de l'Académie d'Aix
Théâtre du Jeu de Paume

LES BORÉADES
by Rameau
conductor Marc Minkowski
Les Musiciens du Louvre
Grand Théâtre de Provence
[Concert version]

Concerts included

VARIATRIONS GOLDBERG
by Bach
piano Alexandre Tharaud
Théâtre de l'Archevêché

2015

ALCINA

by Handel
director Katie Mitchell
conductor Andrea Marcon
Freiburger Barockorchester
Grand Théâtre de Provence

DIE ENTFÜHRUNG AUS DEM SERAIL
director Martin Kusej
conductor Jérémie Rhorer
Freiburger Barockorchester
Théâtre de l'Archevêché

A MIDSUMMER NIGHT'S DREAM
Revival of 1991
conductor Kazushi Ono
Orchestre de l'Opéra de Lyon
Théâtre de l'Archevêché

IOLANTA
by Tchaikovsky

Followed by

PERSÉPHONE
by Stravinsky
director Peter Sellars
conductor Teodor Currentzis
Orchestre de l'Opéra de Lyon
Grand Théâtre de Provence

LE MONSTRE DU LABYRINTH
by Jonathan Dove
[World premiere]
director Marie-Eve Signeyrole
conductor Simon Rattle
London Symphony Orchestra
Orchestre des jeunes de la Méditerranée
Grand Théâtre de Provence

SVADBA
by Ana Sokolovic
conductor Dairine Ni Mheadhra
director Ted Huffman
director Zack Winokur
Artists of the Académie d'Aix
Théâtre du Jeu de Paume

WINTERREISE
by Schubert
Revival of 2014
baritone Matthias Goerne

piano Markus Hinterhäuser

2016

COSÌ FAN TUTTE
by Mozart
director Christophe Honoré
conductor Louis Langrée
conductor Jérémie Rhorer
Freiburger Barockorchester
Théâtre de l'Archevêché

IL TRIONFO DEL TEMPO E DEL DISINGANO
by Handel
director Krzysztof Warlikowski
conductor Emmanuelle Haïm
Concert d'Astrée
Théâtre de l'Archevêché

KALÎLA WA DIMNA
by Moneim Adwan
[World premiere]
director Olivier Letellier
conductor Zied Zouari
Artists of the Académie d'Aix
Théâtre du Jeu de Paume

PELLÉAS ET MÉLISANDE
by Debussy
director Katie Mitchell
conductor Esa-Pekka Salonen
Philharmonia Orchestra
Grand Théâtre de Provence

OEDIPUS REX / SYMPHONIE DE PSAUMES
by Stravinsky
director Peter Sellars
conductor Esa-Pekka Salonen
Philharmonia Orchestra
Grand Théâtre de Provence

ZOROASTRE
by Rameau
conductor Raphaël Pichon
Ensemble Pygmalion
Grand Théâtre de Provence
[Concert version]

2017

PINOCCHIO
by Philippe Boesmans
[World premiere]
director Joël Pommerat
conductor Emilio Pomarico
Klangforum Wien
Grand Théâtre de Provence

CARMEN
by Bizet
director Dmitri Tcherniakov
conductor Pablo Heras-Casado
Orchestre de Paris
Grand Théâtre de Provence

THE RAKE'S PROGRESS
by Stravinsky
director Simon McBurney
conductor Eivind Gullberg Jensen
Orchestre de Paris
Théâtre de l'Archevêché

DON GIOVANNI
by Mozart
director Jean-François Sivadier
conductor Jérémy Rhorer
Le Cercle de l'Harmonie
Théâtre de l'Archevêché

ERISMENA
by Cavalli
director Jean Bellorini
conductor Leonardo García Alarcón
Cappella Mediterranea
Artists of the Académie d'Aix
Théâtre du Jeu de Paume

EUGÈNE ONÉGUINE
by Tchaikovsky
conductor Tugan Sokhiev
Orchestra of the Bolshoi Theatre
Grand Théâtre de Provence
[Concert version]

2018

ARIADNE AUF NAXOS
by Strauss

director Katie Mitchell
conductor Marc Albrecht
Orchestre de Paris
Théâtre de l'Archevêché

L'ANGE DE FEU
by Prokofiev
director Mariusz Treliński
conductor Kazushi Ono
Orchestre de Paris
Grand Théâtre de Provence

DIE ZAUBERFLÖTE
by Mozart
Revival of 2014
conductor Raphaël Pichon
Ensemble Pygmalion
Grand Théâtre de Provence

DIDO AND ÆNEAS
by Purcell
director Vincent Huguet
conductor Vaclav Luks
Ensemble Pygmalion
Théâtre de l'Archevêché

SEVEN STONES
by Ondřej Adámek
[World premiere]
concept Ondřej Adámek
director Éric Oberdorff
Accentus / Axe 21
Artists of the Académie d'Aix
Théâtre du Jeu de Paume

ORFEO AND MAJNUN
by Moneim Adwan et al
directors A. Berg, M. Winkel
conductor Bassem Akiki
Artists of the Académie d'Aix
Mediterranean Youth Orchestra

PIERRE AUDI

2019

REQUIEM
by Mozart
director Romeo Castellucci

conductor Raphaël Pichon
Ensemble Pygmalion
Théâtre de l'Archevêché

TOSCA
by Puccini
director Christophe Honoré
conductor Daniele Rustioni
Orchestre de l'Opéra de Lyon
Théâtre de l'Archevêché

JAKOB LENZ
by Wolfgang Rihm
director Andréa Breth
conductor Ingo Metzmacher
Ensemble Modern
Grand Théâtre de Provence

LES MILLE ENDORMIS
by Adam Maor
[World premiere]
director Yonatan Levy
conductor Elena Schwarz
Ensemble Lucilin
Théâtre du Jeu de Paume

LA VILLE DE MAHAGONNY
by Kurt Weill
director Ivo Van Hove
conductor Esa-Pekka Salonen
Philharmonia Orchestra
Grand Théâtre de Provence

BLANK OUT
by Michel van der Aa
[World premiere]
director Michel van der Aa
conductor Klaas Stok
Conservatoire Darius Milhaud (Auditorium Campra)

2020

Annulled because of COVID-19

2021

LES NOCES DE FIGARO
by Mozart
director Lotte de Beer
conductor Thomas Hengelbrock

Balthasar Neumann Ensemble
Théâtre de l'Archevêché

FALSTAFF
by Verdi
director Barrie Kosky
conductor Daniele Rustioni
Orchestre de l'Opéra de Lyon
Théâtre de l'Archevêché

I DUE FOSCARI
by Verdi
conductor Daniele Rustioni
Orchestre de l'Opéra de Lyon
Grand Théâtre de Provence
[Concert version]

TRISTAN UND ISOLDE
by Wagner
director Simon Stone
conductor Simon Rattle
London Symphony Orchestra
Grand Théâtre de Provence

INNOCENCE
by Kaija Saariaho
[World premiere]
director Simon Stone
conductor Susanna Mälkki
London Symphony Orchestra
Grand Théâtre de Provence

COMBATTIMENTO etc.
by Monteverdi and others
director Silvia Costa
conductor Sébastien Daucé
Ensemble Correspondances
Théâtre du Jeu de Paume

L'APOCALYPSE ARABE
by Samir Odeh-Tamimi
[World premiere]
Mise en espace Pierre Audi
conductor Ilan Volkov
Ensemble Modern
Arles: Grande Halle, Parc des Ateliers

LE COQ D'OR
by Rimski-Korsakov
director Barrie Kosky

conductor Daniele Rustioni
Orchestre de l'Opéra de Lyon
Théâtre de l'Archevêché

Concerts included

LONDON SYMPHONY ORCHESTRA
conductor Simon Rattle
Le Bourgeois gentilhomme by Strauss
Das Lied von der Erde by Mahler
Grand Théâtre de Provence

LONDON SYMPHONY ORCHESTRA
conductor Susanna Mälkki
conductor Clément Mao-Takacs
The Oceanides by Sibelius
Cinq reflets de l'amour de loin by Kaija Saariaho
Violin Concerto in D by Stravinsky
Symphony no.7 by Sibelius
Grand Théâtre de Provence

2022

RÉSURRECTION
by Mahler
director Romeo Castellucci
conductor Esa-Pekka Salonen
Orchestre de Paris
Vitrolles: Stadium de Vitrolles

SALOMÉ
by Strauss
director Andréa Breth
conductor Ingo Metzmacher
Orchestre de Paris
Grand Théâtre de Provence

IDOMENEO, RE DI CRETA
by Mozart
director Satoshi Miyagi
conductor Raphaël Pichon
Ensemble Pygmalion
Théâtre de l'Archevêché

MOÏSE ET PHARAON
by Rossini
director Tobias Kratzer
conductor Michele Mariotti
Orchestre de l'Opéra de Lyon

Théâtre de l'Archevêché
IL VIAGGIO, DANTE
by Pascal Dusapin
[World premiere]
director Claus Guth
conductor Kent Nagano
Orchestre de l'Opéra de Lyon
Grand Théâtre de Provence

LE COURONNEMENT DE POPPÉE
by Monteverdi
director Ted Huffman
conductor Leonardo García Alarcón
Cappella Mediterranea
Théâtre du Jeu de Paume

WOMAN AT POINT ZERO
by Bushra El-Turk
[World premiere]
director Laila Soliman
conductor Kanako Abe
Ensemble Zar
Pavillon Noir

L'ORFEO
by Monteverdi
conductor Leonardo García Alarcón
Cappella Mediterranea
Grand Théâtre de Provence
[Concert version]

NORMA
by Bellini
conductor Riccardo Minasi
Ensemble Resonanz
Grand Théâtre de Provence
[Concert version]

ORPHÉE ET EURYDICE
by Gluck
conductor Raphaël Pichon
Ensemble Pygmalion
Grand Théâtre de Provence
[Concert version]

2023

THE THREEPENNY OPERA
by Brecht and Weill

[co-production with the Comédie-Française]
director Thomas Ostermeier
conductor Maxime Pascal
Orchestre Le Balcon
Théâtre de l'Archevêché

PICTURE A DAY LIKE THIS
by Benjamin and Crimp
[World premiere]
directors Daniel Jeanneteau,
Marie-Christine Soma
conductor George Benjamin
Mahler Chamber Orchestra
Théâtre du Jeu de Paume

COSÌ FAN TUTTE
by Mozart
director Dmitri Tcherniakov
conductor Thomas Hengelbrock
Orchestre Balthasar Neumann
Théâtre de l'Archevêché

WOZZECK
by Berg
director Simon McBurney
conductor Simon Rattle
London Symphony Orchestra
Grand Théâtre de Provence

BALLETS RUSSES
by Stravinsky
conductor Klaus Mäkelä
videos Rebecca Zlotowski, Bertrand Mandico, Evangelia Kranioti
Orchestre de Paris
Stadium de Vitrolles

THE FAGGOTS AND THEIR FRIENDS BETWEEN REVOLUTIONS
by Philip Venables and Ted Huffman
director Ted Huffman
conductor Yshani Perinpanayagam
Pavillon Noir

LE PROPHÈTE
by Meyerbeer
conductor Mark Elder
London Symphony Orchestra
Grand Théâtre de Provence
[Concert version]

OTELLO
by Verdi
conductor Michele Mariotti
Orchestra of the Teatro di San Carlo
Grand Théâtre de Provence
[Concert version]

LUCIE DE LAMMERMOOR
by Donizetti
conductor Daniele Rustioni
Orchestre de l'Opéra de Lyon
Grand Théâtre de Provence
[Concert version]

Concerts

KIRILL GERSTEIN
Ligeti, Brahms, Mahler
Hôtel Maynier d'Oppède

SEXTET MOSAÏC
'Jazz et héritages musicaux de la Méditerranée'
Hôtel Maynier d'Oppède

HANNS EISLER, KIRILL GERSTEIN, HK GRUBER, JOS HOUBEN, EMILY WILSON
'Le Cabaret du pianiste':
Alexander von Zemlinsky, Kurt Weill
Hôtel Maynier d'Oppède

ASMIK GRIGORIAN, LUKAS GENIUSAS
'Macrocosmes, Microcosmes':
Romances de Tchaikovsky and Rachmaninoff
Conservatoire Darius Milhaud

ORCHESTRE BALTHASAR NEUMANN
'Un Orchestre, deux cheffes'
Hôtel Maynier d'Oppède

LAKECIA BENJAMIN
'Sur les pas des Coltrane': Hommage à Alice et John Coltrane
Hôtel Maynier d'Oppède

LONDON SYMPHONY ORCHESTRA
conductor Simon Rattle
'Chant de la nuit, promesse de l'aube':
Ces belles années by Betsy Jolas
Symphony no.7 by Mahler
Grand Théâtre de Provence

NOÉ CLERC TRIO

'Jazz Migrations'
Hôtel Maynier d'Oppède

CHRISTIAN GERHAHER, GEROLD HUBER
'Un Soldat sous la lune': Lieder by Robert Schumann
Conservatoire Darius Milhaud

PRETTY YENDE, VANESSA GARCIA DIEPA
'Harmonies du soir': Mélodies by Rossini, Donizetti, Liszt etc.
Hôtel Maynier d'Oppède

MAHLER CHAMBER ORCHESTRA
conductor George Benjamin
'George Benjamin, Affinités électives':
Kammerkonzert by Ligeti
Walden by Hans Abrahamsen
Chansons madécasses by Ravel
Two Inger Christensen Songs by Hans Abrahamsen
At First Light by George Benjamin
Conservatoire Darius Milhaud

LONDON SYMPHONY ORCHESTRA
conductor Susanna Mälkki
'Triptyque de la plus haute intensité':
Concerto for Orchestra by George Benjamin
Mathis der Maler Symphony by Paul Hindemith
Piano Concerto no.3 by Rachmaninoff
Grand Théâtre de Provence

GHARBI TWINS
Hôtel Maynier d'Oppède

ORCHESTRE BALTHASAR NEUMANN
conductor Thomas Hengelbrock
Missa Solemnis by Beethoven
Grand Théâtre de Provence

ORCHESTRE DES JEUNES DE LA MÉDITERRANÉE
conductor Duncan Ward
A Little Summer Suite by Betsy Jolas
Escales by Jacques Ibert
Création collective by OJM
Variations on an Egyptian Folktune by Gamal Abdel-Rahim
Concerto pour violoncelle no.1 by Saint-Saëns
La Valse by Ravel
Grand Théâtre de Provence

World Premieres

1954

LES CAPRICES DE MARIANNE
by Henri Sauguet
director Jean Meyer
Orchestre des concerts du Conservatoire
Théâtre de l'Archevêché

1961

LAVINIA
by Henry Berraud
director Daniel Sorano
conductor Serge Baudo
Orchestre des concerts du Conservatoire
Théâtre de l'Archevêché

1971

BÉATRICE DE PLANISSOLES
by Jacques Charpentier
director Dominique Delouche
conductor Jacques Charpentier
Orchestre de Paris
Théâtre de l'Archevêché

1977

SIRIUS
by Stockhausen
Cloître Saint-Louis, Lycée Vauvenargues
[Concert]

1989

LE ROUGE ET LE NOIR
by Claude Prey

director Mireille Laroche
conductor Philippe Nahon
La Péniche-Opéra
Ars Nova
Grand Théâtre d'Aix

2002

LE BALCON
by Peter Eötvös
director Stanislas Nordey's
conductor Peter Eötvös
Ensemble Intercontemporain
Théâtre de l'Archevêché

2008

PASSION
by Pascal Dusapin
director Giuseppe Frigeni
conductor Frack Ollu
Ensemble Modern
Théâtre du Jeu de Paume

2010

UN RETOUR
by Oscar Strasnoy
director Thierry Thieû Niang
conductor Roland Hayrabedian
Artists of the Académie d'Aix
Grand Saint-Jean

2011

THANKS TO MY EYES
by Oscar Bianchi
director Joël Pommerat
conductor Franck Ollu
Ensemble Modern
Artists of the Académie d'Aix
Théâtre du Jeu de Paume

AUSTERLITZ: EINE KINDHEITSREISE
by Jérôme Combier
director Jérôme Combier
director Pierre Nouvel
Ensemble Ictus

2012

WRITTEN ON SKIN
by George Benjamin
director Katie Mitchell
conductor George Benjamin
Mahler Chamber Orchestra
Grand Théâtre de Provence

2013

THE HOUSE TAKEN OVER
by Vasco Mendonça
director Katie Mitchell
conductor Etienne Siebens
Orchestre Asko / Schönberg
Artists of the Académie d'Aix
Grand Saint-Jean

2015

LE MONSTRE DU LABYRINTH
by Jonathan Dove
director Marie-Eve Signeyrole
conductor Simon Rattle
London Symphony Orchestra
Orchestre des jeunes de la Méditerranée
Grand Théâtre de Provence

2016

KALÎLA WA DIMNA
by Moneim Adwan
director Olivier Letellier
conductor Zied Zouari
Artists of the Académie d'Aix
Théâtre du Jeu de Paume

2017

PINOCCHIO
by Philippe Boesmans
director Joël Pommerat
conductor Emilio Pomarico
Klangforum Wien
Grand Théâtre de Provence

2018

SEVEN STONES
by Ondřej Adámek
concept Ondřej Adámek
director Éric Oberdorff
Accentus / Axe 21
Artists of the Académie d'Aix
Théâtre du Jeu de Paume

ORFEO AND MAJNUN
by Moneim Adwan et al
directors A. Berg, M. Winkel
conductor Bassem Akiki
Mediterranean Youth Orchestra

2019

LES MILLE ENDORMIS
by Adam Maor
director Yonatan Levy
conductor Elena Schwarz
Ensemble Lucilin
Théâtre du Jeu de Paume

BLANK OUT
by Michel van der Aa
director Michel van der Aa
conductor Klaas Stok
Conservatoire Darius Milhaud (Auditorium Campra)

L'APOCALYPSE ARABE
by Samir Odeh-Tamimi
Mise en espace Pierre Audi
conductor Ilan Volkov
Ensemble Modern
Arles: Grande Halle, Parc des Ateliers

2021

INNOCENCE
by Kaija Saariaho
director Simon Stone
conductor Susanna Mälkki
London Symphony Orchestra
Grand Théâtre de Provence

2022

IL VIAGGIO, DANTE
by Pascal Dusapin
director Claus Guth
conductor Kent Nagano
Orchestre de l'Opéra de Lyon
Grand Théâtre de Provence

WOMAN AT POINT ZERO
by Bushra El-Turk
director Laila Soliman
conductor Kanako Abe
Ensemble Zar
Pavillon Noir

2023

PICTURE A DAY LIKE THIS
by George Benjamin
directors Daniel Jeanneteau, Marie-Christine Soma
conductor George Benjamin
Mahler Chamber Orchestra
Théâtre du Jeu de Paume

The Académie: World Premieres

2008
Christian Bertrand, SATKA (flute, clarinet, violin, cello, piano and percussion)

2009
Francesco Filidei, CONCERTINO DI AIX (wind quintet, string quartet and piano)

2010
Mark Andre, IV 8 (string trio)
Charlotte Bray, VERRE DE VENISE (tenor and string quartet) – co-commission Britten-Pears Young Artist Programme, Aldeburgh
Jonathan Harvey, SONGS AND HAIKU (soprano and piano)
Felix Ibarrondo, BOTSBI (two mezzo-sopranos and two sopranos)
Betsy Jolas, RUHT WOHL (piano and viola)
Piotr Moss, LIEN ENTRE LES JOURS (quartet and voice)
Oscar Strasnoy, UN RETOUR (opera)

2011
Karol Beffa, MES HEURES DE FIÈVRE (voice, viola and piano)
Oscar Biancchi, THANKS TO MY EYES (opera)
Francisco Coll Garcia, SGUARDO VERSO L'INTERNO (quintet with clarinet) – co-commission Britten-Pears Young Artist Programme, Aldeburgh
Zad Moultaka, MAADANN (eight voices, piano, cimbalom and percussion)
Yann Robin, CRESCENT SCRATCHES (string quartet)

2012
Mauro Lanza, DER KAMPF ZWISCHEN KARNEVAL UND FASTEN (string octet)
Magic Malik, EMPATHIE FORCÉE (string quartet, flute and electronics)
Vasco Mendonça, BOYS OF SUMMER (mezzo-soprano and string trio) – co-commission Britten-Pears Young Artist Programme, Aldeburgh
Gilbert Nouno, PUNKT! (string quartet, mezzo and electronics)

2013

Laurent Durupt, SUPER8 (string octet)
François Meïmoun, UNTITLED (string quartet)
Vasco Mendonça, THE HOUSE TAKEN OVER (opera)

2014

Jérôme Combier, PARLER LONGUEMENT DE FANTÔMES (string quartet and mezzo-soprano)
Sebastian Rivas, STAINS ON THE CARPET (quintet with double bass)
Francesca Verunelli, SKY AND DECAYING SINUSOIDS (double bass and electronics)

2015

Hye-Yeon Choi, NO NONSENSE (soprano, baritone and piano)
Andrzej Kwiecinski, PER NON PENSARE (mezzo-soprano and piano four hands)
Thomas Lacôte, TORPEURS (soprano, baritone and string quartet)
Sarah Lianne Lewis, ALTHOUGH YOU SIT IN A ROOM THAT IS GRAY (baritone and piano)
Sarah Lianne Lewis, RELATIVITY AND REVELATION (mezzo-soprano, piano and Tibetan bowls)
Samy Moussa, THE SICK ROSE (tenor and piano)
Alexandre Ouzounoff, VENT NOIR (mezzo-soprano and piano)

2016

Moneim Adwan, KALÎLA WA DIMNA (opera)
Gilbert Amy, LE POÈTE INACHEVÉ (cello and baritone)
Benjamin Attahir, ASFAR (piano trio)
Nuno da Rocha, ECCE PUER (mezzo-soprano, baritone and piano)
Benjamin de la Fuente, RICOCHETS (string octet, drums and recorded tape)
Sébastien Hervier, D'ABORD, LA FIN (DONC) (drums and recorded tape)
Jug Markovic, ULTRATERRENO (soprano, mezzo-soprano and piano)
François Meïmoun, TSIMTSOUM (quintet with two violas)
Rene Orth, A DIALOGUE BETWEEN DEATH AND YOUTH (soprano, baritone and piano)
Luca Vago, DREDD (string quartet)

2017

Ondřej Adámek, THROWING (vocal ensemble and percussion)
Sivan Eldar, THE WHITE PRINCESS (two sopranos, percussion and electronics)
Matthew Herbert, REQUIEM (string quartet and electronics)
Raphaël Languillat, SAUVE, ÉTERNEL (mezzo-soprano, baritone and harp)
Oliver Leith, THE BOW (electronics)

Oliver Leith, FOLK'S QUESTIONS (tenor, bass baritone and piano)
Camille Pepin, LYRAE (string quartet, harp and percussion)
Pascal Robert, OBSCURE LUMIÈRE (string quartet)

2018

Ondřej Adámek, SEVEN STONES (opera)
Charlotte Bray, IN BLACK LIGHT (viola)
Bastien David, IMPATIENCE (string quartet)
Samy Moussa, FANFARE
Diana Soh, SSSH (string quartet)
Fabien Touchard, ICI MÊME (tenor and piano)

The Académie: Laureates

2006

Anastasia Boldyreva (Russia), mezzo-soprano
Anna Stéphany (France/United Kingdom), mezzo-soprano
Daniel Schmutzhard (Austria), baritone
Tomasz Slawinski (Poland), bass
Minetti Quartet (Austria)

2007

Ina Kringelborn (Norway), soprano
Gabriela Scherer (Switzerland), mezzo-soprano
James Elliott (United Kingdom), tenor
Edwin Crossley-Mercer (France), baritone
Modigliani Quartet (France)

2008

Emmanuelle de Negri (France), soprano
Carolina Ullrich (Chili), soprano
Kevin Skelton (USA), tenor
Audun Iversen (Norway), baritone
Trio Con Fuoco (France)

2009

Mari Eriksmoen (Norway), soprano
Rosanne van Sandwijk (Netherlands), mezzo-soprano
Pavel Kolgatin (Russia), tenor
Waltteri Torikka (Finland), baritone
Navarra Quartet (United Kingdom)

2010

Elena Galitskaya (Russia), soprano
Andrea Hill (Canada), mezzo-soprano
Gijs Van der Linden (Belgium), tenor

Christian Eberl (Germany), baritone
Alphonse Cemin (France), pianist
Zaïde Quartet (France)

2011

Andreea Soare (Romania), soprano
Léa Trommenschlager (France), soprano
Rupert Charlesworth (United Kingdom), tenor
Damien Pass (Australia), baritone
Michalis Boliakis (Greece), pianist
Quatuor Girard (France)

2012

Sabine Devieilhe (France), soprano
Lin Shi (China), mezzo-soprano
Rodrigo Ferreira (Brazil), countertenor
Tomasz Kumiega (Poland), baritone
David Smith (United Kingdom), pianist
Giocoso Quartet (Romania)

2013

Julie Fuchs (France), soprano
Kitty Whately (United Kingdom), mezzo-soprano
Konstantin Shushakov (Russia), baritone
Scott Conner (USA), bass-baritone
Edwige Herchenroder (France), pianist
Tana Quartet (France)

2014

Chloé Briot (France), soprano
Katharina Melnikova (Belarus), soprano
Andri Björn Róbertsson (Iceland), bass-baritone
Krzysztof Bączyk (Poland), bass
Hélio Vida (Brazil), pianist
Van Kuijk Quartet (France)

2015

Lise Davidsen (Norway), soprano
Beate Mordal (Norway), soprano
Jonathan Abernethy (New Zealand), tenor
John Chest (USA), baritone
Nicolas Royez (France), pianist
Berlin-Tokyo Quartet (Germany/Japan)

2016

Ying Fang (China), soprano
Léa Desandre (France/Italy), mezzo-soprano
Guillaume Andrieux (France), baritone
Evan Hugues (United States), bass-baritone
Florian Caroubi (France), pianist
Quatuor Arod (France)

2017

Catherine Trottmann (France), mezzo-soprano
Paul-Antoine Bénos-Djian (France), countertenor
Jakub Józef Orliński (Poland), countertenor
Fabien Hyon (France), tenor
Enrico Cicconofri (Italy), pianist
Sōra Trio (France/Latvia)

2018

Marie-Laure Garnier (France), soprano
Fleur Barron (Ireland), mezzo-soprano
Trystan Llyr Griffiths (United Kingdom), tenor
Célia Oneto Bensaid (France), pianist
Oleksandr Yankevych (Ukraine), pianist
Esmé Quartet (South Korea)

Notes

CHAPTER ONE
LILY AND GABRIEL

[1] Maurice Escande (1892-1973). The future sociétaire and General Administrator of the Comédie-Française (in the 1960s), had just joined the troupe following a distinguished career in the army (he was injured at the Somme in 1916).
[2] See Gabriel Dussurget (ed. Renaud Machart), *Le Magicien d'Aix: Mémoires intimes* (Arles, 2011), p.33.
[3] See Alain Lompech, 'Gabriel Dussurget', in *Le Monde*, 30 July 1996.
[4] See Simon Trowbridge, *The Comédie-Française from Molière to Éric Ruf* (Oxford, 2020), p.204-05.
[5] See *Le Magicien d'Aix*, p.128.

CHAPTER TWO
CREATING THE FESTIVAL

[1] The 1923 building was abandoned by the Casino in 1993 and demolished in 2003 during the construction of the Sextius Mirabeau quarter.
[2] See Renaud Machart, 'Notes', *Le Magicien d'Aix*, p.207.
[3] *Festival d'Aix, 1948-2008* (Arles, 2008), p.30.
[4] Quoted in 'History of the Festival', Festival d'Aix-en-Provence website, at https://festival-aix.com/en/festival-daix/history/history-festival [accessed 10/9/2022].
[5] See 'History of the Festival', Festival d'Aix-en-Provence website.
[6] *Festival d'Aix, 1948-2008* (Arles, 2008), p.35.
[7] Ibid., p.31.
[8] Quoted in *Le Magicien d'Aix*, p.139.
[9] *Festival d'Aix, 1948-2008*, p.31.
[10] See 'Edmonde Charles-Roux parle de la comtesse Lily Pastré', in *Culture 13*, at http://www.culture-13.fr/agenda/edmonde-charles-roux-parle-de-la-

comtesse-lily-pastre.html [accessed 10/9/2022].
[11] *Festival d'Aix, 1948-2008*, p.25.

CHAPTER THREE
A GOLDEN DECADE

[1] *Le Magicien d'Aix*, p.140.
[2] A.P., 'The Aix Festival: Two Mozart Operas in Provence', in *The Guardian*, 21 September 1950.
[3] See *Festival d'Aix, 1948-2008*, p.30.
[4] Jardin Campra. Today the festival uses this garden area adjoining the main building for dressing-rooms, a green room and a café for the artists and staff. It is also used for first night parties and receptions.
[5] Robert Kemp, 'À Aix-en-Provence', in *Le Monde*, 16 juillet 1952.
[6] See *Le Magicien d'Aix*, p.157.
[7] 'Music at Aix: The British Share in Festival Works, Aix-en-Provence, July 29', in *The Times*, 30 July 1952.
[8] See Yves Florenne, 'Figaro à Aix-en-Provence', in *Le Monde*, 31 juillet 1953.
[9] 'Music at Aix', in *The Times*, 30 July 1952.
[10] Britten and Pears stayed with Tony Mayer (the French Cultural Attaché in London) in Ménerbes for part of their stay. Dussurget wrote in his memoirs that they stayed with him: this was probably on the night of their concert, 24 July.
[11] 'Music at Aix', in *The Times*, 30 July 1952.
[12] See Yves Florenne, 'Boyd Neel - Recital Benjamin Britten', in *Le Monde*, 28 juillet 1952.
[13] 'Music at Aix', in *The Times*, 30 July 1952.
[14] See *Le Magicien d'Aix*, p.147.
[15] *L'Avant-Scène Opéra*, January 1985.
[16] See *Le Magicien d'Aix*, p.152-53.
[17] Ibid., p.153.
[18] See Yves Florenne, 'Platée', in *Le Monde*, 25 juillet 1956.
[19] 'Rameau's *Platée* Lives Again', in *The Times*, 27 July 1956.
[20] Colin Mason, 'Mozart and the Moderns at Aix-en-Provence', in *The Guardian*, 2 August 1956.
[21] 'Wagner in a Roman Amphitheatre', in *The Times*, 7 August 1958.
[22] Jeremy Noble, 'Aix Festival', in *The Observer*, 28 July 1957.
[23] See Claude Rostand, 'Igor Markevitch et Pierre Boulez à Aix', in *Le Monde*, 31 juillet 1959.

CHAPTER FOUR
EXPANSION

[1] Dussurget's work at the Opéra de Paris falls outside the scope of this study but is a subject that warrants attention. It seems that the Opéra de Paris has forgotten him entirely for he is not mentioned on its website, not even in the pages devoted to the company's modern history.
[2] See *Le Magicien d'Aix*, p.132-33.
[3] 'Internationalism in Aix Festival Operas', in *The Times*, 8 August 1961.
[4] Andrew Porter, 'Festival at Aix-en-Provence', in *The Financial Times*, 3 August 1960.
[5] *Le Magicien d'Aix*, p.148.

CHAPTER FIVE
THE END OF THE FESTIVAL'S FIRST ERA

[1] *Le Monde*, 31 juillet 1988.

CHAPTER SIX
A CELEBRATION OF SONG

[1] See Stanley Sadie, 'Aix's pseudo-classical fantasy', in *The Times*, 3 August 1974.
[2] William Mann, 'Mozart as we like to hear him', in *The Times*, 18 August 1977.
[3] Lefort would win the lawsuit.

CHAPTER SEVEN
A PREMATURE DEPARTURE

[1] Stanley Sadie, 'Alcina', in *The Times*, 3 August 1978.
[2] See *Le Monde*, 21 juillet 1978.
[3] See Jacques Lonchampt, 'À Aix: l'échec des Noces de Figaro', in *Le Monde*, 17 juillet 1979.
[4] See Mihaï de Brancovan, 'Les Concerts', in *La Nouvelle revue des deux mondes* (Octobre 1979), p.203-14.
[5] W.S.M., 'Aix', in *The Times*, 5 December 1979.
[6] John Higgins, 'Superb Sounds in the Mistral Gallery', in *The Times*, 27 July

1981.

CHAPTER EIGHT
OLD RAMEAU, YOUNG MOZART

[1] During the 1970s, Louis Erlo, more than any other artistic director, championed the operas of Rameau. At Lyon, he mounted productions of *Castor et Pollux*, *Platée*, *Les Paladins*, *Les Fêtes d'Hébé* and *Zoroastre*.
[2] For background on Rameau's *Les Boréades*, see Simon Trowbridge, *Rameau: A Life*, 3rd ed. (Oxford, 2023), p.256-62.
[3] There was one previous concert performance of the work, incomplete, given by the Orchestre de l'ORTF under Pierre-Michel Le Conte in Paris in October 1964. The performance seems to have had a negligible impact.
[4] John Eliot Gardener, '*Les Boréades*', in the booklet of his complete recording of the work (Erato, 1990).
[5] *The Times*, 10 August 1985.
[6] Ibid.
[7] Marc Minkowski with Antone Boulay, *Chef d'orchestre ou centaure: Confessions* (Paris, 2022), p.193.
[8] Nicholas Kenyon, 'Flowering of French Baroque', in *The Times*, 4 March 1983.
[9] Gerald Kaufman, 'Finding Enlightenment at Aix', in *The Guardian*, 6 August 1982.
[10] Edward Greenfield, '*Les Boréades* on Radio 3', in *The Guardian*, 21 April 1975.
[11] See 'Le prochain festival d'Aix-en-Provence: de Rameau à Berio', in *Le Monde*, 4 mars 1983.
[12] Edward Greenfield, 'Gardiner Makes Rameau Blossom', in *The Guardian*, 25 July 1983.
[13] Hilary Finch, 'Crackling Mozart', in *The Times*, 4 August 1983.
[14] Jacques Lonchampt, 'Jeunesse de Mozart', in *Le Monde*, 18 juillet 1984.
[15] See *Le Monde*, 20 juillet 1984.

CHAPTER NINE
AN IMPROVED THEATRE

[1] See Jacques Lonchampt, 'Au nouveau théatre d'Aix-en-Provence: des Noces en demi-teintes', in *Le Monde*, 12 juillet 1985.
[2] Hilary Finch, 'Wasteful obsession with time', in *The Times*, 30 July 1985.
[3] Ibid.
[4] David Murray, 'Respectful Giovanni Fails to Strike Sparks in Aix', in *The*

Financial Times, 29 July 1986.
[5] Ibid.
[6] David Murray, 'Tancrède, Aix-en-Provence', in *The Financial Times*, 30 July 1986.
[7] Max Loppert, 'Lully and Mozart at Aix', in *The Financial Times*, 28 July 1987.
[8] Max Loppert, 'Gluck Outshines Rain and Neglect', in *The Financial Times*, 23 July 1987.
[9] David Murray, 'Così fan tutte at the Aix-en-Provence Festival', in *The Financial Times*, 28 July 1988.

CHAPTER TEN
ANCIENT AND MODERN

[1] Louis Erlo, in the *Festival d'Aix-en-Provence 1989* programme, p.5.
[2] Gerald Larner in *The Guardian*, July 26, 1989.
[3] Hilary Finch, 'Meeting and Mingling', in *The Times*, 25 July 1989.
[4] Olivier Rouvière, *Les Arts Florissants de William Christie* (Paris, 2004), p.95.
[5] Adrian Noble, interviewed in *The Sunday Times*, 19 October 1997.
[6] Mihaï de Brancovan, 'L'été des festivals', in *Revue des deux mondes*, Octobre 1989, p.227-234.
[7] David Murray, 'Fairy Tales Under the Stars', in *The Financial Times*, 22 July 1989.
[8] See 'L'avenir d'Aix', in *Le Monde*, 4 août 1989.
[9] See 'Le séduisant programme d'Aix-en-Provence: un festival réduit, mais toujours brillant', in *Le Monde*, 7 avril 1990.
[10] Max Loppert, 'Les Indes galantes, Aix-En-Provence', in *The Financial Times*, 24 July 1990.
[11] See *Le Monde*, 17 juillet 1990.
[12] Max Loppert, 'Une Heure Avec… : Aix-en-Provence', in *The Financial Times*, 25 July 1990.
[13] L'ogre et la gazelle: Gabriel Bacquier et Barbara Hendrickx aux prises dans Don Pasquale', in *Le Monde*, 31 juillet 1990.
[14] See *Le Monde*, 12 juillet 1991.
[15] Quoted in Alan Riding, 'Baroque Eclipses Mozart at Aix Festival', in *The New York Times*, 17 July 1991.
[16] Quoted in Trowbridge, *Rameau*, 3rd ed., p.116.
[17] For an analysis of *Castor et Pollux* see Trowbridge, *Rameau*, 3rd ed., p.114-21, 261-65.
[18] Nicholas Kenyon, 'The Twins Are Heavenly as Ever, Castor et Pollux in Aix-en-Provence', in *The Observer*, 14 July 1991.
[19] 'Le songe d'une nuit d'Aix, le coup d'éclat que le Festival attendait:

Shakespeare résonne de toutes ses musiques dans l'opéra de Britten', in *Le Monde*, 21 juillet 1991.
[20] Quoted in James Morgan, 'As They Say in Europe', in *The Financial Times*, 27 July 1991.
[21] David Murray, 'A Midsummer Night's Dream, Aix-en-Provence Festival', in *The Financial Times*, 24 July 1991.

CHAPTER ELEVEN
FUNDING WOES DEEPEN

[1] See 'L'Été festival Aix-en-Provence, Interrogations aixoises: Quel avenir pour le Festival d'art lyrique?', in *Le Monde*, 21 juillet 1992.
[2] Ibid.
[3] Rodney Milnes, 'Listen with Eyes Closed', in *The Times*, 26 July 1993.
[4] See 'Une splendeur perdue: accumulant les déficits depuis quatre ans, le Festival d'art lyrique d'Aix-en-Provence traverse la plus importante crise de son histoire', in *Le Monde*, 17 juillet 1994.
[5] Ibid.
[6] Quoted in John Rockwell, 'Critic's Notebook: Decrescendo in Opera Series at Aix Festival', in *The New York Times*, 16 July 1994.
[7] Quoted in Andrew Clark, 'Will the Axe Fall on Aix? The Festival is Facing the Biggest Crisis in its 46-year History', in *The Financial Times*, 15 July 1994.
[8] Ibid.
[9] John Higgins, 'New Caution Pays Off in Aix', in *The Times*, 28 July 1995.
[10] John Higgins, 'Pinched Tenor's Thin Gruel', in *The Times*, 2 August 1995.
[11] Quoted in 'Grandes et petites manoeuvres autour du Festival d'Aix-en-Provence', in *Le Monde*, 25 juillet 1995.
[12] Louis Erlo, in the *Festival d'Aix-en-Provence 1996* programme, p.9.

CHAPTER TWELVE
RENAISSANCE

[1] Quoted in Alan Riding, 'Trying to Give Opera a Festival Like No Other', in *The New York Times*, 28 June 1998.
[2] Ibid.
[3] Amelia Gentleman, 'Arts News: Young Conductor Woos Opera Buffs: British Wunderkind Excels at Mozart', in *The Guardian*, 11 July 1998.
[4] Andrew Clark, 'Miraculous Mozart in Aix: Peter Brook Has Triumphantly Scaled the Mountain of Expectation', in *The Financial Times*, 23 July 1998.
[5] Rodney Milnes, 'Aix Revitalised by Youthful Participants', in *The Times*, 21 July 1998.

⁶ Tom Sutcliffe, 'Out of Step with the Full Monte', in *The Evening Standard*, 4 June 1998.
⁷ See *Le Monde*, 29 juin 1998.
⁸ Renaud Machart, 'L'enchantement aérien d'une Flûte aixoise et européenne', in *Le Monde*, 13 juillet 1999.
⁹ See Ibid.
¹⁰ David Murray, 'Dishing Up a Memorable Feast', in *The Financial Times*, 14 July 2000.
¹¹ Renaud Machart, 'Un Retour d'Ulysse à Aix, tout de fluide beauté', in *Le Monde*, 12 juillet 2000.
¹² Alex Ross, 'Orpheus Ascending', in *The New Yorker*, vol.78, Iss.11, 13 May 2002, p.98.
¹³ Michel Parouty, 'The Long Journey to Love', in *Les Echos*, 11 Jul 2000.
¹⁴ Hugh Canning, 'Triumphant Return', in *The Sunday Times*, 16 July 2000. Other examples: John Allison (*The Times*, 17 July 2000): 'Il ritorno d'Ulisse in patria has to be the operatic event of the year, if not more. [...] Ulysses's ritorno to Ithaca also marked Adrian Noble's ritorno to opera with a staging so beautiful and truthful in its simplicity that it mirrored the stillness of the score.' David Murray (*The Financial Times*, 14 July 2000): 'It made a profound experience, a revelation of Monteverdi's operatic art beyond anything I've seen or heard.'
¹⁵ See Marie-Aude Roux, 'Entretien avec le directeur du festival d'art lyrique d'Aix-en-Provence, in *Le Monde*, 21 juin 2001.
¹⁶ Rupert Christiansen, 'An Enthralling Turn for the Better', in *The Daily Telegraph*, 31 July 2001.
¹⁷ Ibid.
¹⁸ See Renaud Machart, 'Benjamin Britten et les fantômes de l'innocence bafouée: Le Tour d'écrou, opéra de chambre écrit d'après le roman éponyme de Henry James, traite d'un thème récurrent dans l'œuvre du compositeur britannique: l'enfance dévoyée', in *Le Monde*, 12 juin 2001.
¹⁹ Rupert Christiansen, 'A Powerhouse of Excitement', in *The Daily Telegraph*, 9 July 2002.

CHAPTER THIRTEEN
LISSNER PART TWO

¹ Quoted (in French) in Clément Hervieu-Léger, 'L'Obsession du récit', in Sarah Barbedette and Pénélope Driant (eds.), *Patrice Chéreau: Mettre en scène l'opéra* (Actes Sud, 2017), p.96.
² Quoted in Sarah Barbedette and Pénélope Driant (eds.), *Patrice Chéreau: Mettre en scène l'opéra* (Actes Sud, 2017), p.161.
³ Rupert Christiansen, 'At last, a Così without cliché', in *The Daily Telegraph*,

21 July 2005.

CHAPTER FOURTEEN
IN LISSNER'S SHADOW

[1] Michael Henderson, 'Daniel Harding: Conducting His Life with Brio', in *The Observer*, 30 July 2006.
[2] Rupert Christiansen, 'From the House of the Dead, Aix Festival: A Stark, Moving Miracle', in *The Daily Telegraph*, 20 July 2007.
[3] Rupert Christiansen, 'When a Movie Maestro Focuses on the Opera Stage', in *The Daily Telegraph*, 10 July 2008.
[4] Jean-Louis Validire, 'À Aix, Pascal Dusapin assouvit sa Passion', in *Le Figaro*, 1 July 2008.

CHAPTER FIFTEEN
A FESTIVAL OF NEW OPERAS

[1] John Allison, 'The premiere of George Benjamin's *Written on Skin*, inspired by 12th-century Occitan legend, was the haunting highlight of this year's Aix festival', in *The Daily Telegraph*, 18 July 2012.
[2] See *Le Monde*, 30 juin 2014,
[3] See Sarah Connolly, 'Nightmare in Aix: Sarah Connolly on a shocking first night', in *Theartsdesk.com*, 8 July 2014, at https://theartsdesk.com/opera/nightmare-aix-sarah-connolly-shocking-first-night (accessed 29 June 2023).

Index

Abbado, Claudio, 122, 132, 133, 135
Abbaye de Silvacane, 52
Abernethy, Jonathan, 185
Abetz, Otto, 16
Académie européenne de musique, Aix
   (Renamed Académie du Festival
   d'Aix in 2013), 12, 130, 131,
   132, 133, 136, 137, 138, 139,
   140, 142, 143, 144, 145, 147,
   149, 150, 154, 156, 157, 159,
   161, 166, 168, 170, 172, 175,
   176, 177, 178, 180, 182, 185
Academy of St Martin in the Fields
   (London), 74, 75, 77
Acis and Galatea
   (Handel), 172
Acquart, André, 74
Actéon
   (Charpentier), 107
Adámek, Ondřej, 186
Adams, Donald, 113
Adani, Mariella, 39
Adlgasser, Anton, 111
Aeschlimann, Robert, 136
Affaire Makropoulos, L'
   (Janáček), 139, 144, 145
Agathonos, Anna, 140
Agnew, Paul, 137
Aillagon, Jean-Jacques, 148, 151, 152, 153
Aimard, Pierre-Laurent, 159
Ainsley, John Mark, 135, 166, 172
Aix en Juin, 177, 178
Akademie für alte Musik, 169
Alarie, Pierrette, 30
Albeniz, Isaac, 148
Albinoni, Tomaso, 31, 41
Albrecht, Marc, 186

Alceste
   (Gluck), 169
Alcina
   (Handel), 71, 181
Alden, Christopher, 180
Aler, John, 87, 90, 98
Alexander, Ninon, 23
Alexander, Roberta, 90
Algeria, 15
Allain, Juliette, 184
Allam, Roger, 102
Alliol-Lugaz, Colette, 96
Alsina, Carlos-Roque, 90
Altinoglu, Alain, 148
Alva, Luigi, 39
Amériques
   (Varèse), 143
Amiens, Guillaume d', 41
Amour des trois oranges, L'
   (Prokofiev), 101, 104, 153, 154
Amours de Ronsard, Les
   (Milhaud), 35
Amsterdam, 175
Amy, Gilbert, 75, 77, 90
Anacréon
   (Rameau), 107
Anderson, June, 100
Ange de feu, L'
   (Prokofiev), 186
Ángeles, Victoria de los, 30
Anouilh, Jean, 37
Aperghis, Georges, 148
Apollo
   (Stravinsky), 143
Apollo e Dafne
   (Handel), 143
Appleby, Paul, 185
Après-midi d'un faune, L'

(Debussy), 52
Aquilon et Orithie
 (Rameau), 23
Araiza, Francisco, 67
Arditti Quartet, 94
Arena, Maurizio, 85
Argenta, Nancy, 94, 102
Ariadne auf Naxos
 (Strauss), 47, 91, 93, 95, 186
Arias, Alfredo, 106, 115
Arié, Raphaël, 29
Ariettes oubliées
 (Debussy), 107
Ariodante
 (Handel), 179
Armida
 (Rossini), 99, 100
Arne, Thomas, 65
Ars Nova, 104
Art sans la barre
 (Béjart), 81
Arts Florissants, Les, 101, 102, 104, 106, 107, 113, 116, 123, 126, 142, 144, 173
Asko Schönberg Ensemble, 176
Aspromonte, Francesca, 185
Association du Festival d'Aix, 108
Attwood, Thomas, 65
Atys
 (Lully), 98, 101
Aubert, Pauline, 23
Auden, W. H., 115, 185
Audi, Pierre, 176, 180, 190
Auriacombe, Louis, 39
Auvity, Cyril, 142
Auvray, Jean-Claude, 63, 76
Ave verum corpus
 (Byrd), 100
Avemo, Kerstin, 158, 170
Avignon Festival, 98, 178
Bach, Johann Sebastian, 25, 29, 62, 68, 94, 105, 139, 144, 180
Bacquier, Gabriel, 44, 49, 64, 67, 72, 104, 107
Bączyk, Krzysztof, 181, 186
Baer, Olaf, 100
Baez, Joan, 60, 62
Bagatelles
 (Beethoven), 40
Bagouet, Dominique, 97

Baïz, Josette, 177
Baker, Janet, 72
Balcon, Le
 (Eötvös), 145, 149, 150
Baldwin, Dalton, 43, 60, 66
Balibar, Jeanne, 161
Balladur, Édouard, 117
Ballet du Grand Théâtre de Genève, 93
Ballet Preljocaj
 (Aix), 133
Ballets des Champs-Elysées
 (Paris), 17
Ballets russes, 28, 46, 49
Balthus, 28, 52
Bär, Olaf, 166
Barat, Pierre, 76
Baráth, Emöke, 176
Barbaux, Christine, 74, 92, 97
Barber, Samuel, 66
Barbier de Séville, Le
 (Rossini), 34, 38, 90, 158
Barbizet, Pierre, 47
Barrault, Jean-Louis, 16, 28, 37
Bartók, Béla, 22, 29, 40, 46, 132, 135, 143, 148
Bartoletti, Bruno, 45
Basilique Sainte-Marie-Madeleine, 54
Bastin, Jules, 74, 75, 104
Battesti, Jean-Michel, 130
Baudo, Serge, 46, 48, 49, 52, 54, 66
Baudry, Elisabeth, 98
Bausch, Pina, 132, 135
Bayreuth Festival, 131
Béatrice de Planissoles
 (Jacques Charpentier), 55
Bedford, Steuart, 113
Beethoven, Ludwig van, 29, 30, 40, 43, 48, 52, 86, 107, 123, 158, 159, 171
Béjart, Maurice, 81
Bella mia fiamma, addio
 (Mozart), 143
Belle Hélène, La
 (Offenbach), 137, 139
Bellèvre, Jean-François, 139
Bellorini, Jean, 185
Belshazzar
 (Handel), 167
Benjamin, George, 164, 173, 174

Bennett, Michael, 134
Benoit, Jean-Christophe, 61, 65, 69
Bérard, Christian, 15
Berbié, Jane, 44, 48
Bérénice
  (Racine), 44
Berg, Alban, 22, 36, 40, 49, 66, 96, 139, 143, 145, 151
Berganza, Teresa, 34, 39, 44, 45, 71, 72, 74, 77, 88, 112
Berio, Luciano, 86, 88, 89
Berkeley, Leonard, 32
Berliner Philharmoniker, 145, 161, 164, 166
Berlioz, Hector, 47, 48, 52, 65, 86, 110, 171
Bernfeld, Jay, 133
Berraud, Henry, 42, 46
Bertin, Pierre, 16, 30
Bertrand, Jean, 20, 51, 53
Besard, Jean-Baptiste, 46
Beuron, Yann, 148, 169
Bianchi, Oscar, 172
Bibliothèque nationale de France, 81
Bignens, Max, 65, 73, 74
Bigonnet, Roger, 20, 21, 24, 26, 28, 51, 52, 64, 190
Birtwistle, Harrison, 143
Bizet, Georges, 25, 38, 39, 185
Blake, Rockwell, 88, 125
Blanc, Dominique, 182
Blanchard, Jean-Marie, 123
Blanchard, Roger, 74
Blazat, Anne-Marie, 76
Blegen, Judith, 85
Blixt, Karolina, 171
Blochwitz, Hans Peter, 100, 122
Bluzet, Dominique, 141
Bodelman, Laci, 66
Boden, Samuel, 180
Boesmans, Philippe, 158, 185
Boeuf sur le toit, Le
  (Milhaud), 86
Boisseau, Marc, 104
Boito, Arrigo, 112
Boldyreva, Anastasia, 159
Bolton, Ivor, 170
Bondy, Luc, 146, 147, 153, 154, 155, 158
Bonner, Yvette, 150

Bonporti, Francesco Antonio, 43
Bontoux, Bertrand, 142
Booth, Juliet, 113
Borciani, Paolo, 23
Boréades, Les
  (Rameau), 81, 82, 83, 84, 85, 86, 105, 126, 180
Borodin Quartet, 52
Borodin, Alexander, 52
Boruzescu, Miruna, 85
Boruzescu, Radu, 176
Bouffes du Nord
  (Paris), 129, 153, 156
Boulanger, Nadia, 29
Boulez, Pierre, 11, 22, 38, 40, 41, 49, 88, 89, 132, 133, 135, 136, 139, 143, 148, 151, 152, 153, 159, 160, 165, 166
Boulin, Sophie, 98
Bour, Ernest, 24, 25, 29, 42
Bourdet, Gildas, 89, 95
Bourseiller, Antoine, 62
Boussard, Vincent, 165, 175
Bowman, James, 75, 113
Boyd Neel Orchestra, 33
Bozonnet, Marcel, 132, 133
Brahms, Johannes, 40, 43, 60, 66, 139, 143, 148
Brasseur, Elisabeth, 37, 47
Braunschweig, Stéphane, 132, 138, 140, 147, 151, 153, 160, 165, 168
Brendel, Alfred, 107
Bretano Lieder
  (Strauss), 126
Brewer, Bruce, 75
Bridge, Frank, 15
Briot, Chloé, 180, 185
Britannicus
  (Racine), 15
British Council, 86
Britten, Benjamin, 15, 32, 33, 34, 36, 41, 42, 43, 46, 49, 50, 52, 54, 66, 101, 104, 109, 112, 113, 115, 123, 132, 133, 134, 145, 146, 147, 158, 159, 174, 182
Brochen, Julie, 150, 160
Brook, Irina, 149
Brook, Peter, 102, 112, 129, 131, 132, 133, 134, 135, 136, 137, 138, 149, 150, 156, 169, 181

Brooklyn Academy of Music
  (New York), 143
Brower, Angela, 186
Brown, Trisha, 136, 165, 171
Browne, Sandra, 88
Bruckner, Anton, 22
Bruguière, Dominique, 146
Brunel, Richard, 168, 173
Bruyère, Jean-Michel, 175
Buchvald, Claude, 139, 140
Bufoir, Jacques, 93
Bullock, Julia, 185
Bumbry, Grace, 68
Buratto, Eleonora, 185
Bureau des concerts de Paris, 16
Burrowes, Norma, 67
Burrows, Stuart, 60
Burt, Robert, 142
Buxtehude, Dieterich, 98
Bychkov, Semyon, 90, 93, 96, 105
Byrd, William, 32, 100
Byström, Malin, 173
Caballé, Montserrat, 60, 62, 63, 66, 68, 76
Cachemaille, Gilles, 90, 92, 135, 137
Cacoyannis, Michaël, 99
Cahusac, Louis de, 83
Calvario, Philippe, 154
Calvet Quartet, 24
Camden Festival
  (London), 112
Camerata Salzburg, 167, 168
Campanello di note, Il
  (Donizetti), 68
Campion, Thomas, 41
Campo, Antonio, 36, 44
Campra, André, 11, 19, 33, 43, 63, 71, 73, 80, 95, 96, 107, 118
Camus, Albert, 28
Canadian Opera Company, 171
Cannes Film Festival, 17
Cantafora, Arduino, 115
Capecchi, Renato, 26, 29, 34
Čapek, Karel, 139
Cappechi, Renato, 110
Cappella Mediterranea, 176, 185
Caprices de Marianne, Les
  (Sauguet), 35, 42
Carissimi, Giacomo, 65
Carmeli, Boris, 69

Carmen
  (Bizet), 39, 185
Carnaval d'Aix, Le
  (Milhaud), 86
Carnaval de Venise, Le
  (Campra), 63, 71
Carnet d'un disparu
  (Janáček), 145, 146
Carreras, José, 61, 68
Carsen, Robert, 112, 113, 114, 115, 116, 118, 121, 122, 125, 175, 176, 182
Casadesus, Jean-Claude, 25, 61, 74
Casadesus, Robert, 25, 48
Casino
  (Aix), 11, 20, 26, 51, 52, 53, 55, 129, 156
Cassandre, 24, 25, 28, 55
Castor et Pollux
  (Rameau), 36, 64, 105, 109, 110
Castronovo, Charles, 171
Cauchetier, Patrice, 66
Cavalli, Francesco, 175, 176, 185
Cena Furiso
  (Monteverdi), 137
Cenerentola
  (Rossini), 86, 88, 140, 144
Centre Acanthes, 70, 75, 77, 81, 88, 89, 90, 94, 98, 130
Centre de pédagogie lyrique, 74
Centre international de créations théâtrales
  (Paris), 129
Centre lyrique de Wallonie, 76
Cercle de l'Harmonie, Le, 168, 173, 175, 185
Ceremony of Carols
  (Britten), 52
Cézanne, Paul, 19, 23, 131, 141, 161
Chabrier, Emmanuel, 25
Chamber Symphony no. 1
  (Schönberg), 35
Chambre régionale des comptes de Provence-Alpes-Côte d'Azur, 124
Chance, Michaël, 90
Chant du Rossignol, Le
  (Stravinsky), 143
Charbonneau, Pascal, 173
Charles, Ray, 72
Charles-Roux, Edmonde, 15, 23, 25,

26, 27, 28, 30, 109, 126, 149, 167
Charpentier, Jacques, 55
Charpentier, Marc-Antoine, 52, 55, 104, 107, 173
Chartreuse de Villeneuve-lès-Avignon, 98
Château d'Ansouis, 31, 52, 65
Château de Barbe-Bleue, Le (Bartók), 132, 133, 135
Château de Chantilly, 16
Château de Fonscolombe, 40
Château de la Mignarde, 24
Château de Lourmarin, 31
Château de Montredon, 14
Château du Tholonet, 31
Château, Christiane, 62, 64
Chekhov, Anton, 99
Chen Shi-Zheng, 140
Chéreau, Patrice, 93, 99, 155, 156, 157, 158, 165, 166, 175, 177
Cherubini, Luigi, 30, 66
Chevalier, Françoise, 90
Chevalier, Jean-Pierre, 61, 76
Child of Our Time (Tippett), 100
Chirac, Jacques, 123, 151, 152
Chmoulevitch, Vsevolod, 133
Choel, Bruno, 97
Chœur Accentus, 159
Chœur de chambre Accentus, 148
Chœur du Conservatoire (Paris), 37, 47
Chojuacka, Elisabeth, 94
Chopin, Frédéric, 40, 43, 159
Chorale Elisabeth-Brasseur, 75
Chorégies d'Orange Festival, 17
Christie, William, 43, 98, 101, 102, 104, 106, 107, 110, 111, 116, 118, 121, 122, 123, 125, 126, 139, 141, 142, 144, 149, 153, 155, 171, 173
Christophers, Harry, 95
Chuberre, Bertrand, 142
Cimarosa, Domenico, 29, 46, 68
Cinq concerts à la une, 90
Cinq études (Milhaud), 35
Cinq pièces pour piano (Schönberg), 49
Cité du Livre (Aix), 143

City of Birmingham Symphony Orchestra, 140, 143
Clancy, Deirdre, 102, 103
Clark, Graham, 140
Claudel, Paul, 67
Clavé, Antoni, 32
Clayette, Pierre, 52, 93
Clayton, Allan, 174
Clemenza di Tito, La (Mozart), 61, 99, 158, 171
Cloître Saint-Louis (Aix), 40, 43, 46, 60, 69, 75, 77, 85, 86
Cloos, Hans Peter, 117
Cluytens, André, 35
Cochet, Jean-Laurent, 52
Cocteau, Jean, 43
Coda, Eraldo, 29
Coelho, Eliane, 95
Cohen, Joël, 65
Colao, Paolo, 165
Collège Mignet (Aix), 131
Collegium Aureum, 49
Collegium Musicum Italicum, 31
Collegium Vocale, 136
Collot, Serge, 49
Colonna, Monica, 135
Combattimento di Tancredi e Clorinda, Il (Monteverdi), 46, 86
Comédie-Française, 15, 16, 17, 25, 30, 37, 44, 61, 133
Commanderie de la Bargemone, Saint-Cannat, 65
Commins, Daniel, 165
Comte Ory, Le (Rossini), 122
Concert d'Astrée, 183
Concert no. 4 (Rameau), 23, 40
Concert no. 5 (Rameau), 23
Concert no. 6 (Rameau), 39
Concerto da camera (Honegger), 35
Concerto for Orchestra (Bartók), 148
(Hindemith), 40

Concerto for Piano
  (Schumann), 125
Concerto for Piano no. 12
  (Mozart), 126
Concerto for Piano no. 24
  (Mozart), 25
Concerto for Strings
  (Stravinsky), 43
Concerto for Three Pianos
  (Mozart), 52
Concerto Köln, 140, 144
Concerto pour basson
  (Rivier), 48
Concerto pour piano
  (Poulenc), 29
Confédération générale du travail
  (CGT), 152
Connolly, Sarah, 172, 179, 180
Conseil d'administration
  (Aix Festival), 89, 123, 125, 128
Conservatoire
  (Paris), 11, 21, 41, 58, 180
Conservatoire Darius-Milhaud
  (Aix), 75
Cook, Howard, 111
Copley, John, 72
Corboz, Michel, 65, 92
Corneille, Pierre, 66
Corneille, Thomas, 97
Cornwell, Joseph, 142
Cortis, Marcello, 26, 28, 29, 32, 34, 36, 44, 52
Così fan tutte
  (Mozart), 11, 17, 18, 21, 23, 28, 34, 36, 39, 41, 46, 51, 52, 55, 61, 67, 76, 99, 101, 122, 140, 156, 157, 165, 167, 183
Coster, Janet, 68
Cótrubas, Ileana, 63
Couderc, Bertrand, 157
Couperin, François, 25, 33, 40, 49, 107, 126
Courjal, Nicolas, 184
Cours Mirabeau
  (Aix), 18, 19, 20, 31, 118, 141
Création du Monde, La
  (Milhaud), 36
Création, La
  (Haydn), 100
Crespin, Regine, 132

Crimp, Martin, 155, 174
Crochot, Michel, 44, 46, 47, 48
Croft, Richard, 169
Crook, Howard, 98
Crucifixus
  (Lotti), 100
Cuccaro, Constanza, 61, 66
Cuenod, Hugues, 60, 65
Cum invocarum
  (Campra), 107
Curlew River
  (Britten), 54, 132, 134, 145
Currentzis, Teodor, 182
Cusack, Niamh, 102
D'Alembert, Jean le Rond, 83
D'Alep à Séville, 148
Da Ponte, Lorenzo, 18, 32, 38, 59, 91, 145, 157
Dahl, Tracy, 97
Dahlberg, Tove, 158
Dalayman, Katerina, 168
Dalbavie, Marc-Andre, 133
Dale, Laurence, 106
Dam, José van, 87, 96, 98, 100
Damiani, Davide, 158
Damnation de Faust, La
  (Berlioz), 47
Danco, Suzanne, 26, 29, 36
Daniecki, John, 112
Daniel, Paul, 158
Danse des morts, La
  (Honegger), 67
Daphnis et Chloé
  (Ravel), 52, 118
Dardanus
  (Rameau), 49
Dautremay, Jean, 66
David et Jonathas
  (Charpentier), 104, 173
Davidsen, Lise, 186
Davies, Neal, 173
Davis, Colin, 60, 171
Dawson, Lynne, 94, 98, 102
De Gaulle, Charles, 17, 42
De Keersmaeker, Anne Teresa, 153, 155
De la maison des morts
  (Janáček), 165, 166, 167
Dean, Stafford, 66, 69
Debussy, Claude, 25, 31, 49, 52, 66,

82, 107, 139, 143, 148, 159, 183
Decker, Willy, 166
Degout, Stéphane, 12, 138, 140, 147, 148, 157, 183, 185
Degroat, Andy, 115
Délégation musicale régionale, 74
Deletré, Bernard, 102, 111
Deller Consort, 49
Deller, Alfred, 49
Delman, Jacqueline, 32
Delouche, Dominique, 55
Delunsch, Mireille, 137, 143, 147, 148, 154, 169
Denève, Stéphane, 171
Denize, Nadine, 62, 65, 66, 74
Denley, Catherine, 90
Deplus, Guy, 49
Derain, André, 30, 32, 34
Dervaux, Pierre, 39, 43, 44, 46, 48
Desandre, Léa, 12, 184, 185
Desarzens, Victor, 24
Deschamps, Jérôme, 151, 155
Desderi, Claudio, 139, 140
Deshorties, Alexandra, 137, 140
Desjardins, Christophe, 139, 143
Désormière, Roger, 29, 33, 37
Dessay, Natalie, 122, 126, 147, 171
Deux Garçons, Les
 (Aix), 20
Devia, Mariella, 97
Devieilhe, Sabine, 12, 175, 186
Dickson, Stephan, 85
Diderot, Denis, 66, 83
Dido and Aeneas
 (Purcell), 43, 46, 72, 93, 107, 132, 133, 160, 161
Didon
 (Campra), 43
DiDonato, Joyce, 155
Diener, Melanie, 135
Dieu
 (Henry), 81
Directeur de théâtre, Le
 (Mozart), 60
Divertimento for Strings
 (Bartók), 29
Doat, Jan, 33
Domaine Musical, Le
 (Paris), 49
Dominguez, Amaya, 170

Don Giovanni
 (Mozart), 25, 26, 29, 36, 39, 44, 51, 55, 65, 76, 94, 95, 110, 114, 115, 116, 131, 132, 133, 134, 135, 136, 137, 138, 149, 169, 175, 184
Don Pasquale
 (Donizetti), 72, 105, 107, 108
Donath, Hélène, 112
Donizetti, Gaetano, 64, 68, 69, 72, 77, 107
Donnedieu de Vabres, Renaud, 156
Douste-Blazy, Philippe, 123, 124, 125, 128
Dove, Jonathan, 140, 150, 182
Dowland, John, 33, 65
Doyen, Jean, 23
Dryden, John, 93
Dubosc, Catherine, 96, 104, 106, 107
Duesing, Dale, 160
Dufay, Guillaume, 41
Dufourt, Hugues, 90
Duggelin, Werner, 64
Duhamel, Jacques, 55
Duisit, Marie, 98
Dumait, Olivier, 147, 150
Dumay, Augustin, 133
Dumbarton Oaks
 (Stravinsky), 35
Dunn, Oliver, 176
Dupont, Jacques, 49
Durand, Jean-Georges, 82
Dusapin, Pascal, 148, 167, 168
Dusechkin, Kirill, 154
Dussurget, Gabriel, 11, 14, 15, 16, 17, 18, 19, 20, 21, 22, 23, 24, 25, 26, 27, 28, 29, 30, 31, 32, 33, 34, 35, 36, 37, 38, 39, 40, 41, 42, 43, 44, 45, 46, 47, 48, 49, 51, 52, 53, 54, 55, 56, 58, 59, 62, 63, 64, 65, 77, 80, 81, 98, 105, 110, 114, 118, 122, 126, 130, 131, 134, 141, 190
Dutilleux, Henri, 33, 47, 54, 77
Dutoit, Charles, 118
Duval, Denise, 43
Ebers, Clara, 25, 26
Éclat
 (Boulez), 89
Éclat-Multiples
 (Boulez), 143

École des Arts et Métiers
  (Aix), 48
Eda-Pierre, Christiane, 41, 48, 64, 71,
  72
Edy, Anders, 77
Église de la Madeleine
  (Aix), 64
El Hadj Djeli Sory Kouyate, 144
Elektra
  (Strauss), 175, 177
Elena
  (Cavalli), 176, 185
Eliasson, Goran, 140
Elijah
  (Mendelssohn), 105
Elisabetta, regina d'Inghilterra
  (Rossini), 62
Elisir d'amore, L'
  (Donizetti), 64
Encina, Juan del, 41
Enfance du Christ, L'
  (Berlioz), 48
Enfant et les sortilèges, L'
  (Ravel), 175
Engerer, Brigitte, 148
England, 31, 67, 125
English Bach Festival, 110
English Baroque Soloists, 82, 83, 85,
  86, 87, 90, 92, 94, 98
English Chamber Orchestra, 67, 68,
  99, 100, 105, 115, 117
English National Opera, 63
  (London), 92
English Opera Group, 54, 93
English Voices, 170
Ensemble Alim Qassimov, 144
Ensemble baroque de Paris, 41, 46
Ensemble Dastan, 144
Ensemble instrumental de France, 52
Ensemble instrumental de Provence,
  43, 46
Ensemble Intercontemporain, 88, 139,
  143, 150, 152
Ensemble Modern, 168, 172
Ensemble Musicatreize, 159
Ensemble Orchestral de Paris, 99,
  100, 104, 110, 113
Ensemble Shewkat Mirzaëv, 144
Ensemble vocal de Paris, 33
Ensemble vocal et instrumental de
  Lausanne, 65
Entführung aus dem Serail, Die
  (Mozart), 29, 51, 96, 97, 105, 106,
  151, 153, 155, 165, 182
Eötvös, Peter, 145, 149, 150
Equilbey, Laurence, 139, 140, 148,
  159
Erede, Alberto, 43, 62
Erismena
  (Cavalli), 185
Erlo, Louis, 75, 80, 81, 82, 86, 89, 90,
  91, 92, 94, 95, 96, 97, 98, 99, 101,
  102, 103, 104, 105, 106, 108, 109,
  110, 111, 112, 114, 115, 116, 117,
  118, 119, 120, 121, 122, 123, 124,
  125, 126, 128, 130, 131, 190
Ernman, Malena, 158
Escande, Maurice, 15
Eslava, Juan Jose, 133
Etcheverry, Micaëla, 76
Études Symphoniques
  (Schumann), 107
Eugène Onéguine
  (Tchaikovsky), 149
Euripides, 66
Europe galante, L'
  (Campra), 118
European Community Youth
  Orchestra, 122
Euryanthe
  (Weber), 116, 117
Evangelatos, Daphne, 96
Evans, Wynford, 90
Exultate Jubilate
  (Mozart), 68
Exurge Domine
  (Campra), 43
Eyre, Richard, 145
Fairy Queen, The
  (Purcell), 101, 103, 113, 114, 126,
  141
Fall, Jean-Claude, 74, 88, 100, 112
Falla, Manuel de, 148, 152, 153, 160
Falstaff
  (Verdi), 44, 48, 55, 96, 146
Fasano, Renato, 31
Fassini, Alberto, 68
Fauré, Gabriel, 43, 52, 60, 77, 86,
  107, 148
Fedele, Ivan, 148

Fegnard, Jean-François, 64
Fercioni, Gian Maurizio, 97
Ferro, Gabriele, 107
Festival d'Arles, 62
Festival d'automne
 (Paris), 58
Festival d'Avignon, 17
Festival de Saint-Maximin-la-Sainte-
 Baume, 49
Festival Production Centre
 (Venelles), 129
Fêtes vénitiennes
 (Campra), 43
Février, Jacques, 47
Fikret, Nazan, 147
Filippetti, Aurélie, 178
Finances, budgets and public subsidies
 (Aix Festival), 11, 26, 51, 53, 54,
 55, 62, 81, 86, 99, 105, 108,
 109, 114, 116, 119, 120, 121,
 122, 128, 129, 130, 138, 144,
 156, 167
Finley, Gerald, 113
Finta giardiniera, La
 (Mozart), 89, 112, 126, 175
Finzi, Gerald, 66
Fitzgerald, Ella, 64
Five Movements
 (Webern), 36
Fleuret, Maurice, 89
Foccroulle, Bernard, 159, 164, 165,
 166, 167, 168, 169, 170, 173, 174,
 175, 177, 178, 179, 180, 181, 182,
 183, 186, 190
Ford, Bruce, 112
Fouchécourt, Jean-Paul, 106, 145
France-Musique, 54
Francescatti, Zino, 48
François, Guy-Claude, 96, 97
Freiberger, Venceskawa, 85
Freiburger Barockorchester, 169, 170,
 179, 181, 182, 183
Frémeau, Jean-Marie, 74
Freshwater, Geoffrey, 102
Frigeni, Giuseppe, 168
Frizza, Riccardo, 161
Fry, Gareth, 181
Fuchs, Julie, 172, 180, 185
Gabrieli, Giovanni, 43
Gagnidze, George, 176
Gall, Hugues, 108
Gambill, Robert, 160
Gandolfi, Romano, 107
Ganeau, François, 30, 39, 52
Ganzarolli, Wladimiro, 48
Garanča, Elīna, 157
Garaventa, Ottavio, 62
García Alarcón, Leonardo, 172, 176,
 185
Gardiner, John Eliot, 81, 82, 83, 85,
 86, 87, 90, 91, 92, 94, 96, 98, 101,
 126
Gardino, Jolanda, 23
Gardon, Mathieu, 180
Gatti, Daniele, 158
Gautier, Georges, 77, 104
Gavazzeni, Gian Andrea, 29
Gavoty, Bernard, 23
Gay, Pierre, 53, 58
Gayraud, Christiane, 47
Gedda, Nicolai, 35, 36, 37
Gelmetti, Gian-Luigi, 90
Gendron, Maurice, 16
Genet, Jean, 145, 149, 150
Gens, Véronique, 102, 111, 135, 144,
 145, 170
Genz, Christoph, 138
Genz, Stephan, 143
Gerbaud, Christine, 140
Gessendorf, Mechthild, 97
Gibbons, Orlando, 32
Gibbs, Armstrong, 66
Gide, André, 182
Gielen, Michael, 42, 46
Gielgud, John, 112
Gierlach, Wojciech, 140
Gilles, Jean, 52
Gillett, Christopher, 113
Gillibrand, Nicky, 181
Gimenez, Raul, 107
Ginefri, Noëlle, 149
Giordani, Tommaso, 43
Giovannetti, Julien, 23
Gisler, Andreas, 142
Gitton, Jean, 29
Giulini, Carlo Mario, 32, 33, 34, 40,
 41
Giustino
 (Vivaldi), 29
Gluck, Christoph Willibald, 31, 32,

36, 96, 98, 169, 170
Glyndebourne Festival, 44, 45, 48, 54, 68, 112, 121, 138
Goerne, Matthias, 180
Goldberg Variations (Bach), 94, 180
Goldoni, Carlo, 41
Golove, Jonathan, 133
Gomez, Jill, 89
Goncharova, Natalie, 47
Goretta, Claude, 92, 93
Gorget-Chemin, René, 47
Götterdämmerung (Wagner), 60, 168
Gottlieb, Peter, 76
Gould, Christopher, 148
Gounod, Charles, 35, 39, 43, 66
Gracis, Patrizia, 107
Graham, Colin, 94
Graham-Hall, John, 113
Granados, Enrique, 148
Grand Macabre, Le (Ligeti), 75
Grand orchestre de l'Institut national belge de radiodiffusion, 40
Grand Saint-Jean, 138, 140, 143, 147, 148, 154, 155, 158, 161, 170, 172, 175, 176
Grand Théâtre de Bordeaux, 123
Grand Théâtre de Genève, 108, 112
Grand Théâtre de Provence (Aix), 73, 160, 165, 167, 169, 173, 177, 178, 180, 181, 182, 183, 184
Grande Écurie et la Chambre du Roy, 96, 98
Gras, Hans, 95
Graun, Carl Heinrich, 29
Greenberg, Sylvia, 95
Greenwood, Paul, 102
Gregory, Anthony, 181
Gregotti, Vittorio, 165
Grenier, Jean-Pierre, 37, 39
Grétry, André, 38
Grieg, Edvard, 148
Grillet, Hervé, 99, 120
Grimaud, Hélène, 126
Grochowski, Gerd, 168
Groupe Grenade (Aix), 177

Groupe instrumental de Paris, 52
Grüber, Klaus Michael, 137, 151, 152, 153, 160
Gruberov, Edita, 85
Gualda, Sylvio, 94
Gubisch, Nora, 137, 146, 148
Guillaumot, Bernard, 91
Guinand, Patrick, 75
Guion, Olivier, 89
Guirlande de Campra, La, 33
Gullberg Jensen, Eivind, 185
Guller, Youra, 14
Gunn, Nathan, 165
Gurre-Lieder (Schönberg), 143
Guryakova, Olga, 149
Guschlbauer, Theodor, 85, 88, 100
Guy, Michel, 64, 69
Hablowetz, Silvia, 133
Hadley, Jerry, 115
Haefliger, Ernst, 30
Hagegard, Erland, 85
Hagen, Reinhard, 122
Haider, Friedrich, 110
Haïm, Emmanuelle, 143, 183
Hall, Peter, 25, 74
Halsey, Simon, 182
Hamel, Michel, 47
Hampson, Thomas, 92
Handel, George Frideric, 33, 43, 71, 72, 73, 86, 88, 90, 116, 119, 123, 125, 139, 143, 153, 155, 167, 172, 179, 181, 183
Hanjo (Hosokawa), 153, 155
Hannigan, Barbara, 168, 174, 183, 184
Harding, Daniel, 133, 135, 137, 139, 143, 147, 149, 151, 153, 154, 157, 158, 160, 165, 166, 185
Harmonie municipale d'Aix-en-Provence, 77
Harnoncourt, Nikolaus, 166
Harth, Roger, 61, 68, 69
Haskil, Clara, 14, 23
Hasse, Johann Adolf, 74
Hatley, Tim, 145
Haugland, Aage, 97
Hayashi, Yasuko, 61
Hayashi, Yusuko, 66

Haydn, Joseph, 29, 31, 38, 41, 46, 52, 85, 100, 104, 107, 139, 143, 159, 167, 168
Haydn, Michael, 111
Hayrabedian, Roland, 159, 170
Heiffer, Claude, 94
Heldenleben, Ein
  (Strauss), 86
Helfer, Claude, 49
Hellekant, Charlotte, 146
Hemleb, Lukas, 158
Hendrickx, Barbara, 107
Henry, Pierre, 81
Henze, Hans Werner, 40
Heppner, Ben, 168
Heras-Casado, Pablo, 181
Hercules
  (Handel), 86, 153, 154, 155
Herlitzius, Evelyn, 177
Hieber, Eva Maria, 110
Hilliard Ensemble, 105
Hinterhäuser, Markus, 180
Hippolyte et Aricie
  (Rameau), 86, 87, 88, 111, 171
Histoire du soldat, L'
  (Stravinsky), 46
Histoire vraie de la Périchole
  (Offenbach), 160
Hoare, Peter, 140
Hogwood, Christopher, 125
Holcroft, Sam, 176
Holland Festival, 41
Homoki, Andreas, 173
Honegger, Arthur, 33, 35, 36, 67, 107
Honoré, Christophe, 183, 184
Horne, Marilyn, 76, 77
Hosokawa, Toshio, 153, 155
Hôtel Boyer d'Eguilles
  (Aix), 24
Hôtel d'Espagnet
  (Aix), 31
Hôtel de Caumont
  (Aix), 75, 77
Hôtel de Valbelle
  (Aix), 76
Hôtel de Ville
  (Aix), 20, 32, 33, 94, 107, 128, 159
Hôtel du Pigonnet
  (Aix), 36
Hôtel Maynier d'Oppède
  (Aix), 35, 36, 38, 40, 41, 43, 46, 130, 132, 133, 137, 146, 148, 159, 161, 167, 168, 177
House Taken Over, The
  (Mendonça), 176
Howarth, Judith, 110
Howells, Herbert, 100
Huc-Santana, André, 37
Hunt, Lorraine, 112, 137
Hurrell, Susanna, 185
Hutinet, Philippe, 93
Hymn to Saint Cecilia
  (Britten), 49
Hysing, Kathrine, 93
I Musici, Rome, 43
Ibert, Jacques, 15
Idoménée
  (Campra), 43
Idomeneo
  (Mozart), 47, 95, 169
Idomeneo suite
  (Mozart), 25
Impatience, L'
  (Rameau), 65
Improvisation I sur Mallarmé
  (Boulez), 40
Incoronazione di Poppea, L'
  (Monteverdi), 44, 137, 140
Indes galantes, Les
  (Rameau), 37, 105, 106, 107, 111, 126
Infedeltà delusa, L'
  (Haydn), 167
Intermittents du spectacle, Les
  (Strikes), 151, 178, 179, 180
Into the Little Hill
  (Benjamin), 174
Iolanta
  (Tchaikovsky), 182
Ionesco, Irina, 138
Iphigénie en Aulide
  (Gluck), 96
Iphigénie en Tauride
  (Gluck), 32
IRCAM
  (Paris), 70
Israel in Egypt
  (Handel), 88
Italiana in Algeri, L'

(Rossini), 54, 160, 161
Ivaldi, Christian, 65
Jacobs, René, 136, 139, 140, 144,
  165, 169
Jacquillat, Jean-Pierre, 52
James, Eirian, 100, 113
Janáček, Leoš, 139, 140, 145, 146,
  149, 150, 165, 166
Jardin Campra
  (Aix), 30, 179
Jaroussky, Philippe, 181
Jarry, Gérard, 49
Jarsky, Irène, 76
Järvefelt, Göran, 93, 95
Jas de Bouffan
  (Aix), 23
Jaujard, Jacques, 21
Jeanneteau, Daniel, 146
Jenkins, John, 65
Jephté
  (Carissimi), 65
Jeux
  (Debussy), 143
Jo, Sumi, 122, 126
Joël, Nicolas, 65, 88, 123
Johannsson, Bardi, 159
Johnston, Jennifer, 161
Joissains, Alain, 75
Jones, Gemma, 102
Jones, Richard, 179
Jordan, Armin, 64, 97, 99, 104, 115,
  126
Jordan, Philippe, 147
Josquin des Prez, 41, 49
Joxe, Louis, 21
Joy, Geneviève, 47
Jude, Josèphe, 148
Julie
  (Boesmans), 158
Kaemmerlen, Geneviève, 142
Kagel, Mauricio, 77
Kaiser, Joseph, 170
Kalman, Jean, 117, 142, 181
Kalmar, Carlos, 106, 107
Kammerkonzert
  (Berg), 36
Kannen, Gunther von, 97
Karajan, Herbert von, 22, 36, 40, 42,
  52
Karthäuser, Sophie, 169

Kavrakos, Dimitri, 107
Keenlyside, Simon, 136
Kemmer, Marlette, 95
Kempff, Wilhelm, 29, 40
Kennedy, Roderick, 113
Kenny, Yvonne, 88
Kentridge, William, 169, 172, 180
Kerdoncuff, François, 148
Kerns, Robert, 48
Ketelsen, Kyle, 170, 173, 185
Kiarostami, Abbas, 167, 168
Killick, David, 102
King Arthur
  (Purcell), 91, 93, 101, 114
King, Malcolm, 77
Kinmouth, Patrick, 121, 125
Knodt, Erich, 104
Kochno, Boris, 15, 17
Kodaly, Zoltán, 33, 52
Kodama, Mari, 126
Kontrapunkte
  (Stockhausen), 40
Korngold, Erich Wolfgang, 148
Kostinen, Juha T., 133
Kozena, Magdalena, 145
Krips, Joseph, 17
Krönungsmesse
  (Mozart), 77
Kruysen, Bernard, 66
Kunde, Gregory, 172
Kunstenfestival des arts, Bruxelles, 146
Kusej, Martin, 182
Kwon, Hellen, 104
La Scala
  (Milan), 33, 34, 44, 63, 92, 155
Laage, Béatrice de, 131
Labèque, Katia, 75
Labèque, Marielle, 75
Lacroix, Christian, 165
Lafont, Jean-Philippe, 95
Lagrange, Michele, 104
Lalique, Suzanne, 44, 47
Lambert, Henri, 14, 16, 21
Lamford, Chloe, 181
Lancelot, Francine, 102
Landino, Francesco, 41
Landowski, Marcel, 58, 88
Lang, Jack, 108, 109, 117, 120
Lang, Petra, 143
Langheinrich, Ulf, 159

Langrée, Louis, 96, 167, 170, 171, 183
Langridge, Philip, 71, 75, 84, 95
Laporte, Christophe, 142
Laroche, Mireille, 104
Larsson, Anna, 160
Larsson, Lisa, 135, 137
Laterme, Vincent, 161
Lausanne Chamber Orchestra, 24
Lausanne Festival, 58
Lavaudant, Georges, 96, 97, 106
Lavelli, Jorge, 63, 64, 65, 67, 71, 73, 74, 75, 103, 106, 146, 181
Lavinia
  (Berraud), 46
Lazaridis, Stefanos, 72
Le Conte, Pierre-Michel, 21
Le Corre, Hélène, 138, 147
Le Maigat, Pierre-Yves, 96
Le Poulain, Jean, 61, 68
Le Roux, François, 96, 106, 107, 111
Le Texier, Vincent, 104
Le Tholonet, 39, 49, 52, 60, 73
Le Touzel, Sylvestra, 102
Leclair, Jean-Marie, 40
Leçons de ténèbres pour le mercredy
  (Couperin), 107
Leçons des Ténèbres
  (Charpentier), 52
Lee, Noël, 66
Lefort, Bernard, 58, 59, 60, 61, 62, 63, 64, 65, 66, 67, 68, 71, 72, 73, 74, 75, 76, 77, 80, 81, 86, 160, 177, 190
Lehnoff, Nicolaus, 61
Leonard, Isabel, 184
Lepage, Robert, 171
Leppard, Raymond, 71, 72
Les Baux-de-Provence, 35, 36
Les Milles (Internment Camp)
  (Aix), 15
Leveugle, Daniel, 52, 55
Levine, Michael, 112, 113, 181
Liaisons dangereuses, Les
  (Prey), 75, 76, 77
Lidholm, Ingvar, 77
Lied von der Erde, Das
  (Mahler), 60
Lieder
  (Webern), 89

Ligeti, György, 75, 159
Lindenstrand, Sylvia, 66, 67, 68
Lindsey, Kate, 183
Lissner, Stéphane, 123, 124, 125, 128, 129, 130, 131, 132, 133, 134, 135, 136, 137, 138, 139, 140, 141, 142, 144, 145, 146, 149, 151, 152, 153, 154, 155, 156, 159, 160, 161, 164, 166, 167, 190
Little, Tasmin, 143
Llorca, Denis, 99, 100, 122
Lloyd, Robert, 62, 66, 68, 85
Lo Piccolo, Maurizio, 140
Locke, Matthew, 32
Loeb, Rebecca Jo, 174
Lohengrin
  (Wagner), 92
Lombard, Alain, 61, 65, 123
London, 15, 17, 33, 36, 63, 82, 93, 112, 113, 131, 175
London Oriana Choir, 100, 107
London Philharmonic Orchestra, 48
London Symphony Orchestra, 171, 175, 176, 182
Loose, Emmy, 26, 29, 30
Lopez-Cobos, Jésus, 76
Lopez-Cobos, Jésus, 66
Lorengar, Pilar, 36, 45
Loriod, Yvonne, 16
Lotti, Antonio, 100
Lovett, Leon, 100
Loy, Christof, 170
Lublinand, Eliane, 49
Luchetti, Veriano, 66
Luisa Miller
  (Verdi), 61, 68
Lully, Jean-Baptiste, 43, 96, 97, 98, 101
Lungu, Irina, 171, 176
Lupa, Krystian, 160
Lutosławski, Witold, 77
Lyon, Ed, 171
Maag, Peter, 47
Macbeth
  (Shakespeare), 44
Machaut, Guillaume de, 41, 65
Mâche, François-Bernard, 90
MacKane, Armand, 62
Mackerras, Charles, 67, 71, 72, 99
Madeira, Jean, 39

Maestra di capella, Il
   (Cimarosa), 68
Magee, Garry, 158
Magicien d'Aix, Le
   (Dussurget), 15, 22
Magnificat
   (Bach), 68
Maheu, Jean, 69
Mahler Chamber Orchestra, 133, 135, 143, 145, 147, 148, 149, 154, 158, 161, 165, 166, 174
Mahler Youth Chamber Orchestra, 133, 136, 143
Mahler, Gustav, 22, 60, 123, 139, 143, 158, 161
Maïer, Henri, 123
Maîtrise Gabriel Fauré de Marseille, 52
Makeïeff, Macha, 155
Malclès, Jean-Denis, 37, 38, 46
Malgoire, Jean-Claude, 96, 97, 98
Malheurs d'Orphée, Les
   (Milhaud), 46, 55
Malipiero, Gian Francesco, 44
Malraux, André, 42, 52, 88
Mandarin merveilleux, Le
   (Bartók), 143
Mannion, Rosa, 116, 122
Manoury, Philippe, 133
Marais, Marin, 49, 65
Maraisienne, La
   (Marais), 65
Marcello, Benedetto, 26, 28, 29, 31, 32, 36, 44, 46
Marchaud, Louis, 49
Marcon, Andrea, 179, 181
Marder, Marc, 148
Maréchal, Marcel, 122
Margiono, Charlotte, 99
Margita, Stefan, 166
Mariage secret, Le
   (Cimarosa), 29, 30
Mariinsky Academy, 154
Marini, Giorgio, 115, 116
Markeas, Alexandraos, 133
Marriner, Neville, 74
Mars, Jacques, 62
Marseille, 14, 16, 18, 23, 25, 152
Marteau sans maître, Le
   (Boulez), 40

Martin, Frank, 77
Martin, Marvis, 88
Martin, Stephane, 121
Martinon, Jean, 33
Martinoty, Jean-Louis, 83, 84
Masini, Gianfranco, 63, 100
Mason, Anne, 99
Mass in A-flat
   (Schubert), 75
Mass in B minor
   (Bach), 94
Mass in C minor
   (Mozart), 100
Mass in G major
   (Poulenc), 49
Massard, Robert, 45
Massenet, Jules, 74
Massin, Béatrice, 102
Masterson, Valerie, 63, 67, 71, 72, 74, 75, 77, 112
Mattei, Peter, 135, 137, 149, 158
Matteuzi, William, 122
Mauriac, François, 26
Mauti-Nunziata, Elena, 66
Mazarin Quarter
   (Aix), 19, 131
Mazel, Lorin, 52
Mazzola, Enrique, 146
McBurney, Simon, 179, 180, 181, 185
McDonald, Anthony, 116
McFadden, Claron, 111
McGreevy, Geraldine, 146, 148
McLaughlin, Marie, 147
McVicar, David, 171
Médecin malgré lui, Le
   (Gounod), 43
Médée
   (Cherubini), 66
Mefistofele
   (Boito), 112
Mehta, Bejun, 174
Meier, Waltraud, 177
Mellon, Agnès, 111
Membra Jesu Nostri
   (Buxtehude), 98
Mendelssohn, Felix, 88, 102, 105
Mendonça, Vasco, 176
Menotti, Gian Carlo, 29
Mercure, Jean, 37, 67, 75, 99

Mercuriali, Angelo, 30
Meresz, Yan, 139
Meriweather, Annette, 69
Mesplé, Mady, 47
Messe de Requiem
  (Campra), 96
Messiaen, Olivier, 16, 29, 52, 99, 107, 159
Messiah, The
  (Handel), 90, 123
Messier, Jean-Marie, 128, 148, 149
Meyer, Jean, 25, 26, 28, 29, 30, 35, 36, 43, 44, 52, 95
Michael, Audrey, 92
Micheau, Janine, 37
Midsummer Night's Dream, A
  (Britten), 101, 109, 112, 114, 126, 182
  (Shakespeare), 15
Mijanovic, Marijana, 142
Milhaud, Darius, 23, 35, 36, 46, 86, 180
Milianti, Alain, 89, 95
Miller, Lajos, 69
Miller, Marlin, 147
Minetti Quartet, 159
Ministry of Culture, 21, 42, 53, 55, 58, 59, 62, 75, 81, 86, 88, 89, 105, 108, 109, 117, 120, 123, 124, 125, 130, 148, 151, 156, 178
Ministry of Foreign Affairs, 21
Minkowski, Marc, 83, 118, 137, 139, 144, 145, 151, 155, 165, 169, 175, 180
Minutillo, Hana, 146
Mireille
  (Gounod), 35
Mishima, Yukio, 155
Missa di Gloria
  (Puccini), 66
Missa Solemnis
  (Beethoven), 123
Mitchell, Katie, 174, 176, 180, 181, 183, 186
Mitridate
  (Mozart), 86, 88, 89
Mitterrand, François, 105, 117, 123
Moffo, Anna, 36
Molière, 43, 97
Mollvik, Christine, 139

Monde de la lune, Le
  (Haydn), 38, 41, 168
Mondonville, Jean-Joseph Cassanéa de, 46, 126
Monk, Gregory, 147
Monoyios, Ann, 98
Monstre du labyrinth, Le
  (Dove), 182
Montague, Diana, 92
Monteverdi Choir, 83, 85, 86, 90, 94, 98
Monteverdi Players, 82
Monteverdi, Claudio, 11, 29, 31, 41, 44, 45, 46, 48, 60, 65, 80, 86, 91, 92, 132, 136, 137, 139, 141, 142, 143, 144, 145, 148, 166, 168, 170
Morel, Marisa, 23
Mortimer, Vicki, 174
Motet de Sainte Suzanne
  (Couperin), 33
Mouton, Jean, 49
Mozart, Wolfgang Amadeus, 11, 17, 18, 20, 21, 23, 24, 29, 30, 31, 33, 34, 36, 39, 40, 41, 43, 45, 46, 47, 51, 52, 59, 60, 61, 62, 64, 66, 67, 68, 73, 77, 80, 81, 84, 85, 86, 88, 89, 91, 92, 94, 95, 96, 99, 100, 101, 105, 107, 109, 110, 111, 112, 123, 124, 125, 126, 132, 134, 135, 137, 143, 145, 151, 156, 157, 158, 164, 165, 166, 167, 169, 170, 171, 175, 181, 182, 183
Munch, Charles, 29
Münchner Philharmoniker, 22
Munich, 175
Murphy, Suzanne, 95
Murray, Ann, 71, 74, 75, 77
Murray, Sean, 102
Musée des Tapisseries
  (Aix), 19, 23, 25
Musée Granet
  (Aix), 19
Musée instrumental du conservatoire de Paris, 43
Musiciens du Louvre, Les
  (Grenoble), 118, 144, 169, 180
Musik Musikaisphe Exequien
  (Schütz), 100
Musique dans la rue
  (Aix), 54, 59, 60, 177

Mussbach, Peter, 151, 154
Muti, Riccardo, 155
Nagano, Kent, 104, 115
Nahon, Philippe, 104
Nancy, Gilles, 109, 114, 115
Naouri, Laurent, 145, 148
Nâzeri, Châhrâm, 144
Nédélec, Ronan, 150
Negri, Emmanuelle de, 184
Nelson, Judith, 64, 90
Neveu, Ginette, 16
New York, 175
New York Baroque Dance Company, 83
Nez, Le
(Shostakovich), 172
Nguyen Thien Dao, 90
Nielsen, Carl, 148
Nigl, Georg, 168
Nilsen, Birgit, 60
Nîmes, 17
Nironet, Jean, 98
Noble, Adrian, 102, 103, 105, 139, 141, 142, 149, 158
Noces, Les
(Stravinsky), 46
Noelte, Rudolph, 109, 110, 146
Noiret, Michèle, 170
Nordey, Stanislas, 150
Norman, Jessye, 66, 86, 87, 93, 126
Norrington, Roger, 110
Noseda, Gianandrea, 176, 177
Nouvel orchestre philharmonique de Radio-France, 77, 85, 86, 88, 89, 93
Novelette
(Lutosławski), 77
Nozze di Figaro, Le
(Mozart), 18, 32, 34, 36, 39, 44, 51, 52, 55, 61, 73, 91, 103, 109, 110, 145, 165, 173
Nuits d'été, Les
(Berlioz), 86
Nuñez-Camelino, Manuel, 180
Nuovo Quartetto Italiano, 24, 25, 33, 36
O King
(Berio), 89
Oberdorff, Éric, 186
Obolensky, Chloë, 134

Ockeghem, Johannes, 105
Ockenden, Rebecca, 142
Ode à Napoléon
(Schönberg), 52
Ode to Saint Cecilia
(Purcell), 32, 72
Oedipus Rex
(Stravinsky), 184
Offenbach, Jacques, 137, 160, 169
Ogier, Daniel, 83, 84
Oida, Yoshi, 133, 134
Oliveira, Hugo, 170
Ollendorff, Fritz, 30
Ollu, Franck, 168, 172
Ono, Kazushi, 155, 158, 171, 172, 182, 186
Opéra Bastille
(Paris), 123, 131
Opera da Camera di Milano, 48
Opéra de Bordeaux, 90
Opéra de Lille, 90
Opéra de Lyon, 35, 75, 80, 82, 90, 91, 92, 95, 96, 99, 101, 107, 124
Opéra de Marseille, 58, 62, 90
Opéra de Montpellier, 123
Opéra de Nice, 95, 99
Opéra de Paris, 36, 37, 39, 42, 47, 58, 63, 72, 76, 95, 120, 123, 128
Opéra du Rhin, 64
(Strasbourg), 61, 63, 90, 95
Opéra-Comique
(Paris), 43, 48, 101
Opolais, Kristine, 170
Orchestre de chambre de la Monnaie, 155, 158
Orchestre de chambre de La Sarre, 49
Orchestre de chambre de Toulouse, 39
Orchestre de chambre de Versailles, 43, 50
Orchestre de chambre Gürzenich de Cologne, 30
Orchestre de gamelan du village de Sebatu
(Bali), 143
Orchestre de l'Association des Concerts Pasdeloup, 39
Orchestre de l'Opéra de Lyon, 95, 97, 98, 104, 115, 147, 171, 172, 182
Orchestre de la chambre de Hollande, 41, 45

Orchestre de la Société des concerts du Conservatoire (Paris), 24, 25, 29, 31, 32, 33, 35, 37, 43, 48, 52, 122
Orchestre de Lille, 74, 88
Orchestre de Lyon, 66
Orchestre de Nice, 100
Orchestre de Paris, 24, 52, 53, 54, 60, 88, 105, 123, 137, 146, 148, 154, 177, 185, 186
Orchestre de Strasbourg, 61
Orchestre de Sudwestfunk de Baden-Baden, 24, 33, 40
Orchestre des cadets du conservatoire (Paris), 21
Orchestre des jeunes de l'Union européenne, 86
Orchestre des jeunes de la Méditerranée, 177, 178, 182
Orchestre des solistes de l'Association des Concerts Colonne, 46
Orchestre du Capitole de Toulouse, 64, 65, 67, 68
Orchestre du Teatro comunale di Bologna, 158
Orchestre européen du Festival d'Aix, 122, 125
Orchestre Jean-Marie Leclair, 40
Orchestre lyrique de l'ORTF, 60, 61, 62
Orchestre national de France, 118
Orchestre national de la RTF, 29
Orchestre philharmonique de Radio-France, 72
Orchestre philharmonique de Strasbourg, 21, 96
Orchestre philharmonique du Festival d'Aix, 48
Orchestre Pro Arte de Munich, 62
Orfeo
   (Monteverdi), 29, 48, 91, 92, 132, 136, 165
Orgonasova, Luba, 104
Orlando
   (Handel), 116, 117, 119
Orlando furioso
   (Ariosto), 116
Orphée
   (Gluck), 36
   (Rameau), 23

Orphée aux enfers
   (Offenbach), 169
Oustrac, Stéphanie d', 158
Paasikivi, Lilli, 160
Pabst, Peter, 140
Padmore, Mark, 111, 137
Palais Garnier
   (Paris), 106
Palestrina, Giovanni Pierluigi da, 105
Palladio Theatre
   (Venice), 112
Palmer, Felicity, 116
Panerai, Rolando, 34, 36, 44, 45
Parade(s), 178
Paradis et la Péri, Le
   (Schumann), 94
Parc Rambot
   (Aix), 40, 41, 48
Paris, 11, 14, 15, 16, 17, 19, 21, 28, 32, 33, 37, 46, 49, 58, 63, 67, 70, 84, 87, 98, 120, 131, 170, 175, 176
Parnasse, Le
   (Couperin), 40
Parsons, Geoffrey, 60
Parti socialiste (PS), 117
Pascal, Luis, 96
Pasquier Trio, 24
Pass, Damien, 180
Passaggio
   (Berio), 86, 89
Passerelles, 165, 177
Passion
   (Dusapin), 167, 168
Pastorale d'été
   (Honegger), 36
Pastré, Lily, 14, 18, 20, 21, 23, 27
Paulus
   (Mendelssohn), 88
Pavillon Vendôme
   (Aix), 86, 88, 89
Pears, Peter, 32, 112
Pearson, William, 75
Peduzzi, Laurent, 95
Peduzzi, Richard, 146, 147, 154, 155, 157, 166
Pelléas et Mélisande
   (Debussy), 49, 55, 183
   (Fauré), 86
Penchenat, Jean-Claude, 96, 97

Péniche-Opéra, La, 104
Peretti Della Rocca, Jean-Pierre de, 89
Pergolese, Jean Baptiste, 31, 43
Pergolèse, Umberto de, 61
Pergolesi, Giovanni Battista, 60, 61, 62, 64, 68
Pérotin, 105
Perrin, Cécile, 148
Perséphone
  (Stravinsky), 182
Persson, Miah, 146, 148
Peter Grimes
  (Britten), 179
Petersen, Marlis, 170
Petibon, Patricia, 173, 179, 181
Petit, Roland, 17
Petite messe solennelle
  (Rossini), 107
Petite renarde rusée, La
  (Janáček), 149, 150
Petitjean, Stéphane, 137, 148
Petkov, Dimiter, 66
Petrenko, Mikhail, 177
Philharmonia Orchestra
  (London), 36, 183, 184
Philip, Michel, 64
Piau, Sandrine, 102, 179
Picheral, Jean-François, 108, 109, 115, 119, 120, 121, 123, 124, 125, 128
Pichon, Raphaël, 180
Pido, Evelino, 122, 126
Pier'Alli, Pierluigi, 92
Pierro, Nahuel di, 184
Pierrot lunaire
  (Schönberg), 92, 151, 152, 160
Pignolet, Michel, 49
Piland, Jeanne, 95, 97, 99
Pilarczyk, Helga, 40
Pinnock, Trevor, 64
Pinocchio
  (Boesmans), 185
Pintilié, Lucian, 84, 85
Pizzetti, Ildebrando, 29, 77
Pizzi, Pier Luigi, 76, 87, 111
Place de Saint-Jean-de-Malte
  (Aix), 33
Place des Cardeurs
  (Aix), 62, 64, 72
Place des Quatre-Dauphins
  (Aix), 23, 36, 61, 64, 68, 72, 85, 89
Planès, Alain, 139, 146, 159
Plasson, Michel, 60, 64, 65
Platé, Roberto, 106
Platée
  (Rameau), 37, 38, 63
Platonov
  (Chekhov), 99
Plenel, Edwy, 179
Podles, Ewa, 90
Poème de l'extase, Le
  (Scriabin), 143
Pointier, Henri, 19
Polgar, Laszlo, 135
Pommerat, Joël, 172, 185
Ponnelle, Jean-Pierre, 74
Porpora, Nicola, 74
Porporino, 74
Poschner-Klebel, Brigitte, 100
Poulenard, Isabelle, 106
Poulenc, Francis, 16, 21, 29, 33, 34, 42, 43, 48, 49, 77
Pousseur, Henri, 40, 41
Preston, Stephen, 64
Prévost, Jean-Simon, 69
Prey, Claude, 75, 76, 101, 104
Price, Margaret, 112
Prince de bois, Le
  (Bartók), 148
Prison, La
  (Landowski), 88
Pritchard, John, 48
Pro Musica Antiqua
  (New York), 41
Prodigal Son, The
  (Britten), 54, 104
Prohaska, Anna, 181
Prokofiev, Sergei, 101, 104, 148, 153, 154, 177, 186
Psyché
  (Lully), 96
Puccini, Giacomo, 66, 107
Pujol, Jean-Louis, 76, 80
Purcell, Henry, 11, 17, 31, 32, 33, 43, 44, 49, 60, 65, 66, 72, 80, 91, 93, 94, 101, 102, 103, 107, 113, 114, 132, 133, 160, 170
Purves, Christopher, 174
Putnam, Ashley, 88

Py, Olivier, 169, 178, 180
Pye, Tom, 134
Pygmalion
    (Rameau), 107, 171, 184
Quator pour la fin du temps
    (Messiaen), 52
Quatre pièces pour clarinette et piano
    (Berg), 49
Quatre pièces religieuses
    (Kodaly), 52
Quatuor Parisii, 148
Quatuor Tokyo, 159
Quatuor Via Nova, 52
Queen Elizabeth Hall
    (London), 82
Queen's Theatre
    (London), 93
Quilico, Gino, 92, 95, 107
Quintans, Ana, 173
Quintette Boccherini, 31
Rachmaninoff, Sergei, 148, 159
Racine, Jean, 15, 44, 87, 88
Radok, David, 158
Radu, 85
Raffard, Éric, 142
Ragon, Gilles, 98
Raimond, Jean-Bernard, 119, 123
Raimondi, Ruggero, 157
Rake's Progress, The
    (Stravinsky), 101, 115, 185
Rameau, Jean-Philippe, 11, 23, 25, 29, 31, 36, 37, 38, 39, 40, 43, 46, 49, 61, 63, 64, 65, 80, 81, 82, 83, 84, 85, 86, 87, 88, 92, 96, 105, 106, 107, 109, 110, 111, 126, 171, 180, 184
Ramey, Samuel, 115
Randle, Thomas, 102, 104
Rape of Lucretia, The
    (Britten), 174
Rapp, Jacques, 104
Rassemblement pour la République
    (RPR), 117, 119, 123, 125
Rattle, Simon, 12, 22, 133, 139, 143, 145, 160, 165, 168, 182
Ravel, Maurice, 23, 40, 43, 52, 86, 107, 118, 139, 143, 148, 159, 175
Raynaud, André, 66
Re pastore, Il
    (Mozart), 105

Redel, Kurt, 62
Régy, Claude, 146
Reinhart, Gregory, 96, 104
Relais culturel d'Aix, 54
Remigio, Carmela, 135
Renaud, Madeleine, 16
Rendall, David, 99
Requiem
    (Gilles), 52
    (Howells), 100
    (Mozart), 94
    (Verdi), 48
Requiem allemande, Un
    (Brahms), 148
Respighi, Ottorino, 107
Retour, Un
    (Strasnoy), 170
Rewerski, Mariana, 170
Rheingold, Das
    (Wagner), 160
Rhodes, Jane, 45
Rhorer, Jérémie, 168, 173, 182, 185
Ricciarelli, Katia, 76, 77
Richter, Tobias, 97
Rigaud, Christine, 138, 147
Rigoletto
    (Verdi), 175, 176
Rimes pour diverses sources sonores,
    (Pousseur), 40
Ring des Nibelungen, Der
    (Wagner), 93, 145, 157, 160, 165, 167, 168
Ris et Danceries, 102, 106, 111
Ritorno d'Ulisse in patria, Il
    (Monteverdi), 141, 149, 154
Rituel in memoriam Bruno Maderna
    (Boulez), 143
Rivalland, Françoise, 148
Rivenq, Nicolas, 106
Rivier, Jean, 40, 48
Rivoli, Gianfranco, 48, 72
Roberto Devereux
    (Donizetti), 68
Robinson, Faye, 61, 69
Robson, Martin, 142
Rodgers, Joan, 81, 85, 88, 90
Roger, Bruno, 167
Rogers, Noëlle, 62
Rolfe Johnson, Anthony, 90, 95
Roméo et Juliette

(Berlioz), 48, 65
(Prokofiev), 177
Rosbaud, Hans, 11, 12, 21, 22, 23,
  24, 25, 26, 28, 29, 30, 31, 32, 36,
  37, 39, 40, 42, 135
Rosbaud, Paul, 22
Rosenkavalier, Der
  (Strauss), 96, 105
Rosenthal, Manuel, 15
Ross, Finn, 181
Rossi, Franco, 23
Rossini, Gioachino, 34, 38, 54, 62,
  75, 76, 77, 80, 85, 86, 88, 99, 100,
  105, 107, 122, 140, 160, 161, 180
Rostropovich, Mstislav, 54, 88
Roubert, Jean-Loup, 130
Rouge et le noir, Le
  (Prey), 101, 104
Rousseau, Jean-Jacques, 83
Roussel, Albert, 40, 148
Rousset, Christophe, 168
Roux, Michel, 30, 32
Royal Collections
  (Windsor), 111
Royal Library
  (London), 43
Royal Opera House
  (London), 15, 44, 110, 112
Royal Shakespeare Company, 63, 102,
  105, 113, 116
Royal Theater Carré
  (Amsterdam), 171
Royal, Kate, 165
Rozario, Patricia, 95
Rubenstein, Arthur, 43
Rubio, Consuelo, 45
Rudel, Julius, 68
Ruf, Jean-Yves, 176
Ruggeri, Miriam, 106
Ruiten, Lenneke, 183
Rupp, Andrew, 134
Rysanek, Leonie, 66
Saariaho, Kaija, 145
Sacre du printemps, Le
  (Stravinsky), 40
Sado, Yutaka, 151, 154
Sainte-Victoire, 19, 52, 161, 165
Saint-Martin, Jean-Gabriel, 180
Saint-Sauveur, cathedral and cloisters
  (Aix), 19, 30, 32, 48, 54, 60, 62,
    64, 65, 66, 88, 89, 91, 94, 96,
    98, 107
Sakharoff, Clotilde, 48
Salieri Chamber Orchestra, 112
Salle Gaveau
  (Paris), 16, 17
Salonen, Esa-Pekka, 146, 148, 177,
  183, 184
Salusse, Jean, 58
Salzburg, 16, 18, 31, 54, 89, 99, 121,
  137, 145
Sarrazin, Maurice, 32, 34, 38, 41, 44
Sass, Sylvia, 65
Satie, Erik, 65, 107
Sauguet, Henri, 35, 42
Savall, Jordi, 64
Scaltriti, Roberto, 135
Scarlatti, Alessandro, 74
Scarlatti, Domenico, 25, 46
Schaer, Hanna, 133, 147
Scharinger, Anton, 104, 122
Schirrer, René, 98
Schmid-Lienbacher, Edith, 104
Schmidt, Andreas, 110, 115
Schmitt, Charles, 97
Schmucki, Norbert, 64
Schmutzhard, Daniel, 159
Schola Cantorum, University of
  Arkansas, 49
Schönberg, Arnold, 22, 35, 40, 49, 52,
  77, 92, 107, 139, 143, 151, 152,
  153, 160
Schubert, Franz, 33, 43, 52, 60, 66,
  75, 107, 125, 139, 143, 148, 159,
  180
Schuldigkeit des ersten Gebots
  (Mozart), 109, 111
Schumann, Robert, 43, 60, 94, 107,
  125, 148
Schütz, Heinrich, 100
Schwarzkopf, Elisabeth, 60
Sciutti, Graziella, 30, 32, 34, 35, 39,
  45
Scottish Chamber Orchestra, 71, 76
Scottish Opera, 71, 72
Scriabin, Alexander, 139, 143, 159
Scylla et Glaucus suite
  (Leclair), 40
Ségovia, Andrès, 25, 33
Segovia, Claudio, 63

Selig, Franz-Josef, 182
Sellars, Peter, 167, 169, 182, 184
Semele
  (Handel), 119, 125
Semenchuk, Ekaterina, 149
SEMETA, 108, 115, 119, 124
Sémiramis
  (Rossini), 75, 76
Sénéchal, Michel, 34, 37
Senna festeggiante, La
  (Vivaldi), 43
Sept dernières paroles du Christ en croix, Les
  (Haydn), 104
Sept lieder de jeunesse
  (Berg), 66, 96
Sequi, Sandro, 48
Serenade for Tenor, Horn and Strings
  (Britten), 50
Serenata notturna
  (Mozart), 30
Serva padrona, La
  (Pergolesi), 60, 61
Service éducatif du Festival, 177
Servillio, Toni, 161
Seven Sonnets of Michelangelo
  (Britten), 34
Seven Stones
  (Adámek), 186
Sextius-Mirabeau Quarter
  (Aix), 73, 109, 115, 160, 165
Shaham, Rinat, 133
Shakespeare, William, 44, 102, 112
Shéhérazade
  (Ravel), 143
Shicoff, Neil, 74
Shimanovitch, Ekaterina, 154
Shimell, William, 155, 168
Shostakovich, Dmitri, 52, 172
Shtoda, Daniil, 149
Sibelius, Jean, 107, 148, 171
Siebens, Etienne, 176
Siegfried
  (Wagner), 167
Siegfried Idyll
  (Wagner), 126
Signeyrole, Marie-Eve, 182
Silbermann, Alfred, 48
Silja, Anja, 140, 152
Simone, Roberto de, 90

Simoneau, Léopold, 29, 34, 45
Simple Symphony
  (Britten), 43
Sinfonia Varsovia, 95
Sirius
  (Stockhausen), 69
Sirius Centre
  (Aix), 69
Sivadier, Jean-François, 171, 184
Six pièces
  (Webern), 40
Six pièces for orchestra
  (Webern), 143
Six symphonies pour petit orchestre
  (Milhaud), 46
Sixteen, The, 95, 96, 97, 98, 99, 100
Sjón, 186
Skibine, Georges, 47
Skovhus, Bo, 170
Skram, Knut, 67
Skrowaczewski, Stanislas, 75
Slawinski, Tomasz, 159
Sly, Philippe, 184
Smith, Jennifer, 84, 94, 145
Soares-Holanda, Marcio, 142
Sogno di Scipione, Il
  (Mozart), 105
Sokhiev, Tugan, 154
Soloists Charlotte Margiono, 107
Soloviy, Sofia, 168
Soltesz, Stephen, 95
Solti, Georg, 40, 86
Solyom, Janos, 66
Sonata for Piano no. 1
  (Boulez), 49
Sonata for Piano no. 23
  (Beethoven), 43
Sonata for Piano no. 31
  (Beethoven), 107
Sonata for Violin and Piano no. 3
  (Beethoven), 48
Sonata for Violin and Piano no. 6
  (Beethoven), 48
Sonata for Violin and Piano no. 7
  (Beethoven), 48
Sonate pour deux pianos et percussion
  (Bartók), 46
Sorano, Daniel, 46
Souzay, Gérard, 30, 43, 44, 60, 66
Soyer, Roger, 64, 65, 98

Spectre de la Rose, Le
 (Berlioz), 48
Spering, Andreas, 175
Špicer, Krešimir, 142, 158
St Matthew Passion
 (Bach), 105
Staatsoper, Berlin, 154
Stabat Mater
 (Rossini), 107
Stafford, Ashley, 94
Stains, Zachary, 142
Steffek, Henry, 44
Stenhamar, Wilhelm, 148
Stéphany, Anna, 159
Stephens, Suzanne, 69
Stern, David, 131, 132, 138, 190
Stich-Randall, Teresa, 34, 36, 39, 44, 47
Stilwell, Richard, 66
Stockhausen, Karlheinz, 40, 69
Stockhausen, Markus, 69
Stoklossa, Eric, 166
Strasbourg, 22, 31, 34, 61, 63, 64
Strasnoy, Oscar, 170
Strauss, Johann, 25, 31
Strauss, Richard, 43, 47, 86, 91, 95, 96, 107, 126, 148, 175, 177, 186
Stravinsky, Igor, 35, 40, 42, 43, 46, 47, 49, 84, 101, 114, 115, 139, 143, 152, 153, 158, 160, 171, 182, 184, 185
Strehler, Giorgio, 74
Streit, Kurt, 104
String Trio
 (Schönberg), 49
 (Webern), 49
Strong, Pablo, 147
Strosser, Pierre, 95, 133
Strozzi, Barbara, 170
Stundytė, Aušrinė, 186
Suite for Harpsichord no. 5
 (Purcell), 65
Suites for Orchestra
 (Bach), 144
Symphonie de psaumes
 (Stravinsky), 184
Symphonie fantastique
 (Berlioz), 52
Symphony for Wind Instruments
 (Stravinsky), 40

Symphony no. 1
 (Beethoven), 30
 (Dutilleux), 33
Symphony no. 10
 (Mahler), 143
Symphony no. 3
 (Beethoven), 86
Symphony no. 33
 (Mozart), 85
Symphony no. 35
 (Mozart), 25, 31
Symphony no. 39
 (Mozart), 60
Symphony no. 4
 (Mahler), 159
Symphony no. 40
 (Mozart), 144
Symphony no. 48
 (Haydn), 85
Symphony no. 5
 (Mahler), 161
Symphony no. 8
 (Dvořák), 143
Symphony no. 83
 (Haydn), 143
Symphony no. 9
 (Schubert), 143
Symphony no. 92
 (Haydn), 31, 143
Symphony op. 21
 (Webern), 40
Szmytka, Elzbieta, 99
Szot, Paulo, 173
Tallis, Thomas, 105
Tancrède
 (Campra), 95
 (Rossini), 75
Tani, Jennifer, 140
Tanovitsky, Alexei, 154
Tappy, Éric, 60, 62, 81
Tarver, Kenneth, 135
Tate, Jeffrey, 99, 100, 104, 117, 122, 123
Tchaikovsky, Pyotr Ilyich, 148, 149, 182
Tcherniakov, Dmitri, 169, 175, 185
Tear, Robert, 133
Teatro Comunale de Gênes, 76
Teatro di San Carlo, 90
Teatro La Fenice, 90

Teatro Real
   (Madrid), 129
Teatro Regio de Turin, 76
Telemann, Georg Philipp, 41, 43, 46, 49
Téléphone, Le
   (Menotti), 29, 30, 47
Teshigawara, Saburo, 172
Tézier, Ludovic, 171
Thamin, Jean-Louis, 72, 85
Thanks to My Eyes
   (Bianchi), 172
Tharaud, Alexandre, 180
Thau, Pierre, 62
Thaw, David, 37
Théâtre Daunou
   (Paris), 16
Théâtre de l'Archevêché
   (Aix), 24, 25, 29, 32, 34, 35, 39, 40, 43, 44, 46, 48, 52, 53, 55, 59, 61, 64, 65, 66, 68, 73, 74, 75, 76, 83, 86, 87, 88, 89, 90, 91, 93, 94, 96, 99, 101, 107, 108, 109, 112, 114, 117, 118, 119, 125, 126, 129, 130, 132, 136, 137, 139, 140, 145, 147, 148, 149, 152, 154, 158, 160, 165, 167, 169, 171, 173, 175, 180, 183, 185
Théâtre de la Madeleine
   (Paris), 153
Théâtre de la Ville
   (Paris), 67
Théâtre des Champs-Élysées
   (Paris), 17, 18
Théâtre du Bois de l'Aune
   (Aix), 175
Théâtre du Capitole de Toulouse, 123
Théâtre du Châtelet
   (Paris), 58, 123
Théâtre du Jeu de Paume
   (Aix), 139, 140, 141, 143, 144, 146, 148, 149, 152, 155, 158, 159, 166, 167, 172, 175, 176, 180, 186
Théâtre Gymnase
   (Paris), 150
Théâtre Marigny
   (Paris), 28
Théâtre Montansier
   (Versailles), 48
Théâtre municipal d'Avignon, 76
Théâtre national de Strasbourg, 66
Théâtre romain
   (Arles), 62, 66, 86
Théâtre Royal de la Monnaie de Bruxelles, 96, 136, 158, 159, 164, 169
Théâtre Sarah-Bernhardt
   (Paris), 16
Theresienmesse
   (Haydn), 85
Thibaut de Chambure, Geneviève, 43
Thielemann, Christian, 100
Thieû Niang, Thierry, 170
Thompson, Adrian, 146
Tilling, Camilla, 145, 148, 155, 158
Timbres, espace, movement
   (Dutilleux), 77
Tippett, Michael, 100
Titus, Alan, 62
Tombeau de Couperin, Le
   (Ravel), 23, 86
Tomé, Job, 170
Tomlinson, John, 85, 90
Torelli, Giuseppe, 43
Tosca
   (Puccini), 15
Toubon, Jacques, 117, 125
Tournafond, Françoise, 97, 106
Tournus, Michel, 49
Tout un monde lointain...
   (Dutilleux), 54
Trauernacht
   (Bach), 180
Traviata, La
   (Verdi), 65, 71, 151, 152, 153, 154, 171
Tréguier, Christian, 98
Treliński, Mariusz, 186
Tribun, Le
   (Kagel), 77
Trionfo del tempo e del disinganno, Il
   (Handel), 183, 184
Trois fragments de Wozzeck
   (Berg), 40
Trois pièces for orchestra
   (Berg), 143
Trois pièces pour clarinette seule
   (Stravinsky), 49

Troyens, Les
 (Berlioz), 49
Tucker, Mark, 94
Turangalîla-Symphonie
 (Messiaen), 29
Turco in Italia, Il
 (Rossini), 85, 180
Turn of the Screw, The
 (Britten), 145, 146, 150, 158
Turocy, Catherine, 83
Ulivieri, Nicola, 135
Une Situation Huey P. Newton
 (Bruyère), 175
Uppsala University Choir, 77
Upshaw, Dawn, 100, 115
Urmana, Violetta, 135
Valade, Pierre-André, 133
Valentini-Terrani, Lucia, 88, 90
Valletti, Cesare, 34
Valse, La
 (Ravel), 118
Van Kerckhove, Hendrickje, 158
Van Mechelen, Reinoud, 184
Vaness, Carol, 112
Varcoe, Stephen, 94
Varèse, Edgard, 139, 143
Variations on a Theme of Frank Bridge
 (Britten), 36, 46
Veasey, Joséphine, 60
Venelles, 144, 161
Venice, 16, 64, 142
Venice Film Festival, 92
Verdi, Giuseppe, 20, 48, 59, 61, 65,
 66, 71, 73, 77, 92, 96, 146, 151,
 171, 175, 176
Vergier, Jean-Pierre, 97
Vernet, Isabelle, 107
Vesperae solennes de Dominica
 (Mozart), 77
Vessières, André, 47
Viala, Jean-Luc, 104
Vidal, Elisabeth, 98
Vienna, 175
Vienna Philharmonic, 17
Vienna State Opera, 44
Vignoles, Roger, 148
Vilar, Jean, 17
Villazon, Rolando, 154
Ville d'Aix-en-Provence, 21, 53, 58,
 73, 75, 86, 89, 108, 109, 118, 119,
 120, 122, 124, 128, 138, 141, 156
Ville de Paris, 123
Villegier, Jean-Marie, 98
Vincent, Jean-Pierre, 66, 76, 94
Vingt regards sur l'Enfant Jesus
 (Messiaen), 16
Vink, Elena, 112
Violin Concerto
 (Brahms), 143
Viollier, Renée, 37
Visée, Robert de, 49
Vishnevskaia, Galina, 88
Vitrolles, 176
Vivaise, Caroline de, 157
Vivaldi, Antonio, 29, 31, 33, 41, 43,
 46
Vivendi, 128, 148
Voix humaine, La
 (Poulenc), 43
Voltaire, 75, 110
Von Otter, Anne-Sofie, 90, 98, 137,
 168
Von Stade, Federica, 107
Wagner, Richard, 59, 60, 92, 113,
 126, 137, 145, 157, 158, 164, 165,
 168
Wagner-Pasquier, Eva, 131
Wahl, Bernard, 43, 50
Wakhévitch, Georges, 22, 35
Walkerie, Die
 (Wagner), 165
Wall, Erin, 157
Wall, Jean, 15
Wand, Gunter, 30
Ward, Anthony, 141
Warlikowski, Krzysztof, 183
Warsaw, 186
Warsaw Sinfonietta, 107
Watkinson, Carolyn, 92
Watson, Katherine, 184
Watson, Lillian, 113
Weber, Carl Maria von, 113, 116, 117
Webern, Anton, 36, 40, 49, 88, 89,
 139, 143
Weidinger, Christine, 90
Weikert, Ralf, 68, 69, 74, 76, 88
Weiss, Kenneth, 161, 166
Weitz, Pierre-André, 169
Welsh National Opera, 154
Wernicke, Herbert, 137, 146

Werther
   (Massenet), 74
Westbroek, Eva-Maria, 165
Whately, Kitty, 176
White, Willard, 125, 140, 146, 160
Wieder-Atherton, Sonia, 148
Wiener Festwochen, 153
Wiener Piano Trio, 159
Winterreise
   (Schubert), 180
Wispelwey, Pieter, 159
Wixell, Ingvar, 61, 68
Wolf, Hugo, 148
Wolk, Emil, 113
Woodington, Albie, 102
Woodrow, Pipa, 147
Workmann, William, 49
Wozzeck
   (Berg), 151, 152, 153
Written on Skin
   (Benjamin), 173, 175
Wyn Davies, Catrin, 135
Xenakis, Iannis, 94, 159
Yakar, Rachel, 87

Yannopoulos, Dino, 66
Yepes, Ana, 106
Young Person's Guide to the Orchestra, The
   (Britten), 41
Yultchieva, Monâjât, 144
Zachwatowicz, Krystina, 71
Zaffini, Clément, 43, 46
Zaïde
   (Mozart), 167, 182
Zareska, Eugenia, 29, 30
Zauberflöte, Die
   (Mozart), 38, 41, 46, 48, 55, 84, 85, 88, 101, 103, 118, 119, 121, 122, 126, 132, 137, 138, 139, 147, 160, 168, 169, 178, 180
Zémire et Azor
   (Grétry), 38, 47
Zobel, David, 148
Zola, Émile, 19
Zoller, Paul, 173
Zoroastre
   (Rameau), 184

THE AUTHOR

Simon Trowbridge was born in Oxford in 1961. He was educated at King's College, London, and University College, London. He is the author of a history of the Comédie-Française and a biography of the composer Jean-Philippe Rameau.

www.ingramcontent.com/pod-product-compliance
Lightning Source LLC
Chambersburg PA
CBHW020520080526
44583CB00013B/672